JAMES M. HUNT
Babson College

JOSEPH R. WEINTRAUB
Babson College

The
COACHING
MANAGER

DEVELOPING TOP
TALENT IN BUSINESS

SAGE Publications
International Educational and Professional Publisher
Thousand Oaks ▪ London ▪ New Delhi

For information:

Sage Publications, Inc.
2455 Teller Road
Thousand Oaks, California 91320
E-mail: order@sagepub.com

Sage Publications Ltd.
6 Bonhill Street
London EC2A 4PU
United Kingdom

Sage Publications India Pvt. Ltd.
M-32 Market
Greater Kailash I
New Delhi 110 048 India

Printed in the United States of America

Library of Congress Cataloging-in-Publication Data

Hunt, James (James M.)
 The coaching manager : developing top talent in business / by James M. Hunt and Joseph R. Weintraub.
 p. cm.
Includes bibliographical references and index.
 ISBN 0-7619-2418-3 (c) 0-7619-2419-1 (p)
 1. Mentoring in business. 2. Executives--Training of. 3. Leadership.
4. Management. I. Weintraub, Joseph R. II. Title.
 HF5385 .H86 2002
 658.3′124--dc21

                                2002003067

This book is printed on acid-free paper.

02 03 04 05 10 9 8 7 6 5 4

Acquisitions Editor:	Marquita Flemming
Editorial Assistant:	MaryAnn Vail
Production Editor:	Sanford Robinson
Copy Editor:	Karla Freeman
Typesetter:	Siva Math Setters, Chennai, India
Indexer:	Molly Hall
Cover Designer:	Michelle Lee

Contents

Preface

This book is about how business leaders, whom we often refer to simply as "managers," help their employees learn and develop through coaching. The most important point we make here is that when managers communicate a genuine interest in helping rather than evaluating their employees, they create opportunities for everyone to learn. We believe that managers, in addition to focusing on business results, will gain much by focusing on being helpful. A great deal has been written about the notion of the "servant" leader (Greenleaf, 1998). Although our point about being helpful is certainly consistent with that notion, we focus on something more pragmatic. We're talking about managers who try to help employees, as a *routine* part of their management activities, learn and become more productive in the process. Is this at all reasonable? Can large numbers of managers pull this off? Do they really want to help? This is something of a paradigm shift for many people. It was for us.

While this book was being written, the world around us was changing. Our personal and psychological sense of safety was rocked. We came to believe that, more than ever, we need people in our lives who can help us understand and grow from the challenges that we face, professionally and personally. The coaching managers we write about here create workplaces that make learning, growth, and adaptation possible. They combine business leadership with a genuine interest in helping those with whom they work.

We had stumbled on this impulse to help 6 years previously, in our work as management professors at Babson College. Babson is a business specialty school, located just outside of Boston, known for its work in entrepreneurship. Our students are an impressive lot, but like many people who are attracted to careers in business, they tend to be results-focused and pragmatic. In the late 1980s and 90s, business schools came under severe criticism from accreditation boards, the press, large corporations, and society at large for the single-minded focus of the standard business curriculum. Business students are traditionally taught the tools of analysis: finance and accounting, operations management, and strategy. The product of such an education may be a great thinker but may not necessarily be good at communicating his or her ideas, influencing others to work toward shared goals, or collaborating with others on a team. The results of this excessive focus on analysis can be seen in poor decision making about mergers, strategy, new product development, and a range of other business challenges. Without some ability to personally execute and to get others committed to the work at hand, analysis alone is a rather empty and sometimes dangerous skill. Perhaps just as important, the poor interpersonal skills of many managers and employees made working in some business organizations just plain unpleasant. We wanted to do something about all this.

Building on the previous work of one of the authors (Weintraub), the Undergraduate Programs Office and the Management Division at Babson made the commitment to hold assessment centers for all 1st- and 3rd-year undergraduate students. Assessment centers were pioneered in the U.S. Army and refined in AT&T and several other large organizations. In essence, when one participates in an assessment center, one has the opportunity to try out a piece of work (in this case, work with teams) and be observed by trained assessors, or "coaches." The coach then gives feedback to the participant on his or her performance.

We decided that the coaches for our assessment centers would have greater credibility if they came from the business community, given the career goals of our students. Who better to ask to serve in this role than our alumni and MBA students, all of whom have substantial business experience? The call was put out for volunteers. We knew that we would need as many as 800 each year. The volunteers had to commit to an 8-hour training program and a daylong assessment center program, during which they would coach one of our undergraduates.

For each of the last 6 years, hundreds of businesspeople have given their time, gladly. Why did they come? They wanted to help. Some were extraordinary managers and entrepreneurs who routinely coached their employees and saw the positive impact of their efforts to help people develop in their businesses. Others wanted to help but found that their work organizations actively discouraged coaching and mentoring. This seemed like a possible outlet for their interests. Finally, others just wanted to help. Their stories and the data that we have collected with their help provide the foundation for this book.

We began to think about what we were seeing: managers helping people learn. We wanted to know more and began to talk to our coaches about their "real" work—how they coached. We found that what they were doing was different from mentoring. They told us that they focused on helping everyone learn, not just those with whom they had special relationships. In particular, they tried to help good and even stellar performers. They did not focus their helping efforts solely on those with problems. The research on coaching by managers, strangely enough, suggests that the most talented people in business organizations are typically least likely to receive any coaching. We were seeing people whose daily practice in their business careers contrasted with this finding. We concluded that the impulse was widely distributed, though under-expressed, in the business community.

On the basis of what we were learning about coaching and its relationship to the development of talent and ultimately, organizational effectiveness, we developed executive programs for a variety of high-technology, manufacturing, communications, and financial services companies. In those programs, we also talked about helping and learned a great deal about what we could say in this regard that was useful and not so useful. Participating organizations were beginning to realize that when managers help employees, they are also helping improve their business results, particularly those associated with motivation, organizational learning, and retention.

This work became our passion, as well as our inspiration. Many people clearly wanted to help others. Too often, they just didn't know how. Our goal became to try to understand how good to great managers made use of coaching concepts to help good to great employees. The managers we talked with had a variety of good ideas about ways to effectively help people develop. Some developed through experience and some through various formal learning activities. In fact, although they did not know each other for the most part, their ideas were remarkably convergent with one another. One of the clearest messages we received from the managers who helped us learn about coaching was that coaching had to be integrated with their daily work as businesspeople. It wasn't seen as something extra they had to do. It was just part of their normal business routine.

We set as our goal the articulation of a model of coaching that reflected what these managers told us they do. We drew heavily on what we had learned from all our interactions with thousands of coaching managers over the years. When appropriate, we also drew on the research and writing of scholars and practitioners who had tried to develop a better understanding of the concepts of learning, personal development, coaching, and leadership. We wanted the model to accurately reflect what most coaching managers do, while being simple, consistent with what we know about how people learn, and most of all, easy to put into practice.

This book will give the reader a solid understanding of the model that has emerged from this effort and that describes what we call "developmental coaching." Developmental coaching is a helping relationship between a manager and, most often, his or her employees (though coaching managers may coach others in their organizations); its goal is the growth and development of employees. Developmental coaching is most often targeted at those who can best take advantage of it: good to great employees who want to learn and whose continued growth will benefit both themselves and the organization in most cases. Developmental coaching is learning oriented rather than compliance oriented. It takes place within a relationship or a context that encourages employees to take much greater responsibility for their own learning. Developmental coaching is not the job of the manager alone.

Let it be said, however, that there is still more that all of us who are concerned with building productive and humane organizations need to learn about how managers help their people learn and develop. This book presents what researchers would consider hypotheses based on qualitative research and the collected wisdom of practicing managers. These hypotheses will ultimately need to be tested and refined as we move forward. In far too many organizations, managers spend little or no time helping their employees develop. As a result, many managers don't know how to go about it. They assume it is difficult, that they don't have time, that if they start coaching they'll end up handholding, and consequently, they don't learn how to coach.

We hope to challenge these assumptions that so greatly inhibit coaching managers by describing the practice of coaching in a straightforward fashion and by making sure that learning is the shared responsibility of everyone within a work group or team. In doing so, we hope to make coaching and learning much more accessible to employees at all levels. Work and working organizations dominate our lives. The contact we have with our managers is for most of us, the most important contact we have during the at least 8 hours we work each day. If managers are not helping employees learn and develop, then significant negative consequences accrue for individuals, businesses, and society as a whole.

The reader we seek to reach is the current or future practicing manager. We believe our work is appropriate and should be useful to anyone who is trying to help his or her people learn. In addition, however, we believe that the model of developmental coaching we present will be of value to change agents, both internal and external to the organization. Coaching helps individuals and organizations learn and therefore, change. Some of the best coaching managers we have known over the years have been entrepreneurs and corporate entrepreneurs, people who are in the innovation business. We hope this book will be a great help to them. Finally, we believe that our work will also be of use to graduate students from all disciplines in MBA programs; students in other graduate programs studying leadership, organizational development, and human resource management courses; and participants in executive education programs.

The plan for the book is as follows. Chapter 1 describes what we mean by developmental coaching and in particular, how coaching can promote opportunities for experiential learning, a great untapped resource in most business organizations. Most managers don't realize how helpful coaching can be because they don't understand how people learn on the job. Chapter 2 provides an overview of the developmental coaching model. If you're in a hurry or need immediate help, Chapter 2 may get you where you need to be. Chapter 3 describes what we've learned about the mind-set of an effective coaching manager. If you're not sure you personally fit the bill or if you have questions about the qualifications required of a coaching manager, this chapter should help. Coaching, however, works best with people who want to be coached (Goleman, 2000). Who are those people? Who can take best advantage of coaching? Chapter 4 addresses these questions.

Chapter 5 describes the "coaching friendly context" and what you can do to make such a context possible. The coaching friendly context is the foundation that a coaching manager must lay if coaching is to be something other than the "pleasant part of the performance appraisal meeting." Chapters 6 through 11 describe the coaching model in detail. As we move through the model, we will be as pragmatic as we can, offering examples and self-assessment tools that should help you deepen your skills.

Chapters 12, 13, and 14 describe special applications of the coaching model. In Chapter 12, we discuss the use of developmental coaching to promote ongoing career development for employees, extending the line of sight for coaching from today or tomorrow to next year, and beyond. We hope this will be helpful to the many managers who are increasingly being asked to help employees manage their careers. In Chapter 13, we address the thorny issue of coaching for employees with performance problems. We can't give you a quick and easy response to this challenge because there is none. We believe that coaching is neither necessarily the best and certainly not the only approach to dealing with performance problems. Nevertheless, it may be worth a try. We discuss the implications of our model for dealing with performance problems and offer several examples for its application.

Chapter 14 offers advice to managers at all levels who have sent employees off for management or executive education experiences. Companies spend a tremendous amount of money on training or other formal classroom interventions, yet the learning return on this investment is not always what we might hope. The reason is that the educational activity and learning from that activity are not integrated once the employee returns to the workplace. The coaching manager needs to connect the tasks of the business with what the employee has learned in his or her time at the university. If the coaching manager does not work to help capture what has been learned, it is, sadly, very likely to be lost.

Acknowledgments

Writing this book has been a labor of love for both of us, in no small measure because of the extraordinary people we've worked with and felt support from along the way. This book is about people who do their job very, very well: coaching managers. Most of these managers are graduates of Babson College, either the undergraduate or the MBA program. They have given of their time and opened their hearts to us and have our heartfelt thanks. The Babson College Alumni Association has been instrumental in this project throughout. We particularly want to thank Patrick McGonagle, Dan Riley, and Janet Roberts, from the Alumni Association, and Anne Heller, from the Babson Alumni Office, for helping us to build connections with this incredible group of businesspeople. We have also had a chance to test many of these ideas with participants from a variety of companies, in programs at the Babson College School of Executive Education and in our consulting practices. We are grateful for their ideas, criticisms, and most important, for the interest these companies and their leaders show in trying to develop the talent in their organizations.

The Babson College Coaching for Leadership and Teamwork Program (www.Babson.edu/coach) has provided an ongoing laboratory in which we have been able to deepen our understanding of helping, coaching, and learning from experience. More than 2,000 Babson alumni and MBA students have participated in the coaching program since its inception, and we wish to thank them all. In particular, Paul Callen and Amy Weil provided their wisdom and advice as key members of our Coaching Program Advisors. Several of our coaches, Katherine Corey and Linda Rudolph, also offered great insight into the world of the coaching manager. We also want to thank Steve Schiffman, Dean of the Undergraduate Program at Babson College, for his support of this unique program. Melissa Coveney, Karen Cruickshank, and the entire staff of the Undergraduate Programs Office have all been our colleagues in this endeavor and have our deepest gratitude. From the very beginning of our work, we have received the full support of Babson's Development Office, most notably Tom Krimmel, Christine Meng, and Pat Miranda, as well as from the

College Marketing Department, especially Barbara Blair, Michael Chmura, Mark Ford, and Nancy Sullivan. We also owe a debt of gratitude to Marquita Flemming and MaryAnn Vail from Sage Publications. Their interest in promoting this project represents a vote of confidence that we hope we have earned.

James Hunt has been supported throughout by a generous grant from the Charles E. McCarthy Family Term Chair, which has provided funding for research and writing. Bob Bonnevie, faculty member of the Management Division and President of the Palmer Group, has been our partner in developing and teaching our coach training programs over the past 7 years. We greatly appreciate his wisdom and friendship. Faculty colleagues from Babson who have directly supported our efforts include Allan Cohen, Anne Donnellon, and Elaine Landry. They kept us going through the most difficult moments. We've also had intellectual support from scholars from other colleges and universities, including Kathy Kram, Iris Berdrow, and Fred Evers. We also want to acknowledge John Aboud of Organizational Dimensions and Bill Curran from Perkin Elmer for their guidance along the way. Finally, we want to thank our respective families: our wives and daughters, Chris and Molly Hunt and Carol and Sarah Weintraub, as well as Joe's mother, Sylvia Weintraub, for their love and support throughout this process. Chris Hunt and Carol Weintraub deserve special mention for proofreading the manuscript, cover to cover.

1

Introduction:
The Coaching Manager

You probably know the type: the manager of the group down the hall or someone you happened to meet from another company. When you think about a manager like this, you probably feel admiration and maybe even a bit of jealousy. If you know any coaching managers well, you have probably gotten a sense of the impact of their styles on their work and on others around them. Everyone seems to want to work for them. But managers like this seem too "touchy-feely" for you. You may dismiss their concerns as being beyond what is necessary for managers to worry about. Even so, you may still wonder: How do they do it? The people from their groups always seem to have important roles in the next new or interesting projects.

This is a portrait of the coaching manager, someone who uses coaching to develop talent in his or her business unit, as seen from the competition's point of view. It is not an exaggeration. We have talked with people like these, and we know they are out there. We also know that they can play critical roles in addressing some of the most important concerns in business today. Regardless of the state of the economy, if you are in business, you need talented people to do their best. In a down market, it may be easier to fill jobs, but it is probably no easier to fill those jobs with the right people and to keep the right people moving ahead, with commitment.

One of those airport conversations between strangers brought this point home to us recently. We happened to bump into a human resource manager from a well-thought-of marketing firm. Obviously needing to talk, and thinking she could grab some free consultation from a couple of tired business school professors, she explained that her firm was hemorrhaging employees despite the fact that the business overall was doing quite well. Their best people were leaving, drawn away in part by opportunities to earn more money but also by another, less tangible influence. Exit interviews revealed that many departing employees, including some of the very best, just didn't feel that they were learning anything. They went through the same process on very similar projects. They made the same mistakes. They did deliver value for the customer, but over time, they felt as though they were "losing their edge."

The marketing firm the woman worked for inhabits a tough and highly competitive niche (as do most). Hard work is the norm. There is little time for talk. Once you complete a project, you move on to the next. After all, billable hours can be charged only for services to the client. Everything else is overhead. This woman had asked herself and others whether they could devote at least a bit of time to the development of their employees. Perhaps the whole firm would benefit. "Absolutely not!" she was told. The stockholders want results!

Sounds like a painful way to live, doesn't it? Yet this scenario probably sounds familiar. These very bright people are struggling on behalf of their firm, for the firm's survival. They are working and living in a "day-to-day" mode. They believe that they don't have time to stop and think about what they are doing, what they are learning, and how they are developing as "knowledge" workers and as people. They also probably believe that "real development" means classroom education, and that coaching is for the employee with a problem.

Coaching Can Help, for
Employees Who Want to Learn

In this book, we propose an alternative. Over the past 10 years, we have talked about coaching with more than 2,000 practicing managers and entrepreneurs. We could say that we have trained more than 2,000 managers in the practice of coaching, but the reality is, they trained us. When we started this work, we viewed coaching as a rather linear activity in which the manager, serving as coach, provided corrective feedback, ideally in a humane way, to employees who might need to improve their performance. The managers we have worked with have made it clear that effective coaching is much more powerful and useful than merely providing feedback to someone with a performance problem.

Managers, by taking a few simple actions, can create learning discussions that we call *coaching dialogues,* which can help individuals and organizations move out of the "survival mode" toward individual and organizational growth. In all likelihood, many of the best employees in an organization will respond to such coaching because they will feel that they are learning and growing and that the boss cares enough about them to promote this process.

The managers we interviewed also told us that coaching has helped them evolve as leaders. By talking with their employees through coaching, they have a different view of how their teams are functioning and, rather than try to fix every problem themselves, they spend more time building an organization capable of adapting and competing in challenging times.

In contrast with the more linear view of coaching with which we began, we have also reluctantly come to see that coaching will not always help those individuals who have severe performance problems or are a poor "fit" with their organizations. Human resource professionals sometimes talk about coaching as a panacea for performance problems (Waldroop, 1996). Coaching is probably worth a try when someone's performance is poor. However, when an employee has severe performance problems, what might be described as "enabling factors" required for coaching to be effective may be absent. The result is that too many managers spend far too much time (their most valuable resource) trying to coach when coaching may not work. In fact, the amount of time spent trying to "correct" one employee far exceeds the amount of time that most managers spend with good, competent employees. One of the main premises in this book is that managers will accomplish far more by focusing their coaching efforts on the great majority of talented employees—those who are already effective or who show potential—than on employees with performance problems.

Coaching requires a two-way, fairly committed relationship (note that we don't say "totally committed," which wouldn't be realistic and usually isn't necessary). The coach and learner (usually represented in this book as the manager and coachee, or employee) have to be able to engage with one another to achieve the goal of *learning from*—as opposed to rewarding or punishing—the coachee's performance. Both manager and employee must be ready to take a few risks. The coachee must want to learn and be open to learning from the coach, with a minimum of defensiveness. The coaching manager must be willing to let his or her employees struggle with what they don't know. Sometimes, in the interest of learning, coachees must be allowed to make mistakes. Coaching, particularly as described in this book, is then likely to benefit the people who have a desire to become "even better": those who are engaged and excited about their work, who can take some responsibility for their work, who want feedback and seek it out, who want to talk about their development, and whose goals are at least to a degree aligned with the goals of the business unit or the firm. Coaching sets the stage for personal growth for those who want to grow.

Why Don't More Managers Coach?

We have shared the previous conclusion with many managers. Few have objected to our hypothesis. Most good to great employees would like more support with their development, and coaching from the manager is a logical tactic for addressing that need. Unfortunately, it doesn't seem to happen to nearly the degree that it should. Despite the fact that employees are interested in coaching, few are clamoring for it. Something is missing.

Although most managers agree with our point, there is nevertheless a great deal of confusion in the business world about the role that organizations and their managers can and should play in the development of their employees. This confusion has led to inactivity. Managers don't coach, and employees don't ask for coaching. In the world of business, we have created a stigma against learning and against coaching for both the manager and the employee.

We have asked the following question in our coach training sessions since 1996: "How many of you have had your manager devote 100% of a 60-minute (or even a 30-minute) block of time to observing you work on some task and then spend an additional 30 minutes or so talking with you about what he or she saw, in a way you really felt promoted your growth?" Although we occasionally do see a hand go up, most of the time, we do not.

We have also heard the gamut of noncoaching stories: "I found out I'd gotten my raise when it came in my check. I have no idea what I did to deserve that." "I haven't seen or talked to my manager in 6 months. I guess that means I'm doing okay." "I had my performance appraisal over the phone." Our personal favorite: "Coaching is for wimps." Such stories have forced us to ponder the obvious question: Is this any way to treat talented employees? We should add that the sample of companies from which participants in our training programs are drawn include some of the best on the planet.

We interpret all this to mean that real coaching, at least as we define it below, is very rarely practiced, an observation supported by a substantial body of research (Lombardo & Eichinger, 2001). A self-fulfilling prophecy is the result. Little coaching takes place in most organizations, so people don't expect to be coached even though they may wish otherwise. They don't expect coaching, so they don't ask for it—and not surprisingly, because they don't ask, they don't get it. Most likely, they are also confused about coaching and may not know how to ask for it or how to use it. Furthermore, if they were to request coaching from their managers, they would quite likely be talking with people who don't really know how to coach or are afraid to coach. And so it goes. (Of course, if they work for a manager who believes that coaching is for wimps, they'll rightly be afraid to ask.)

Contrast this view with the vision put forth by management authors Evered and Selman (1989). They speculated that if (a) managers and organizations actually encouraged people to ask for coaching and (b) made them feel safe in doing so and (c) if managers could get used to coaching, a potent internal market for coaching would emerge. Employees would start to expect and even demand to be coached, and the stigma, the fear of retribution for admitting that they don't know something, would disappear rather quickly.

We know that most people want to learn (Senge, 1990; McGregor, 1985). Study after study shows that meaningful work, challenge, learning, and career development are high on the list of factors that workers look for in their relationships with employers. The coaching managers we have talked to tell us that this is indeed the case. They have created conditions under which their employees feel relatively comfortable asking for coaching. Some coaching managers have been able to achieve this even while working in companies not necessarily known for promoting the development of employees. We suggest, then, that coaching is a vastly underused resource available to most managers. However, this resource is a skill that one must learn and practice.

Developmental Coaching

In this book, we talk about what we call *developmental coaching*. The model of developmental coaching we describe may be quite different from the mental models that you currently hold about coaching. At the end of this chapter, we ask the reader to take a few minutes to consider the images that come into your mind when you think about coaching.

We define developmental coaching as an interaction between two people, usually a manager and an employee, aimed at helping the employee learn from the job in order to promote his or her development. Learning is primary, though of course, learning usually leads to improved performance. We outline the process of developmental coaching in Chapter 2. Briefly, developmental coaching requires that the employee, with the manager's help, be encouraged to reflect on his or her actions or decisions in relation to a current work challenge: that is, to self-assess one's performance. The manager encourages this self-assessment by asking a few basic questions while withholding criticism or advice, creating the coaching dialogue mentioned above. After the coachee has had time to reflect on his or her performance, the coaching manager may also provide feedback to the learner to help the person get a clearer sense of how that performance appears from another perspective. The two of them then try to understand the difference between current and desired performance, the meaning of that difference, and what needs to be done to address the gap.

Developmental coaching, in contrast to remedial coaching, is not driven by the organization's agenda but rather by the individual's. Real learning, particularly for adults, is almost always driven by the learner's sense of wanting or needing to know. Managers can't make someone else learn. They may be able to insist on compliance, but they can't insist on learning. Adults learn what will be helpful to them as they define needs or goals.

Learning driven by the learner, in an organizational context, may sound quite radical. We are assuming here that in the hiring process, the firm selects people who share some goals or interests in common with the firm. If that overlap of goals exists, the coaching manager can share responsibility for development with the employee. We assume that employees, on balance, have been properly selected and want to learn and grow in a fashion that will help their organizations. Consequently, developmental coaching that creates learning can offer important benefits to the organization.

Coaching and Learning

The idea that managers and employees can share responsibility for learning is a very adaptive one. We make the related assumption that in most organizations, everyone needs to keep learning. Most businesses and not-for-profits confront a range of competitive threats to their survival. These threats include globalization, disruptive technologies, changing societal values, the Internet, and the rest of the list you've grown accustomed to hearing about. The only way for a firm to survive, let alone prosper, is for enough people in the firm to learn how to adapt to and master these challenges so that the organization can respond appropriately.

The underlying theory behind how adults learn and adapt, and how they can in turn help organizations learn and adapt, is well understood. Learning is more than just action, though action is part of learning. Wolfe and Kolb (1984) have described a useful way to understand learning as requiring four interrelated steps. To learn, the individual must act and then make sense of the action and its implications. Action, Step 1 in the learning process, creates experience that registers with the actor in Step 2. This is where development stops in most organizations (Hicks & Peterson, 1997). Unfortunately, there is no guarantee that anything has been learned up to this point in the process.

However, if the experience of an action is subject to self-reflection, discussion, and external feedback, in Step 3 in the process, it is possible for the individual to then draw new conclusions about the nature of that action. The learner generates a new set of ideas, a new theory if you will, regarding the action. The learner thinks about what worked and what didn't work, why, and what might be tried differently. The new theory is subject to experimental testing, in Step 4, as the individual strives to improve his or her performance.

Say that you are trying to help a new product development team get their meeting habits started in the right way. Based on your previous experience, you start with the assumption that a tightly structured agenda can help a group stick to its task. You bring in such an agenda to the first meeting and find that a number of the more creative members of this new team seem to just want to chat with each other. Frustrated, you get angry and become more directive. Your manager, a gifted coach, happens to be observing you. After the meeting, he takes a few minutes to ask you for your thoughts about how it went. You express frustration at your inability to get the crazy creative types to stay on track. He asks you whether you've ever worked with people like this before, and you say no. You then wonder aloud whether your approach to the creative types was perhaps not all that helpful. Your boss, agreeing with you, gives you some feedback to the effect that the creative types seemed to stop paying attention when you became more forceful and directive. A new theory about what is going on occurs to you. Your previous model of effective team leadership, a model that had always worked in the past, may need to be modified. Maybe you need to encourage a team like this to be a little more social with one another as a way of getting started. You resolve to try this next time. You leave this coaching interaction feeling as though you have gained a useful insight into how teams run. You feel as though you're learning something and even feel a little more confident in your ability.

In this example, you have learned to expand your own set of assumptions about how to be an effective team leader. You didn't just keep doing more of what you normally do. Such automatic behavior, continuing to do what we know even when it doesn't work, seems to reflect human nature to a degree, but it is also a hallmark of a failure to learn (Argyris & Schon, 1977). Not surprisingly perhaps, it is all too common in the workplace. We do the same thing over and over again, hoping that this time it will work but ready to blame someone else if it doesn't.

What coaching can do is to help people, both managers and employees, stop and think about what they are doing in the here and now, on their current jobs. Coaching helps people extract readily available learning opportunities, think about what is novel or important (and in most businesses these days, there is plenty of that), and grow "in place." When coaching occurs as we have described it here, the employees feel they are learning, and they are. Employees are also being directly challenged to keep improving their performance, and in that sense, they are being challenged to work at even higher levels of effectiveness. Their performance, and ultimately the firm's competitiveness, can improve in the process.

The Coaching Manager
and Emotional Intelligence (EQ)

Many people use—and abuse—the word *coach*. In particular, many managers feel that providing feedback is all there is to coaching. We struggled for years, with the help of the coaching managers in our programs, to gain a clearer understanding of what was so special about what they were doing. Ultimately, it became obvious that they were promoting self-reflection in others. Effective coaching managers were successful because they not only gave feedback, but gave feedback to people they had *helped make ready for feedback* through the process of reflection. Reflection is the step too often missing in employee development. Reflection allows individual learners to pursue what is important to them, not just what is important to the manager. Reflection allows people to take ownership of their own problems. Learner ownership of the learning process drives development because it fosters and validates the importance of self-directed learning as an important aspect of successful job performance. Isaac Stern, the great violinist, who died in 2001, captured the power of this concept when he described the outcome of his work with his own mentor: "He taught me to teach myself, which is the greatest thing a teacher can do" (Steinberg, 2001).

Readers familiar with the concept of emotional intelligence (EQ) will see important parallels with the work we are describing here (Goleman, 1998). Emotional intelligence represents a breakthrough in our understanding of the factors that lead to superior performance. Individuals with high levels of emotional intelligence have a clearer sense of who they are, are better able to manage their own feelings, have relatively high levels of personal motivation, are able to empathize with others, and are socially skillful.

The research to date indicates that employees who score high on measures of emotional intelligence are likely to be much more effective at their work, regardless of their jobs. Engineers with high levels of emotional intelligence are more likely to end up with more patents. Salespeople with high levels of emotional intelligence are more likely to be superior salespeople. Leaders with high levels of emotional intelligence are more likely to be superior leaders.

Note that there is a link between emotional intelligence and job performance even for those in highly technical skills. There are two reasons for this link. First, the ability to see yourself clearly helps you comprehend and adjust for your own strengths and weaknesses. For example, a great engineer who knows he's lousy at designing a certain kind of manufacturing process is able to admit that to himself and find someone else who can do the job effectively. Second, the interpersonal aspects of emotional intelligence relate directly to the ability to take even a highly technical idea and bring others to the task of working on that idea. Fortunately, it appears that one's emotional intelligence can improve under the right circumstances.

Developmental coaching relies heavily on the idea that learning requires a healthy dose of reflection and self-assessment on the part of the learner. Self-assessment, particularly when coupled with feedback, is very likely to improve self-awareness. Suppose someone, say your boss, asks you to stop and think about your role on a team that produced a new marketing brochure and asks you to talk about your strengths and weaknesses on the project: You are being offered an opportunity to build your capacity for self-awareness. You don't have to talk about emotional intelligence, per se, to promote its development.

The benefits of helping any employee build self-awareness are significant. Most of us have a tendency to believe our skills are superior. Many of us learn, painfully, that not all of our skills are so superior. Miscalculations of this kind can wreck a project or a career. Coaching may not always be able to provide an avenue of rehabilitation for those already in performance trouble. However, a heightened sense of self-awareness, developed in a context of coaching, may help prevent performance problems in the first place.

Beyond self-awareness, coaching offers the opportunity to help build emotional intelligence in other ways as well. Encouragement and support for an employee's strengths, for instance, can enhance an individual's self-esteem and motivation to achieve. The experience of being coached teaches empathy and models effective social skills. Finally, it takes self-regulation, the ability to manage one's emotions, for a manager not to jump in and fix a problem, and it takes self-regulation for an employee to muster up the courage to admit that he or she has made a mistake. Developmental coaching is, then, intimately linked with the ability of an individual and an organization to grow emotionally in ways that can contribute to their success.

Coaching Isn't the Same as Mentoring

Many managers are concerned that coaching, like mentoring, will take a great deal of time and emotional energy. The thought of having to participate in a long-term emotional relationship is anxiety-provoking. We do believe that coaching can create closer relationships between employees and managers. However, coaching relationships don't have to be emotionally intense to create an effective context for learning and development.

Coaching is not the same as mentoring (Kram, 1985). Mentoring typically involves a more ongoing relationship. Effective mentors do use some of the same coaching practices we discuss in this book. However, we believe that coaching doesn't necessarily require the type of emotional bond usually associated with mentoring. In fact, our research suggests that coaching can take place in a rather brief episode, sometimes as short as a few minutes, between relative strangers. Undoubtedly, good chemistry between the manager and the employee can promote coaching and also make the experience of coaching even more satisfying. However, if the manager makes it "psychologically safe" for the employee to openly talk about what he or she wants or needs to learn, that is often enough to create learning.

Coaching: Everybody Learns

There is an additional benefit to coaching at the organizational level. Data from studies such as the Gallup Organization suggest that *organizational,* not just personal, productivity will improve as a result of manager-facilitated learning (Buckingham & Coffman, 1999). The U.S. Army, for example, has made a significant effort to leverage this opportunity (Garvin, 2000). After any military action around the world, all involved army units conduct an "After Action Review" (AAR). The AAR uses a coaching methodology very similar to one described here, in a team context. In the smallest appropriate unit, the unit commander and his or her direct reports "stop the action" by meeting and talking about what happened. Following a highly structured procedure, all involved reflect on what they did well, not so well, and need to do better next time. Later in the book, we describe how the army makes this coaching process work.

However, we stress here that the individuals responsible for creating such learning opportunities are the equivalent of line managers in a business setting. In addition, the army insists that AARs take place after every important activity. They make coaching a priority and part of the routine. Coaching becomes second nature. People expect it, and they know how to make use of it.

The army learns in the process. The officer or facilitator leading the dialogue gathers data from an AAR. (The data do not include "who said what," only key learning points.) Data on what has been learned are pooled to help larger units within the army adapt to new demands and challenges. The army's ability to use a coaching-like intervention to learn on the fly (even under combat conditions) has been a key factor in helping the organization deal with change. The most common duties for the U.S. Army over the past decade, after all, have been peacekeeping, peacemaking, and disaster relief. These dangerous duties are poorly understood and fall outside the traditional training given to soldiers.

When a manager creates a coaching dialogue with an individual or team, he or she is creating an opportunity for everyone, including the firm, to learn. Organizational learning coupled with the growth and development of the best employees can represent a significant competitive advantage for a firm. The cost is not high. It takes a bit of time and thought to capture what has been learned and circulate the insights to the rest of a team or firm.

Making It Work: The Transition to Becoming a Coaching Manager

We are not suggesting that coaching others is necessarily easy. Coaching requires work—specifically, the development of new skills for most managers. Most managers and leaders we know are assertive and results oriented. They tend to jump in and push to get the job done. They are more comfortable that way.

Good managers aren't afraid to confront problems, or at least if they are, they have found a way to control that fear. They are also good at influencing others to work toward a goal or a vision. However, they aren't always as effective at the discipline of stopping and reflecting on their work or the work of others. The push toward action reflects a sense of urgency: "If we don't press ahead and get it done, we might not succeed." The new coaching manager must be willing to take the small amount of time necessary to be effective at harvesting the opportunities for learning at the individual and organizational level, which are readily available in most firms. The challenge for the manager has as much or more to do with changing his or her mind-set as it does with finding more hours in the day.

There does seem to be one ingredient that is critical to the success of the coaching managers we interviewed for this book. They all seem to have an interest in helping others. You can't help people learn if you see them simply as a means to an end. Although most organizational mission statements these days say something about respect for the individual, effective coaching really requires that respect. Inherent in this respect is a bit of trust in the notion that most people want to grow. The coaching manager has to be willing to step back and trust that his or her employees share the same overall goals and want to be entrusted with their own learning.

We concur with other writers, such as Bradford and Cohen (1999), who propose that the most effective leader for our time is *not* the hero who leads the charge up the hill and takes the first bullet! Rather, the most effective model for leadership is one that promotes shared effort toward and responsibility for achieving a goal and also builds organizational capability along the way. Our approach to coaching is consistent with that model.

Your Approach to Coaching
Determines the Outcome of Your Effort

Coaching is a very old form of human activity. It has been a fixture of athletics for centuries. You have almost certainly had occasion to interact with a coach. Before taking a tour of the model of developmental coaching we present in this book, we ask you to reflect a bit on coaches you have known. Take a minute and jot down some notes in response to the following self-assessment questions.

Self-Assessment 1.1:
Your Existing Mental Models of Coaching

As may not be the case in your studies of other subjects, you already know a great deal about coaching. You have probably worked with a coach. You have seen coaches on TV. You have read about them. You may have received coaching from managers or other individuals over the course of your career. These experiences will shape your approach to coaching. You will see how those models compare with the model presented in the remainder of this book.

Think about the best coaches you have known or have some familiarity with:

- What did they do that was most useful?
- In what ways have they influenced your thinking about what coaching really means?

Think about the worst coaches you have known or have some familiarity with:

- What did they do that was not useful?
- In what ways have they influenced your thinking about what coaching really means?

If you were honest with yourself about the influence these models have had on you and your beliefs about coaching . . .

- What beliefs do you bring to the task of coaching in business that you probably need to stick with?
- What beliefs do you bring to the task of coaching in business that you may need to change?

In evaluating your responses, consider the following question: Did the best coaches push for compliance, or did they push for growth and learning? In other words, did the best coaches do nothing more than make sure you did your job? Alternatively, did the best coaches make sure that you learned something while you were doing your job? We suspect that most of you, when thinking about good versus not-so-good coaches, will see the difference.

To clarify this point further, we'll speak more directly to the kinds of learning outcomes you might think about while considering what you learned along with way. Tim Hall has proposed four different kinds of learning outcomes to consider when assessing what we have learned (Hall, 1986). Two of those outcomes are short-term: We may learn to perform our current jobs more effectively, or we may feel differently about our current jobs. These are valuable goals directly relevant to coaching, but there is more. A manager who insists on compliance or only offers feedback may well see at least temporary improvements in performance.

Two of the outcomes are more long-term in nature: We come to see ourselves differently (our identities evolve), and we become more adaptable and more able to deal with change in ourselves and the world around us. Just a bit of prodding can usually help individuals learn to perform their work more effectively, which will make them feel better about what they are doing. We would guess that the learning outcomes you experienced from coaches you found particularly effective left you feeling even more strongly about the experience. Perhaps you felt more confident or had a clearer sense of your strengths and weaknesses, likes, and dislikes. We would also guess that you left the experience feeling more capable of dealing with the world and interested in taking on new challenges. It is our hope that the model of developmental coaching we present in overview form in the next chapter will give you the tools that can help create both the short-term and long-term gains just described. We predict, based on what we've learned from the managers we've worked with, that you will accrue some of the same results yourself.

2

An Overview of Developmental Coaching

IN THIS CHAPTER, YOU'LL LEARN ABOUT THE BASIC MODEL OF DEVELOPMENTAL COACHING, WHICH INCLUDES THE FOLLOWING ELEMENTS:

- A coaching friendly context
- A helpful mind-set
- A "coach-able" learner
- Stopping the action and starting the coaching dialogue
- Knowing what is important
- Observing without inferring
- Providing balanced and helpful feedback
- Collaboratively interpreting what needs to change
- Setting a goal for change and following up

Developmental Coaching: An Example

John and Mary are standing in the airport ticket line in preparation for flights back to the home office. Mary is John's boss at Software, Inc. They happened to be in town at the same time, working with different potential customers. John spent the morning trying to convince Internet Marketing, Inc., a growing e-commerce business, of the merits of a new system being sold by Software, Inc. Their new product helps e-commerce companies manage the mountain of marketing information they accumulate, more effectively than previously thought possible. Mary notes that John doesn't look very happy.

Mary:	So, John, how was it over at Internet Marketing this morning?
John:	Great, that is if you consider losing the sale great.
Mary:	Not so good, huh. What happened?
John:	I blew it, big time.
Mary:	I hear the pain, but what happened?
John:	You know those "dot-com" people haven't got a clue as to what they want in general, let alone how they manage marketing data. I couldn't sell them anything.
Mary:	Well, we've got a few minutes here. Fill me in.
John:	You know how they argue with each other. The CFO and the IT Chief were going at it. The marketing VP looked disgusted. These people acted like I wasn't even in the room.
Mary:	So what did you do?
John:	Kept on trying to get their attention, point out how good our new release was, and how it seemed to me it was a waste of time for them to keep hashing this out. I was pretty blunt with them. You know my style, take no prisoners. . . .
Mary:	Did it work?
John:	No. I couldn't even get their attention. You know, Mary, I'm really frustrated with "potential" accounts like this. I need to nail some of these e-commerce companies, but every time I start pushing, I don't know, it just doesn't work. Maybe this market just isn't going to work out. Maybe it's me.
Mary:	Let's wait a second before we abandon them—or you. Why do you think the direct approach didn't work?
John:	They were just too caught up in their own disagreements, their own problems, to really listen to me. I encouraged them to focus on what we could do for them, but it just didn't work. In part, I know the problem is me. When I get frustrated, I become too direct. I can see that now.
Mary:	It does sound frustrating. What do you think you might have done differently?
John:	I know I should probably have tried to facilitate something, you know, help them figure out the features they want. Make like a consultant to them. I tried to see the

ideas in common that each of them were missing. I know.
. . . We've talked about trying things like that with these
kinds of customers. You have to listen to them, right? And
then keep trying to help them clarify what they're trying
to do so they can see what we might want from them.
Listening isn't my strong suit, as you know.

Mary: I know that has been a problem for you in the past, but
when I've seen you on sales calls recently, I get a clear sense
that you're much more attuned to what the customer is
trying to say. I don't think the gap is as great as it used to
be. What now? Is it really over with them?

John: No, it isn't yet, but I need a different approach. I guess
I have to get better at facilitative selling, learn how to
work with a group like this, and not end up getting
stuck in their indecision. When I listened to all three of
them, I was pretty convinced that with a few product
modifications, we could actually meet all their needs. I
know I shouldn't try to get them to stop arguing, because
somehow what they're arguing about is important to
them.

Mary: You're probably right about that. But what are you going
to do?

John: Well, they did say they'd be willing to talk again. I could
set something up for tomorrow, but I'm going to be
working *way* out of my comfort zone. Any chance you
could come back into town, just to sit in, watch what I do,
give me some feedback? I'm not saying I want you to take
over, just critique.

Mary: I think you're on the right track about both the best
approach and the fact that you've got to find a way to deal
with the frustration that clients like this inflict. Let's get
specific. What are you doing to do differently?

John: First of all, now that I've had a chance to think about it
away from the action, I think I should go back in, ask each
of them to review what they want, write it down on a
board or overhead, and then talk about how we can give
them the win/win/win. The tough part for me is going to
be to listen to them go over the same ground again, but
I'll keep quiet and do it.

Mary: That sounds like the right approach. I'd like to be there
myself, but unfortunately, I have to go to L.A. tonight. I
would like you to get some feedback from someone on
our team and see how it goes. It isn't easy to force yourself to listen as much as I think you'll probably have to,

	especially when the customer doesn't have their act together. Who else can you get in to watch you work and debrief what happened?
John:	I think I could get Jorgi [who works for John] to sit in. He's a good people person, and he's not afraid to tell me what he thinks.
Mary:	Okay, can you brief him in detail on what you're trying to do before the meeting—you know, give him a sense of the kind of approach you're going to be taking?
John:	Yeah, no problem.
Mary:	John, I know this kind of selling is new for you. Do you think you've had enough training in this facilitative approach, honestly? I don't want to set you up for failure here.
John:	No, I know the concepts, I just have to try it.
Mary:	Okay, sounds like a plan. Here's what I'd ask of you. First of all, John, I think this is very important, for both you and the company. Goal one: Get the sale. Goal two: Try working with them as a facilitator, get some feedback from Jorgi, and let's see what you learn from it. Why don't you leave me a voice mail tomorrow night, after the meeting with them? Try to give me a thorough rundown on what you did differently, how it worked, and what you learned from it. If you don't feel as though you made any progress toward your own learning, regardless of the status of the potential sale, consider setting up a third meeting next Monday. I'll be in town, and I'll clear my schedule just to sit in and watch. How does this sound to you?
John:	Fine. We'll get it done.
Mary:	Okay, but remember, we're trying to get two things done—the sale, yes, but also getting you to really move out of your comfort zone with customers like this and try a new approach. Good luck.

The coaching session you've just read demonstrates what can happen when a manager and an employee seize the opportunity to coach, to reflect, and to learn. Such opportunities are often ignored due to a lack of understanding of what can be achieved by a coaching dialogue, time constraints (though this interaction was quite short), frustration with an employee who lost a sale, or the fear that trying to help the employee would not be well received. It didn't take much time, probably about 15 minutes. The results were as follows:

- Although the company did miss a sale, at least for now, John owned the problem. Responding to a simple question, he identified what he may have been doing wrong and the changes he thinks he should make. Note that his manager did not have to give him any critical feedback. No useless conflict occurred.
- John is still going after the sale and may yet land it. However, he may also now become much more valuable to the company. He is a good performer, and if he can learn to work with the most difficult customers, he may become a great performer.
- John also knows that Mary is really trying to help him. He feels that even though he's had a problem with this situation, the situation is being treated as an opportunity to help him grow. His commitment to Software, Inc., is likely to be even stronger than before.

Sound good? We suspect that it does. We also suspect that you are thinking that this game was rigged. It was all too easy. Mary was too good at this (though she didn't do much more than ask a few questions), and John was too open to her approach. We agree, the game was rigged. Mary rigged it. She had worked hard to create an environment in her work group that supported this kind of learning interaction.

In our view, coaching doesn't have to be terribly complicated if the right context has been set, people that are involved bring a coaching mind-set to the task, and they follow a few basic principles. In this chapter, we give you an overview of a developmental coaching model that can be applied in any context. In the following chapters, we then explore each point in greater depth, while providing more examples and self-assessment tools to help you in the learning process. You may be tempted, particularly if you are as busy as we think you are, to stop reading after you have completed this chapter. We hope you keep going. You do need to spend some serious time in advance thinking about how to use the model in your own unique context to recoup your investment.

Why Such a Simple Model?

Having worked with so many managers on the challenges of coaching, we came to realize the obvious: that coaching was not the primary goal of most managers. Managers who do coach have a very simple set of concepts that guide their work. A simple approach to coaching helps the coaching manager prioritize other business demands, while at the same time paying attention to employee development and organization building. Coaching managers don't want to imply to employees that they will help them develop—and then not follow through. They need a model that can be "slipped into" their daily routine. We hope this model meets that challenge.

The complaint of lack of time can also be an excuse. We should note, however, that the time barrier seems much more daunting than it really is. As one participant in a recent coach training program told us, "You just have to do it." However, another participant in the same program said, "I now know that my boss has been coaching me for years, he just never called it that. He just kind of inserted it into our discussions." The real issue for many managers is that they simply don't know how to coach. A simple model that can be practiced can help managers build confidence in their ability to coach. Perhaps the most important reason for presenting the basic, simple model of coaching we use here is that in our experience, it works. Let us reiterate the ultimate goals of coaching. Here are those goals, as we see them:

- To promote employee development through learning
- To build organizational capability through sharing learning with others
- To build better relationships and more effective communications in general in an organization
- To promote employee retention through the provision of experiences that help employees meet their personal goals for growth

Seizing the opportunity to create positive, learning-oriented dialogues represents a simple way to meet those goals.

Having said all this, we must emphasize again that although the model is simple and flexible, using it does take practice. The more you coach, particularly the more you create a demand for coaching among your employees, the more likely you are to become comfortable seizing small coaching moments, as well as using coaching to address major challenges. In addition, the more you create a demand for coaching, the more you can expect your employees to put themselves in the coachee role and generate their own opportunities to create a "coaching dialogue," not only with their manager but also with their peers. The model is presented in graphic form in Figure 2.1.

A Coaching Friendly Context

We said above that Mary rigged the game to make it easier to coach than one might expect. She did so by repeatedly signaling to her employees that they should expect interactions with her and with each other that had the purpose of helping to promote learning. Coaching interactions need to be "safe." Normally, such interactions should have little or nothing to do with evaluation or performance appraisal.

The only personal commitment required of the coaching manager and the employee should be to ask questions and engage in a dialogue that will be

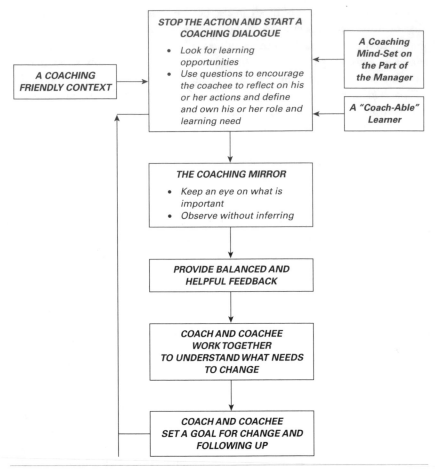

Figure 2.1   An Overview of the Developmental Coaching Model

helpful to the employee and the business. When the coaching manager takes such a stance, and employees believe in it, things change. In a coaching friendly context, employees develop a new set of assumptions about working with their manager. The employee who has learned coaching friendly assumptions holds ideas such as the following:

• It is okay to talk with your manager about a problem, a personal performance goal, or a career goal. You won't be criticized for seeking out coaching. In fact, your manager believes it is part of his or her job to help you learn and improve your performance. You may ultimately receive more critical feedback if you don't seek out and make use of coaching and feedback.

- However, your manager isn't going to solve the problem for you or try to make you grow if you don't want to. Coaching is profoundly different from a pat on the back (though sometimes it does include a pat on the back). Your manager is going to talk about performance goals, listen, ask questions, and challenge you to learn and to try new approaches to your work and your career. In a coaching friendly context, employees expect a lot of questions, but not necessarily a lot of answers.

- Your manager will try, when possible, to put you into situations in which you'll learn, on the job, through challenge and feedback; the feedback will be constructed to help you deepen your ability to assess your own performance, not just to grade your performance.

- Your manager *is* watching your performance, though without any intent to micromanage or usurp your responsibilities. Your manager is watching your performance to gain data that will help provide balanced feedback.

- Even if your manager is responsible for grading your performance through an appraisal system (a periodic event in most firms), coaching will be continuous. It won't take place only during periodic performance appraisal sessions.

Though these assumptions all sound appealing, they may be difficult for your employees to understand or to trust at first. Some may not like to work for a manager who doesn't "tell them the right answer." Others may not want to believe that they need coaching or that coaching has anything to offer. Many of us have gotten used to being quite independent over the years in our organizations. In a coaching friendly context, employees don't experience their managers as trying to undermine their independence. Far from it. In fact, a coaching manager is watching for the purpose of helping employees perform at an ever-higher level of effectiveness. If you want to make it all the way to the top, your manager is there to help you.

If you've never coached before, and if your employees are not used to your asking coaching questions (see below), you may need to signal them in advance that you are going to be trying something new. It may even be necessary to reassure them that coaching does not mean that they are being constantly appraised about their performance. Then you'll have to "walk the talk": follow through on keeping it safe to honestly deal with important questions. Try asking others for coaching and feedback help and in doing so, serve as a model coaching consumer as well as a provider.

The coaching friendly context creates the market for coaching we discuss in Chapter 1 (Evered & Selman, 1989). If it won't hurt them materially or psychologically, people really want to know how they are doing and how they can improve. The great athlete would not think of going to the Olympics without a passion for improving his or her performance and a coach to help in that process. We expect to see coaches, several of them usually, working with any team, even a team with the youngest athletes. If the coach left the sidelines, the team would, rightly, feel abandoned. That is the model for a coaching friendly context.

This stands in stark contrast with the experience that most of us have had with coaching in the business world to date: Coaching takes place during the performance appraisal, if at all. But when the manager has to focus on evaluation and make important compensation decisions, coaching is suspect. The manager, of necessity, is focusing on the needs and goals of the organization, not the employee. (Did you ever get the sense at performance review time that your manager was looking for problems so as to grade you lower and keep the compensation program on track?) Critical feedback, delivered to meet the needs of the organization and not of the individual employee, will be responded to with reactions ranging from skepticism to defensive hostility. Why trust someone's critical feedback when they stand to gain from your failure? The performance appraisal is typically not a coaching friendly context.

Unfortunately, this problem is inherent to coaching that occurs in the supervisory relationship, even when it isn't performance appraisal time. Supervisors are responsible for appraisal and development in most organizations, two activities with conflicting goals, driven by conflicting interests (Beer, 1997). A good solution to the problem has not been found. A number of companies believe it is important to break these two activities apart. In our experience, it is possible to create a coaching friendly context by keeping a separation between the two and signaling when you as a manager are *coaching*, versus appraising and making employment decisions.

Creating a demand on the part of employees for coaching makes managing the conflict between development and evaluation easier. Employees under such circumstances seek out opportunities to learn in discussions with their managers. The coachee becomes a true partner in learning, responsible for his or her own career, able to bring up developmental concerns without fear of reprisal, and active in soliciting coaching help (Phillips, 1998).

A "Coaching Mind-Set" on the Part of the Manager

The coaching friendly context begins, of course, with the coach. Mary had to expand her own repertoire of behaviors beyond the take-charge style that had brought her the success she had achieved prior to becoming more of a coaching manager. The reality for her is that she may not have much of a choice. She needs leaders everywhere. She can't do it all herself.

To coach, in our experience, you have to assume a different frame of mind than when you are engaged in the day-to-day practice of making decisions as a manager. Experience suggests that there are two related components of a coaching mind-set: developing a coaching identity and learning to be helpful rather than evaluative.

It should be acknowledged at the outset that coaching represents a stretch task for many managers. They have typically achieved initial success by "doing." Coaching represents both a shift of one's attention toward the performance of others (probably not that big a stretch for many managers) and a shift of identity to "one who helps others do" (probably a big stretch). Some managers will not achieve this identity transition. They may have a very difficult time becoming comfortable with the role. Perhaps just as important, the motivational distance may be too great. Some managers are only happy if they are in the trenches, doing the work. You probably won't know how you feel about coaching until you have tried it.

We suggest, given the potential power of coaching to enhance performance, that all managers acquaint themselves with the practice. At the very minimum, they will then be in a better position to support an organizational culture that encourages coaching, even if they don't feel inclined to become coaching managers themselves. However, we also suggest that all managers try integrating at least some actual coaching into their work. Many managers avoid coaching because they don't understand it and don't feel competent to coach. Once trained, managers often find that they are much more likely to engage in coaching than they would have predicted.

In addition to focusing on the work of others rather than doing the work yourself, the best coaching represents an act of caring and putting aside your own agenda, feelings, and frustrations to help another individual achieve his or her goals. (As mentioned in Chapter 1, if an organization has done a good job of hiring employees, there will be a significant overlap between the goals of the individual employee and the goals of his or her coach.) We, and others, have asked this question of many managers who have gone through the experience of being coached: "What did your coach do that was helpful?" Our research informants told us that when at their best, "My coach . . ."

- "Seemed to genuinely want to help"
- "Listened; she didn't impose her own agenda"
- "Asked me what I was trying to accomplish"
- "Helped me think the problem through for myself"
- "Told me about my strengths as well as my weaknesses"

This doesn't mean that the coach has to be "soft" and provide only positive feedback. Think again about great athletic coaches. Many are known for being quite tough. However, they are tough in a way that is experienced by the coachee as helpful and motivating. Good coaching leaves an individual feeling (a) motivated to try harder and (b) that he or she has learned something in the process. Good coaches don't leave the coachee feeling as though they were interested only in their own goals. Coaches need to begin by asking themselves the fundamental question: "Do I really feel that what I am about to say will be helpful to the coachee receiving my feedback?"

Interestingly, many managers who have learned to coach have told us that they experienced unanticipated personal growth from their efforts. They report a better understanding of the nature of leadership and teamwork, a positive feeling about themselves from helping others, and enhanced process skills that develop from the act of trying to teach those skills to others. They become better leaders.

The "Coach-Able" Learner

Mary also rigged the game with a little help from human resources and the managers who bring talent into Software, Inc. They look for people who, in addition to being technically good at their jobs, are open to learning about themselves, their interpersonal effectiveness, and the business. John may not sound like the kind of person who typically takes to coaching. He's a hard-charging, independent type who really wants to prove himself every step of the way. John has a great strength, however, in that he realizes that a little effort devoted to learning and self-improvement can help him become even more like the person he aspires to be. In our experience, high-potential employees often possess this characteristic and are willing to take coaching if, and this is important, they see it as valuable. They like coaching best when it helps them stretch and develop a new skill that will increase their range.

Coaching, then, won't work for everyone. We have repeatedly seen good and even excellent coaches who are occasionally unable to get through to an employee. The results of a manager's and an employee's failure to establish a useful coaching relationship are unfortunate. Much time is lost in the process as well. The potential coachee hasn't learned much. Often, he or she will leave the organization and run into similar problems somewhere else.

Good coaching requires a motivated coachee who (a) wants to learn, (b) is able to tolerate the process of reflecting on his or her work, and (c) therefore can deal with feedback that may be appropriately challenging. Imagine a father watching in awe while his daughter is on the receiving end of very tough feedback from her horseback riding coach. One wonders what would happen if the parent were to talk to her that way. ("Can't you keep your head up? You look silly up there. . . .") Why does she put up with such feedback? The answer is quite simple. She signed up for it. She wanted to become very competent at horseback riding. It fits with her goals and her view of herself. She understands that effectiveness doesn't come easy and is willing to pay the price. She doesn't take the feedback personally. She is a "good" coachee.

A manager can't always control who his or her employees will be. However, given the nature of the challenges facing our organizations today, we strongly suggest that, along with other competencies, recruiters and hiring managers look explicitly for people (a) who really want to be part of the organization, (b) who have goals that overlap with the goals of the firm, and (c) who understand that they are going to have to grow, sometimes painfully, during their careers. This may seem obvious, but in our experience, when organizations are defining the competencies they look for in people, they often take a very short-sighted view. They hire for today, even in fast-growing companies, without thinking about the ability of the person to grow, through on-the-job learning and coaching, to meet the demands of tomorrow.

Stopping the Action and Starting the Dialogue: Creating Coaching Opportunities

Coaching moments, moments with the potential for learning, occur all the time in most settings. An employee has a question, a complaint, thinks out loud about a particular issue, or expresses concerns about a problem he or she is having. Most managers confronted with a question will answer it. Confronted with a complaint, they will defend company actions. Overhearing employees chat about a new customer, they may throw in their own opinions. Coaching requires a different approach at such junctures. Coaching requires that the manager stop the action and instigate a dialogue using techniques of inquiry (Senge, Ross, Smith, Roberts, & Kleiner, 1994). In the new economy, we have come to expect that there will never be time to "stop the action." Indeed, a recent issue of *Fast Company* (2000) magazine has on its cover the following command: "Enough Talk! It's Time for Results—Are You Getting It Done?"

We think that is taking the notion of urgency a bit far! Yes, too much analysis does create paralysis, but if you would take just a few minutes to stop and learn, you won't become paralyzed and neither will your subordinates. It doesn't require a 50-minute session in most cases. Coaching just requires punctuating life a bit, stopping to think through what you are doing. It is a useful habit for all managers and a useful habit to encourage in your employees.

Should the manager try to engage employees in a coaching opportunity every time an apparent coaching moment appears? Early in their efforts to become more effective as coaches, we often find that managers may be a bit aggressive in grasping for such moments, overcorrecting in a sense. It is also our experience that employees tend to understand and appreciate the effort. Once it is clear that coaching is a routine part of life in the work group, managers can take their cues from the employees. They, the employees, start to clearly signal when they need or want coaching.

Stopping the action sets the stage for a dialogue between coach and coachee. The question that the coaching manager should keep in mind is this: "What do you, the coachee, want to learn and need to learn?" The coachee and coach need to be engaged early in the process in an effort to mutually define the scope of the coaching effort. Simple questions such as the following are useful ways to get started:

- "What was that experience (the focus of the coaching effort) like for you?"
- "How do you think you did?"
- "What is your own critique?"
- "What could you have done differently?"

In the example at the opening of this chapter, Mary simply cuts through John's complaints and says to him:

- "Lets talk about it, fill me in."
- "What happened?"
- "Did it work?"

The coach asks questions that will help the prospective coachee self-assess his or her performance and, on the basis of that self-assessment, define a learning goal or need. (Of course, the coachee isn't likely to describe the outcome of this process as a learning goal per se in most cases. Typically, the coachee will say something like "I think that approach didn't work. Maybe I should try . . .") Self-assessment represents a foundation for learning. One has to be personally aware of one's own performance and of the gap between that performance and the desired performance, in qualitative and/or quantitative terms.

An Olympic runner, for example, must have a sense of herself while running to be able to diagnose what she needs to do differently. She can't just wait until she has the chance to watch the videos or receive feedback from her coach. A golfer has to personally see what he is doing wrong with his current swing in order to understand how he must alter it. Too many performance appraisals ignore this step. Worse, some managers assume that individuals will distort their self-assessments to make themselves look good. That kind of game playing certainly does occur, but more so in a context that is not coaching friendly. If it isn't safe to tell the truth, most smart employees won't. Fear is the great enemy of critical self-assessment and, therefore, of performance improvement.

If the self-assessment component of the coaching dialogue is successful, a very important issue of ownership is settled. The coachee, not the manager, owns the problem or the challenge. The learning goal belongs to the learner, which is as it should be. The manager can help, but the coachee has defined the issue on his or her terms. Most managers have had the experience of trying to convince an employee to change. Learning theory tells us, however, that we are actually much more likely to change while we are trying to learn something that *we* have decided is valuable to us. You can probably make the assumption, particularly with good employees, that they will learn the easy skills themselves through observation or reading. If you are coaching them, they are probably working on something difficult that takes them out of their comfort zones. They need to take full ownership for that challenge if they are to truly engage with it.

What can a coach do if an employee sees no problem or no need to learn more about his or her performance? Such a response suggests that the individual is not ready for coaching. Feedback that the individual respects will likely be the only force helping him or her to see that there is actually a need for developmental work.

The Coaching Mirror

Self-assessment based on personal reflection alone may not be enough to help employees clearly see how they are doing and what they need to learn to improve their performance. Feedback is a component of coaching episodes. It may be one of the most difficult aspects of coaching. We suggest that coaching managers have the goal of building a "mirror" in which employees can see themselves more clearly. Feedback isn't meant to create change, it is meant to inform. There are two components to the coaching mirror: defining what is important to observe and observing effectively (which can be surprisingly difficult to do).

Knowing What Is Important:
The View From the Business

The coaching manager needs a sense of what good performance looks like in order to know what to look for and what kind of feedback is likely to be helpful.

Tichy (1997) has described this as the requirement for the coach to develop a "teachable point of view." Mary and John were both aware that using facilitation as a technique for helping confused potential customers represented an important model for managing the sales process at Software, Inc. John had been trained in facilitation previous to the interaction we describe in this chapter. Both knew what good performance looked like and as a result, could clearly see the gap between John's performance that day and what he needed to be able to do in the future.

In their efforts to help managers define effective performance, many organizations have developed competency models. Competency models describe what superior performance looks like for a specific role in a specific firm. They are usually built from interviews with superior performers and supervisory reports. Such performance models, though often quite useful, can be both expensive and static. Managers can also build their own quasi-competency models through discussing with their teams what they believe superior performance means. The process of manager and coachee talking together about effective and ineffective performance serves as an important learning opportunity in and of itself. Most managers are surprised to find how little has been communicated to employees about the processes that lead to effective performance.

Note that the organization (through its management) defines the skills that are important to the organization's success. The coachee has to supply the all-important motivation to learn. If the hiring process has been effective, the employee will probably want to learn more about the skills (or attitudes or knowledge) that the organization considers important. Being effective in these areas helps an employee be successful in both the short term and long term.

Observing What Is Important, Effectively

One of the problems associated with giving people feedback is the lack of opportunity to obtain useful data that would be helpful to the coachee. A second problem, however, is that the psychological processes of perception and cognition tend to degrade the data we do obtain.

Mary had several problems in trying to help John in this regard. First, she wasn't at the meeting in question. She had to rely on John's self-assessment. Second, she couldn't be at the follow-up meeting the next day. Luckily, she had created a context that was quite coaching friendly, and as such, John was able to comfortably ask one of his own direct reports to observe him as he tried to apply his facilitation training in a real business situation. Mary will hear how things went, using the eyes and ears of others to help her keep the coaching process going.

Gathering good performance data is increasingly a significant challenge for managers. The big enemy here—no surprise—is time. Managers can't be in two or three or four places at once. Creative thinking, the use of others, and technology can help. A variety of strategies have emerged over the past decade for helping coaches and coachees overcome the problems associated with obtaining data in fast-moving companies. Multi-observer feedback and assessment is one such strategy. In a coaching friendly context, the manager can more readily rely on the reports of others, in addition to the direct report of the coachee. The coach can talk with peers, other managers, and customers about the coachee's performance. Getting the coachee's agreement for such a survey in advance or making such a survey a normal part of your management practice can reinforce its developmental purpose.

Observational data are the best data of all. The coach watches the coachee and, ideally, pays attention to what the coachee did and said, without interpreting the meaning, at least initially. In this critical way, the coach is especially valuable to the coachee, serving as the coachee's eyes and ears and being in a position to offer the coachee fairly accurate feedback.

Unfortunately, even with firsthand data, observer bias quickly becomes a problem. Feelings about the individual being coached; a tendency to identify or "dis-identify" with that person; recent memories of great or terrible performances; race, gender, and cultural and personal style differences between the coach and coachee; these can all make it harder for the coaching manager to focus on what the individual employee is actually doing or saying. The coaching mirror is built from data, not from inference. We spend considerable time on this very important issue in later chapters. The most important point, however, is to acknowledge that such bias exists and is a potential problem for all of us.

Providing Balanced and Helpful Feedback

Feedback represents the coach's view of the gap between an individual's performance and what improved performance might be like, if indeed there is a gap. (In the case of a strong performer, the gap might be "upside down," meaning that the coachee doesn't appreciate that he or she possesses a particular strength.) Feedback serves as a source of information to coachees, helping them assess the gap between desired and current performance. Ideally, feedback holds up an accurate mirror to coachees, so they can see themselves and take ownership of their actions or results. Once coachees have defined learning issues or goals and offered self-assessments of their effectiveness in relation to those areas ("I think I need to be better at . . ."), feedback alone may be enough to help them improve their performance.

John was able, through self-assessment, to see that his failure to use a facilitation approach in working with Internet Marketing, Inc., may have cost him the sale. However, when he goes to use facilitation for the first time in the field, he will be very unsure of himself. Listening seems to be a major challenge for John. He'll need specific behavioral feedback so he can compare his actions with the model of performance effectiveness on which he and Mary agreed. He will need feedback to help him fine-tune his efforts because he probably won't be fully effective as a facilitator his first time out.

In addition to the problems associated with building a useful coaching mirror, there are other barriers to the effective use of feedback. Simply put, nice people don't like to criticize. In this case, however, John has asked for the feedback, and that helps. Again, the coaching friendly context encourages such behavior on the part of employees. However, feedback should always be delivered in a way that will maintain the dignity of the coachee, particularly if it is critical information.

When coaching managers personally deliver feedback, a caring attitude is essential. If coachees define learning goals, they are allowing themselves to be vulnerable to the process of receiving feedback. They have let their defenses down, at least with regard to particular learning needs. It is the coach's job to help maintain an individual's sense of comfort, to the highest degree possible, so their collaborative efforts can continue.

However, this does not mean that such feedback can't be critical. Indeed, it often has to be critical. According to our interviews, coaching managers find that to withhold critical feedback as a means of supporting an employee is often seen as gratuitous. In a coaching friendly environment, critical feedback is taken less personally, particularly if it is directed at the learner's actual goals.

Collaboratively Interpreting the Meaning of Performance Gaps

Assessment of the gap between the desired and actual performance doesn't stop at the behavioral or results level. It is often useful for understanding why coachees acted as they did. This requires that coaches and coachees maintain a collaborative dialogue that will encourage coachees to consider the reasons for their behavior. For example: "Does my failure to take a leadership role on a team mean that I'm not leadership material, or are other factors involved, such as a lack of training?"

Mary was concerned that John might not have a clear sense of the facilitation model that they had agreed on and asked him whether he felt he was ready to try this on his own. He reassured her that he understood the model and just needed to give it a try. A number of other issues could have come up at this point, as stated in the previous paragraph. Suppose that John was the only Mexican American at the meeting and, feeling very much in the minority, was uncomfortable being assertive enough to position himself as a trustworthy facilitator. The real issue wouldn't then be John's lack of knowledge or difficulty in listening effectively, even though on a surface level, the manager might have assumed as much. The coaching manager needs to be ready to listen and to be surprised on occasion by any barriers that the coachee sees to performance improvement.

Setting a Goal for Change and Following Up

John and Mary have agreed on a plan, with specific action items that require follow-up. The plan in this case was fairly simple and informal. John would try out some new behaviors, with a source of feedback in the room to help him debrief later. We have found that plans that emerge from such quick coaching dialogues are surprisingly minimal. Good performers often have an idea about what to do but need some support to get it done—to learn the new and discard the old. In John's case, gaining feedback to assess his progress as he executed his plan for change provided sufficient support for his continued learning. In addition, Mary let John know that she considered this situation important to both the company and to John's career, and she insisted on follow-up. If managers don't pursue the follow-up, they signal to the coachee that the issue isn't important. Follow-up can be minimal, but it needs to take place.

What if John didn't know what to do? How much advice should Mary be prepared to give John to help him develop a plan if he is truly lost? Advice is perhaps the trickiest part of the coaching process. The advice the coach gives about how to change may not fit the needs of the coachee, given the great diversity of learning styles that people bring to the workplace. Advice can also be perceived by coachees as being unrealistic if the coach suggests actions that don't make sense to the coachee or are beyond his or her control. Change requires that the coachee have an opportunity to practice the desired behaviors; just attending a course, for instance, may not be sufficient.

It can be useful to give coachees an opportunity to lead discussions regarding the process by which change should occur. Ask coachees about their thoughts on what they might do differently, what they could try, and other possible sources of advice or information they might seek out. We are not implying that the coach should never give advice, particularly if it is clear that the coach has sound and knowledgeable advice to offer. However, asking coachees about their ideas for change challenges them to keep thinking and to take responsibility for their own learning. If the coachee personally decides on a course of action, he or she is likely to experience a much greater sense of ownership for follow-through and results. The coach then takes the role of validating the coachee's choices (when appropriate), offering "fine-tuning" suggestions, providing resources if possible, and most certainly, providing encouragement.

As You Experiment With Coaching

We have offered the reader an overview of a model of developmental coaching that can work in fast-paced, new-economy companies. As we stated at the outset of this chapter, the model is simple conceptually and doesn't take a great deal of time to execute once you have established a coaching friendly context. However, we work with people on a regular basis just as you, our readers, do. The devil, as they say, is in the details, the multitude of issues and problems and opportunities that emerge as two or more people are trying to work together. To learn to coach, you must try it, self-assess how it goes for you, obtain some feedback, and think about what you need to do to close the gap between current and desired performance. In the chapters that follow, we hope to give you a clearer picture of competency as a coach on the part of a practicing manager.

3

The Coaching Manager and the "Coaching Mind-Set"

IN THIS CHAPTER, YOU WILL LEARN THE FOLLOWING:

- How managers become coaching managers
- The attitudes and beliefs that describe the "coaching mind-set"

We've argued that there isn't enough coaching going on in most business organizations, which means that there aren't enough coaching managers. Yet they do exist, and their stories are important. There seem to be two routes to becoming a coaching manager, both of which have their struggles. Some managers seem to be "natural" coaches, and their struggle is one of finding a credible outlet for their talents. Others learn to coach as they might pick up any other skill, though it appears that even they need to have the proper foundation on which to build coaching skills. Regardless of the pathway, however, managers who do become coaching managers have much in common, particularly with regard to a set of attitudes and beliefs that we describe as the *coaching mind-set.*

We want to go into some detail about the roads that people take to get there. We offer this as a guide that will, we hope, help those who aspire to coach place themselves in the process. However, before describing the paths to a coaching mind-set, we begin with an example of a coaching manager drawn from management literature. This example makes an important point in that it dispels one of the more significant myths that tend to discredit coaching and development.

Coaching Managers Focus on Running a Business

Interestingly, we have found that coaching managers may not define themselves as coaches, and they may not define what they do as coaching. The word *coaching* has obviously become a part of the popular culture, given the attention it has received in the media. However, leaders have been coaching for a long time. The coaching managers we met are businesspeople first. In other words, effective coaching managers don't appear to be more "touchy-feely" than anyone else in the business world. They work hard and tend to be very task and results oriented.

Although some have strong beliefs about the humanistic or even spiritual importance of helping others learn and grow, most enjoy the business life and wouldn't give it up to become social workers (with all due respect to that noble profession). It should come as no surprise that most effective coaches very much like their work. One of the reasons they like to coach is that they are enthusiastic about what they do, and they genuinely want to help others succeed in their fields.

This is an extremely important component of coaching. The coach who is a business leader (not necessarily the CEO, but a formal or informal leader in any size business unit) is likely to have a great deal of what psychologists call "source credibility" (London, 1997). Feedback from someone who is seen as having skills or as having been successful in an area linked with the aspirations of the coachee is likely to be difficult to ignore, even when the feedback is critical in nature. Even more important, if conditions are right, feedback from a credible source is likely to be sought out.

We start this chapter with the description of a business leader who happens to coach, to illustrate the importance of seeing coaching as a part of what effective, passionate business leaders do. Erich Dombrowski was the editor of Germany's largest afternoon paper in post–World War II Frankfurt. That newspaper, *General Anzeiger,* served as the place of employment and learning of management writer Peter Drucker. Drucker has described how he learned the newspaper business from Dombrowski. In the years following the Second World War, Dombrowski had very few resources with which to work. In particular, he had no experienced journalists. He was forced to hire an inexperienced staff. Drucker tells the rest of his coaching story as follows:

> None of us had ever worked on a newspaper. And he [Dombrowski] did two things, one, there was no limit to the responsibility that he heaped on us, and he took the whole editorial staff, 15 people, 16 people, sat down from Saturday evening, when the paper went to press, until Sunday afternoon. And each of us reported [to Dombrowski] and all the others asked questions and criticized. . . . At the end he [Dombrowski] summed up and gave each of us a specific goal. This is what you will have to learn. . . . This is where you have to change the way you do things. . . . This is the additional dimension. And I learned to sit down with

myself once a year at least and look over the work I did over the preceding 6 or 12 months, what did I do well, what could I or should I have done better, what could I or should I have done that I didn't do, and what do I get rid of because it is just surplus baggage, how do I reshape priorities? That is what I learned from him. (Peter Drucker Foundation, 1998)

Drucker has written extensively of his observation that good leaders subordinate themselves to the mission of their organizations. In this case, Dombrowski didn't coach for the sake of coaching or even for the sake of developing his staff. These were not his primary goals. Drucker explains, adding something of a punch line to the above story:

After I went back to Germany in '53 or '54, I cornered him, and I said, "You don't remember, but I want to tell you how much I owe to you, how much I learned from you, how much you made me face up to things, and you have been my mentor and teacher," and he took a long look at me, and said, "This never occurred to me. All I was ever interested in was next month's newspaper." (Peter Drucker Foundation, 1998)

We see here the competitive advantage that can accrue to a business when there is an active effort to build organizational capability through coaching. We also see how coaching represents, at perhaps its best, one manifestation of what might be described as a "bundle" of leadership behaviors or roles (Nannus, 1992). Dombrowski coached, but he also delegated, gave his employees challenging assignments, let them do their best and sometimes fail, and kept his eye on the mission of getting out the newspaper. He also helped his organization adapt to a very difficult and resource-poor environment.

In the process of engaging in these activities, as we would expect of a successful business leader, Dombrowski spent a great deal of time with his people. The young journalists probably did make many mistakes. The tone of Drucker's comments, however, suggests that the editor carefully listened to what they were doing, encouraged them to reflect on their work, encouraged them to help each other, and then gave his own thoughtful feedback. His feedback was not heard as critical, but as informative and challenging. And it was given in the service of helping his employees work toward a goal to which they were presumably committed, that of being effective journalists and newspapermen and -women. Coaching managers are businesspeople first.

The Naturals

How Dombrowski actually learned to be such an effective coach is something of a mystery. We speculate that he might share certain characteristics with the kind of coaching managers we call "naturals." It is certainly doubtful that he received any formal training in coaching. Drucker and all his colleagues at the paper were extremely fortunate that Dombrowski was such a good coach. As we have stated elsewhere, coaching is one of the least-executed leadership skills. In one recent study, coaching and the development of others ranked 66th out of 67 measured leadership competencies (Lombardo & Eichenger, 2001). Why such a poor showing? In the absence of an organizational- or societal-level effort to encourage more coaching in the workplace, the coaching done at that time was probably limited to that which was provided by the naturals. (The same is probably true today for the most part, though the number of individuals who have learned coaching as a skill is increasing.) Naturals are those people who like to help others, are very good at *doing*, and have been that way most of their lives with little or no training.

Judy Giger, marketing manager at Genuity Corporation in Massachusetts, remembers people coming up to her throughout her life, wanting to talk. While working her way up the ladder from small businesses through large ones, she found that people routinely sought her out. For a long time, she didn't know why. Those around her report that she is a good listener. She doesn't remember ever having to learn to listen, however. She likes people. She conveys that outlook with natural warmth and a routine expression of respect for others. She is also good at keeping confidences. Interestingly, she has had more than a few people come up to her over the years and say, "You were my mentor." Much like Erich Dombrowski, this surprises her. She uses her natural coaching style routinely yet does not necessarily think of herself as coaching.

Over the past year, Judy has been asked by her boss to provide support to people in their marketing group who are in the early stages of their careers or are new to the group. It is her responsibility to "bring along the talent." If someone is having trouble with a presentation, dealing with organizational politics, or considering another career move, her role is to do what she has always done: listen, try not to judge or criticize, ask useful questions, observe her "clients" (really her colleagues) doing their work when she can, provide feedback, and on occasion, provide advice. The underlying concept that guides her work is that of helping people figure out what they want to do and what they do well. She then helps them leverage their personal motivation and skills to achieve their personal goals, inside her group or out. If she ends up advising someone in the wrong role to find another job, she considers that a win for everyone. She does not believe in trying to change people.

Judy enjoys this aspect of her work a great deal. However, she has never seriously considered going into human resources or other roles with which one might intuitively associate a natural helper. She likes business, and she likes marketing. She is an example of a natural coach.

Although Judy's story as told so far sounds straightforward, she has had her own struggles. Many naturals find barriers to the expression of their natural talents. They may work for managers who are suspicious of people who seem to be confidants of others within the organization. They may be stymied by managers who fear a loss of control or the keeping of secrets. They may be discredited by managers who think that coaching isn't work at all, but rather a waste of time. Judy's current manager offers two important sources of support. First, she validates the importance of Judy's coaching activities. Judy doesn't have to worry that the time she spends coaching will appear to be time wasted from a business perspective. Second, Judy's manager has actually found a semiformal outlet for the expression of Judy's talents.

The last point can't be emphasized enough. Those who have a strong interest in helping others and yet want to pursue a business career must look for managers and roles that allow them to express that strength. Unfortunately, unless naturals have done a bit of homework, they may not even know that coaching is a valid business activity. They may be concerned about sharing their interests with others for fear of appearing too—yes, "touchy-feely." Naturals, once they have identified their interest in coaching, need to intentionally pursue opportunities for the expression of that interest as part of their own career planning.

The Manager Who Learns to Coach

The low frequency with which we find naturals suggests that we are much more likely to find managers who, if they are coaching, have intentionally learned the skills necessary to coach. We anticipate that their numbers will swell with the growing awareness on the part of business leaders and human resource professionals that the ability to coach represents an essential competency for an effective manager. We emphasize here that these people are probably not without some of the talents one finds in naturals. However, these talents may be less fully refined, and their expression may have been given a lower priority over the course of time.

Our work has shown that those who learn to coach go through a 2-step process. They first identify the need to learn about coaching, and then they must internalize a model of coaching that helps guide their actions. The coaching model they ultimately work with can be an academic one or one they have learned "on the job."

The first step is necessary to point out because the future coaching manager may not even know that coaching is a legitimate business activity. The personal identification of the value of coaching may take place in a number of ways.

Some managers may feel that they just don't have any choice. Like Erich Dombrowski, they may have to work with undeveloped talent. They can't do it all themselves, and they come to realize that becoming a teacher is their only hope. Some may hear about coaching, intuitively think that it is a good idea, perhaps because it fits with their values, and start the learning process. Finally, some identify a need to learn more about coaching through very personal and often difficult experiences.

Stan is an information technology director with a major U.S. consulting firm. He is on the career track to becoming the chief technology office of the firm if he so chooses. His coaching efforts play a significant role in how he runs his group. He takes the development of the members of his team seriously. He was not always aware of coaching or the role that it could play in his leadership style. He had no idea that there was a technique or a model one could use to guide efforts to help others develop. His eyes were opened to the importance of understanding how to help his employees in one very traumatic experience.

Several jobs and companies ago, his manager suddenly and without warning confronted him on the perceived shortcomings of his leadership style. Basing her criticisms on feedback from the management of another group in her organization, she attacked his interpersonal effectiveness in particular (though her attacks were very nonspecific). Stan was left in the dark as to the specific sources of the feedback. She made it clear to him that she felt he had no talent for leadership.

Without concrete details or clear knowledge of "who said what," he was left feeling devastated and helpless. His overriding sense was that his manager, even if she had a point, had not been in the least helpful. He went back to his own group and sought out their feedback, which was largely positive. He then took it on himself to go to a leadership training program that, though he left with some good ideas, also validated the fact that he was actually doing pretty well for a young manager.

There was a problem, however, but it was a cross-functional one. Stan had run into a serious political problem that had nothing to do with his leadership. His manager had been of no help in that regard, either. Her surprising feedback merely generated mistrust in an already highly charged atmosphere. Stan eventually moved on to greener pastures. His insight, however, stayed with him. He did have a problem, but his manager's actions had only exacerbated it. One should expect more from one's manager.

Stan resolved to help his own people in a very different way. He began an effort to create the kind of environment in which his employees could help him (as they had done during his crisis) as well as each other. We'll hear more of his ideas later. Suffice it to say, they include being open to giving and receiving timely, useful, and specific feedback delivered with the dignity of both parties in mind at all times. His motivation to learn was actually quite simple: "I don't ever want to do to anyone else what she [the former manager] did to me." When asked what he worries about, as a manager who coaches, he says, "The thing that keeps me up at night when I'm trying to coach somebody is whether or not I'm having a positive or a negative impact. I still worry about that."

Role modeling is one of the major sources of learning in the career of a leader (McCall, Lombardo, & Morrison, 1988). Managers can learn to coach from managers who coach, such as Dombrowski. Many of our coaching managers have told us that they learned a great deal from their first managers, people gifted at helping them develop. The experience of receiving no or worse yet, destructive coaching early in one's career can also shape an awareness of the importance of humanely helping others to develop.

Whether from the impact of a good or bad manager, the realization of the value of helping has to occur for people to move to the second step: actually internalizing some kind of coaching model. Our experience suggests that many people would like to do more coaching at work but don't because they are anxious. If they don't believe it is important, they won't work to get beyond that anxiety. The comments of one recent participant in a coach training program, an engineer, are illustrative in that regard:

> Coaching appears to be more difficult than it really is. First, I was nervous, but as the session started, I realized I had to and I could do my best to advise [the coachee], drawing from what I learned in the training, at work, and in life. The coachees [learners] made this easy, as they were open to feedback and eager to see how they did. My confidence has built up, and I am ready to go through the coaching process more effectively next time, whenever I need to coach.

We have had new coaching managers tell us that they lost sleep the night before their first coaching efforts. However, as this quote illustrates, the anxiety is largely anticipatory, probably based on the fear of doing the wrong thing and hurting the coachee. As managers come to understand that effective coaching involves sharing responsibility for learning, this anxiety quite abates.

Another coach participant, a research and development manager, stated,

> In the past, I have been afraid to do the wrong thing or give the wrong input, so I kept quiet. I now feel that I know how to have a discussion on nontechnical topics that will be constructive and helpful, rather than upsetting and inflammatory.

This individual has to build a team out of a group of scientists. He knows that if he is going to be successful, he is going to have to help them. In his eyes, a coaching model and a little experience completely reframe the problem.

Being well beyond the anxiety, he can anticipate coaching more in the future. Step 1 on the road to becoming a coaching manager intersects with Step 2.

Through feedback we have received from the coaches who have attended our training programs over the years, we have found that a useful model of coaching needs to be simple and realistic. The language of coaching needs to be clear and businesslike. Perhaps most important, managers need to have a realistic understanding of what coaching is supposed to accomplish, for whom, and how. In our training programs and work in organizations, we find that managers usually become noticeably less anxious about coaching once they understand the following:

- The learner is responsible for much of what takes place in coaching. The coach doesn't have to take responsibility for all aspects of the process or the outcome.
- Coaching does not mean changing someone's personality. Learning takes place incrementally. Small learning gains are usually enough to help people improve their performance toward even stretch goals.
- Coaching doesn't have to take a great deal of time once one has become comfortable with the process and has created a coaching friendly context.
- A manager's ability to coach will usually improve with practice, reflection, and a bit of feedback. Coaching is learned the way one learns any other skill.

Most managers find that they are very effective at executing some aspects of a simple coaching model, but not so effective at others. Stacy McMullen, an information technology manager, runs the Help Desk function at a large multinational retail company. Throughout her career, Stacy has worked to develop her leadership skills in a variety of ways. She decided to learn more about coaching through a course-based training program and to apply what she had learned in working with her employees.

In our coaching training program, she was audiotaped as she delivered her coaching feedback to a coachee. Listening to the tape, she realized that she had not done a good job of using questions to help create a coaching dialogue. Out of her own anxiety and lack of practice, she began to "tell and sell" her point of view to the coachee, rather than asking questions to get the coachee's point of view. She ended up talking far more than the coachee and taking complete responsibility for the conclusions that emerged from the coaching interview. The next day, she was scheduled to hold a meeting with one of her employees to discuss that employee's development goals for the year. She was determined to effect a different outcome.

Stacy decided to literally bite her lip after asking a question, consciously and quietly waiting to see what might happen. This is quite uncomfortable for most people unless they have really worked on their ability to tolerate silence. Nevertheless, it is a great way to keep from dominating a conversation and encouraging the other person to think. After a few awkward silences, the employee began to open up with Stacy. In the space she had created between her questions, the employee began to share his ideas about the strengths and weaknesses of his performance and what he felt he needed to work on. She found herself learning things about her employee that she hadn't known and was quite pleasantly surprised in the process. The result was a development plan that made sense to both of them.

Stacy is a bright, well-motivated manager with good interpersonal skills and an openness to learning. By gaining a conceptual model of coaching, trying out some new behaviors, getting some feedback, and practicing, she was able to learn to coach in a rather short period of time. As with any skill, she'll need to continue practicing, however, for that learning to stick.

Can Anyone Learn to Coach?

So some managers, we believe many, can learn to coach. Can anyone? Probably not. Several basic premises of adult learning are relevant to this question. First, development often involves building on strengths. For Stacy, the ability to coach builds on a set of previously existing strengths. She is a good leader, an effective communicator, and usually patient and mature. Not everyone has such a foundation. As the CEO of a firm that values coaching told us, "I might hire an engineering manager because he is a great engineer. That is his strength. That doesn't mean he'll be a great coach." Does this mean that if there isn't clear evidence of a foundation of interpersonal strengths, you shouldn't give it a try? We think not. A second premise of development is that the learner has to set the goal. If you think it is important for you to learn to coach, there is a much greater likelihood that your efforts will lead to success. Studying biographies tells us that many gifted teachers, counselors, and business and political leaders came from psychologically disadvantaged backgrounds. They made their way through difficult circumstances and were able to have a very positive impact on those around them.

Several of the coaching managers with whom we've worked have suggested to us, though, that the distinction between the natural coach and the coach who has to learn how to coach can represent a false dichotomy. In reality, they have said, the two represent extremes along a continuum. Some people are very gifted and need little additional help to become effective coaching managers. For others, much practice is required.

We have had managers tell us that they really didn't know how to hold a conversation with their employees until they learned how to ask questions and to coach. Not good at small talk, they avoided talking about almost anything at all. They wanted to enhance their ability to just talk with their employees, and coaching represented a vehicle for doing so.

To help you better assess whether or not you are working from a foundation on which effective coaching skills can be built, we describe in some detail what the naturals and those who have learned to coach by more traditional means have in common. As is the case throughout this book, in compiling this list, we draw on our experience in training managers to coach, interviews with coaching managers, and the writings of those who have coached or studied coaching.

The Coaching Mind-Set: An Overriding Attitude of Helpfulness

Managers who become coaching managers, by whatever route, appear to show most if not all the attitudes or behaviors we will be describing (see Box 3.1). Before listing them specifically, we will simply summarize them by the word *helpfulness*. Managers who coach want to *help*, as opposed to fixing or changing others. They like seeing others succeed. They seem to get a kick out of having a chance to admire the good work of others. As one coaching manager told us, "I keep track of them in their careers. I hear about their accomplishments. I like to think that in a way, I have contributed to their success."

Box 3.1

WHAT COACHING MANAGERS HAVE IN COMMON

- They have an overriding attitude of helpfulness when trying to coach others.
- They don't believe in the "sink or swim" theory of employee development.
- They believe that by helping their employees develop, everybody comes out ahead.
- They show less need for control.
- They believe that most people really do want to learn.
- They show empathy in their dealings with others.
- They are open to personal learning, to receiving feedback, and to being coached, even by their employees.
- They set high standards.
- They don't try to "fix" people.
- They don't believe that people are a means to an end.

This attitude of helpfulness will be discussed further in Chapter 5, when we describe the factors necessary for creating a coaching friendly context. Suffice it to say that while a manager is coaching, the employee being coached will be vigilantly observing that manager. The employee will be drawing inferences about why the manager is providing the coaching. If the manager appears to be doing so with self-serving or destructive motives, the employee will react accordingly. He or she will become much more defensive and much less likely to take advantage of the coaching being offered. If the coaching manager can't interact with the employee in a fashion that reflects a genuine interest in being helpful, then that manager might be better off not trying. The importance of helpfulness to the success of a manager or leader doesn't get a great deal of discussion in business today. But note again that helpfulness does not stand in contrast to "toughness" or other attitudes that may be more common expressions of the business culture. The attitude of helpfulness we describe can be bundled with a number of quite hard-nosed and challenging attributes.

Coaching managers don't believe in the "sink or swim" theory of employee development. Morgan McCall (1998) has studied the leadership development practices of a number of companies and has concluded that the "sink or swim" approach to development is probably the most common, even in some very progressive firms. In this approach to development, individuals are given challenging assignments. If they are successful, their careers advance. If not, their careers stall. The individual is given no coaching, mentoring, or other learning supports.

The coaches we have worked with find this a wasteful and invalid practice. As McCall points out, who knows how many more would be successful with a little help? Consider the political mistakes that would not have been made, the time that would not have been lost as an individual made the same mistakes over and over, and the bad habits that even some of the successful sink or swim candidates probably learn along the way, in the absence of feedback.

Interestingly, many of our coaches, when asked why they think coaching is a good idea, say, "Because no one ever coached me!" They struggled to learn and advance in their careers, often without help. They are the victims of a sink or swim mentality and see what has been lost in their own careers. They do believe in giving people challenging assignments, but they also believe in helping out with support, advice, and feedback—in other words, coaching. The "big pit" theory, digging a hole and throwing people in to see who crawls out, is a waste of resources and a poor way of demonstrating that you care!

Coaching managers believe that by helping their employees develop, everybody comes out ahead. In our consulting practices, we have repeatedly run across one of the most insidious barriers to coaching by managers. That barrier is represented by the belief that managers shouldn't try to help their employees develop because in doing so, they will lose the best ones. Employees naturally despise this assumption because it means that they are ultimately just being used by the manager as tools for the manager's self-serving agenda. This assumption and the practices associated with it are particularly dangerous to a business in a tight labor market. Given that employees have options, they will go elsewhere if an opportunity to develop is closed to them.

The coaching managers we have worked with assume that by coaching their employees and aiding their development, they will build the overall capability of their businesses. They also are quite aware that, although they will lose some good people along the way, in the end, they are likely to be even more successful. By taking a developmental approach, their employees are challenged and satisfied. Problems are dealt with more quickly. Morale and commitment are high.

We've asked managers whether or not all this work on development isn't just a bit inconvenient at times. After all, you are always in the business of bringing people along when you operate this way. One coaching manager answered us in jest, "Only when they say they want my job!" For the most part, coaching managers believe that they *should* be preparing people to take their jobs and view it as an essential means of succession planning. They feel it is their obligation to their people and to the business.

Coaching managers show less need for control. At the 1978 Gator Bowl, storied Ohio State Coach Woody Hayes ran onto the football field and hit an opposing player who had previously intercepted a pass. Hayes was subsequently fired (Schwab, 1999). This now rather comic picture speaks to just how difficult it is to be a coach rather than a player. The coaching manager sometimes has to subordinate his or her own wish to be in control and to be on the field, taking care of business, in order to let the team play the game and keep learning. This can be gut-wrenching. Note that the title of this section is *"Show* Less Need for Control." It does not say, "Have Less Need for Control." Self-control is the key.

The tasks of the manager have traditionally been described as those of planning, organizing, directing, and controlling. Managers are held accountable for results. They are rewarded for success and punished for failure. The rewards and punishments with which they must contend are powerful. This emphasis on "results no matter what" can make it hard for managers to coach rather than do.

Given that development requires, among other things, a challenging assignment (Van Velsor, McCauly, & Moxley, 1998), those who are offered such assignments might just fail. Although failure should probably have some consequences, if the consequences are too dire, development will stop. The coaches that we have witnessed doing the best jobs are those who are able to tolerate the potential for at least some failure. They can delegate, turn over a task to another individual, and then stay in the coaching role even when the situation becomes difficult and failure is a very real possibility. That doesn't mean that coaching managers set their employees up for failure or don't step in to help when needed. Rather, they don't rush in at the first sign of trouble.

Perhaps most important, an effective coaching manager has to be able to take time to hold coaching discussions. If managers are focused only on making sure that tomorrow's results are accomplished, they will probably not be thinking about developing people for the longer term. The coach has to be able to raise the priority placed on learning, even in the face of an organization's demands for results.

We have found that at times, coaching managers' need to focus on learning rather than control will, depending on the corporate culture within which the manager is working, lead them to behave in a somewhat protective way toward their developmental activities. Managers may not tell others, even their own bosses, about some of the risks they are taking and about the time they are spending coaching others. It is a shame, but the reality is, in our current business environment, some corporations would not look kindly on the type of investments required for employee development.

Coaching managers believe that most people really do want to learn. The effective coaches we've known have tended to be very good "systems" thinkers. By that we mean that they understand that many people don't appear to want to learn because they have been trained not to. They don't believe, however, that most people really don't want to learn. They believe that it is their obligation to create a context in which learning is possible. More than one coaching manager has told us about a "salvage job" he or she has been working on. This kind of salvage job does not refer to the employee who has a severe performance problem, but rather to the employee who is afraid to learn. Some managers are so hostile toward employee development that they can literally leave a talented employee demoralized, cynical, and greatly inhibited when it comes to learning. A coaching manager involved in a salvage operation might speak of an employee as one might describe a child who was raised in an abusive home: talking about the need to take a lot of time, build some trust, and convince the employee that it is okay to talk about work, your career goals, or what you're having trouble with.

A coaching manager is really much like a gardener. They plant the flowers (hire the right employees), create a context, provide some support, and are there to help out. However, having done that, they don't always expect every effort to bear fruit. Most coaches report that, as they mature, they come to accept that some people don't want to be coached and that they may not be able to make a difference in their development.

Coaching managers show empathy in their dealings with others. As the previous example indicates, effective coaches tend to be able to put themselves in another person's shoes, rather than judging an individual solely on the basis of surface behaviors. They are interested in what makes people work and in the role that work plays in people's lives. One coaching manager, in describing his work, was adamant about the importance of understanding the family or personal lives of his employees. "How can you expect them to take on a tough assignment, one that might really be stressful, when somebody is sick at home or when they are going through a divorce?"

Effective coaches use empathy to help them understand the coachee in his or her totality. This stands in sharp distinction to managers who are so focused on results that they delegate tasks to an already overburdened individual, creating the conditions for failure as well as a lack of learning in the process. Interestingly, however, most of the coaches we've talked with insist that they maintain very high standards with regard to performance. In fact, they use high standards as a tool to keep themselves and their people motivated and focused. They also use the high standards they have set as a framework within which to coach.

Coaching managers are open to personal learning, to receiving feedback, and to being coached, even by their employees. Effective coaches like to learn about themselves, about others, and about their work. They often enjoy being surprised by what they don't know. Coaching is, for them, a tool that helps them foster their own learning. It also helps them know what is going on in their business units, always a desirable outcome.

They also seem to enjoy learning about themselves from others. Frequently, managers who create what we call "coaching friendly contexts" are very likely to encourage employees to coach them. This is a way of modeling the giving and receiving of feedback. However, it is done for more than just the purpose of modeling desired behavior. They genuinely want the feedback. They have come to believe that they really don't know it all and that the perceptions of others, even critical perceptions, are essential to hear and understand.

In this sense, they are comfortable admitting what they don't know and how they might be wrong. This is particularly noticeable when they are gathering performance information about coachees, positive or negative. Rather than taking the attitude, while gathering information, that they have to prove their own positions correct, they're more likely to seek information that will add to or change their perceptions, in an effort to find out what is really going on.

Coaching managers set high standards. We mentioned above that the coaching managers we have interviewed are very rigorous businesspeople. Their rigor is seen in the high standards they set. They expect their employees to be able to meet those standards. The difference is, they are willing to help. They offer help through coaching as well as through other interventions. One of our coaching managers told us, "People are surprised at the fact that I can be tough. The toughness comes out when I make it clear to everyone that I expect this group to be successful, to be the best group in our division. They think that because I'm interested in people, I am inevitably going to be soft. Not true. I set high standards, though I do think they are achievable. I stick to them, I don't back off."

Coaching managers don't try to "fix"people. We have repeatedly noticed that managers who seem to take coaching most to heart also seem to be most accepting of others' strengths and weaknesses. They pay attention to strengths and weaknesses in the hiring process (see Chapter 5) and work hard to create opportunities for people to use their strengths. On the other hand, they can also accept that an employee may not have the right talent for his or her role or the right fit for the business unit. They are able to accept that someone may need to move along to another role or business unit or company and are quite willing to make that happen, even though they may feel bad about the need to do so. To put it simply, they aren't afraid to fire someone if that person is in the wrong job.

Most coaching managers, then, don't assume that coaching can fix everything. They are willing to give coaching a try when serious performance problems arise, but such remedial coaching isn't the primary focus of their developmental efforts. Our observations support the findings of the Gallup Organization's widely reported study of effective managers (Buckingham & Coffman, 1999). The Gallup study found that the best managers, whose activities were statistically linked with higher levels of productivity, economic performance, and employee retention, tried to build on strengths in their coaching, rather than trying to create strength where none existed before.

We have seen this problem from very close range in our coach training programs. Some managers, including some who are clearly well-meaning and interested in other people, show tremendous frustration when their coachees seem unmotivated or abrasive. Despite our best efforts, such coaches will confront coachees on admittedly unappealing behavior without first building relationships with them. The "fix 'em" obsessed managers don't stop to understand people, their contexts, and most important, their goals. The results usually range from unproductive to disastrous. The coachee feels abused and highly defensive. Sadly, we suspect (though we can't prove) that coachees who have been the object of a coach's efforts to fix rather than coach are less likely to seek coaching in the future.

The frustration of the coaches does not abate as they realize that they cannot simply change people. This isn't coaching! The true coach, as stated above, has to be able to tolerate giving over control of the process to learners and be accepting of the fact that things may not always work out for them.

Coaching managers don't believe that people are a means to an end. We can summarize our description of coaching managers by describing their approach to the age-old business paradox: Is the business run for the sake of shareholders, and perhaps customers, or for the employees? Coaching managers dismiss the view of wealth creation or need fulfillment as being dichotomous in relation to the needs of the employees. Their assumption is that the business should meet the needs of both groups: Employees do the work of the organization, but one does not build organizational capability (or "human capital," as it might now be called) simply for the sake of putting out a better product, though that is important. In this view, the development of employees is an inherent part of what makes a business unit worthwhile. Espousing this ideology can create some tension, however (see the earlier comments about human resources).

The Coaching Manager

Would you like to work for the kind of coaching manager we've just described? Unless you are a very exceptional person, the answer is probably an unqualified "yes." Why wouldn't you? These attitudes combine an interest in success with an interest in helping others be successful. Is this just too good to be true? Think about it.

Is there a manager in your organization whom everyone seems to talk about? If it takes place among other managers, is such discussion occasionally tinged with more than a hint of jealousy or envy? Do you ever fear losing some of your good employees to that person? Chances are, he or she is a manager who runs a successful group and is also interested in helping people develop through coaching.

Great organizations tend to be well-known both for being successful and for being interested in their employees. As a result, they don't suffer any shortage of talent. Southwest Airlines, for instance, in one recent year, had over 100,000 job applications for fewer than 5,000 openings. The recruiters and hiring managers get to choose the best individuals from a very large pool.

Managers who coach will likely experience something very similar, on a smaller scale, of course. People want to work for them because those managers help them succeed in both the short term and the long term. The work is challenging and interesting. Growth and career movement are likely outcomes. Coaching managers are able to think about moving people up or across the organization because they know that someone else is waiting in the wings to join their group. They can choose from among the best. In the eyes of potential employees and other company managers, the coaching manager has a sustainable competitive advantage.

Self-Assessment 3.1:
Your Foundation for Learning to Coach

In this self-assessment, consider your own behavior and performance to date and ask yourself how you would answer the following questions. Then, ask someone else in your group to give you feedback on the following questions. Look for areas of consistency and areas of overlap.

1. The basic skills: Rate yourself on the following by giving yourself a score of 5 if you think you do a great job, 3 if you think you do a fair job, and 1 or 0 if you think you do a poor job:

   - Listening
   - Engaging in productive conversation with your employees or others whom you might be in a position to coach (meaning a discussion in which there is a useful give-and-take and the other party doesn't feel particularly defensive)
   - Observing others so as to be able to give them helpful feedback
   - Providing effective feedback, even when it is critical

Questions 2 through 11 all require all "yes" or "no" answers:

2. If you give someone a challenging assignment, do you usually coach that individual?

3. Do you usually give someone a difficult assignment and then wait to see what happens?

4. Do you manage your group in a fashion that demonstrates a belief that developing others in your work group will ultimately help you and your business?

5. Do you worry that by actively developing people, you will lose the very people you need in order to be successful?

6. Do you usually believe that it is appropriate for you to let employees try things their way, in the interest of learning, even if you're not sure you agree?

7. Do you believe that you should stay on top of things and make sure all your employees are doing things right?

8. Do you believe that most people in your group have been encouraged to be learners?

9. Have the people in your group been taught that learning is a lower priority than immediate business results?

10. Do you think you know your employees well enough to understand the problems they are facing in their lives?

11. Are you open to being wrong, to taking critical feedback from others, and to being surprised by what you learn about your employees?

If you scored 10 or higher to Question 1, you have some of the skills necessary for coaching. If you say that your behavior or attitude is usually reflected in a "yes" answer to Questions 2, 4, 6, 8, 10, 11, and 12 and a "no" answer to the rest, you are likely to be well positioned to provide coaching to the members of your business unit. If you asked one or more people in your group to provide feedback to you with regard to these questions, then, in addition to being able to say "yes" to Question 11, you are probably in great shape to begin coaching. In fact, you already have.

4

The "Coach-Able" Learner

IN THIS CHAPTER, YOU WILL LEARN ABOUT THE FOLLOWING:

IN THIS CHAPTER, YOU WILL LEARN ABOUT THE FOLLOWING:

- The evidence suggesting that most people ultimately want to learn on the job
- The indicators that point to an individual's ability to engage in a coaching relationship
- The barriers to "coach-ability" created by potential learners
- Tactics for engaging the coachee

The Question of "Coach-Ability"

In Chapter 3, we described the characteristics of an effective coaching manager. Talk of "characteristics" can be a bit misleading, however. The coaching manager/coachee learner relationship actually functions as a system. Effective coaching is dependent on the nature of the relationships between managers and the people who work for them. One manager might be very effective at coaching someone whom another manager would find to be absolutely recalcitrant. Nevertheless, we do believe that it is possible to draw some tentative conclusions regarding who can benefit from coaching and who might not benefit from coaching, on the basis of the experience of the managers with whom we have worked. As we move forward, however, it is important to keep in mind that we are to an extent the architects of what we see in others.

In this chapter, we will share some of what has been learned regarding the question of coach-ability. The following case example illustrates the two basic questions we must confront. Is coach-ability a reflection of an individual's personality or character? Alternatively, is coach-ability a reflection of the environment within which an individual works and of the way that environment shapes a worker's response to coaching efforts?

Case 4.1: The Reluctant Coachee?

Part I: Aren't You Glad You Got This New Job!

Congratulations. You have just been promoted to director of all credit functions at your company. As part of the package, you find that you are Roger's new manager. (Roger manages the International Credit Group.) You've known Roger for only 3 weeks, but you've already had more than a few complaints. The company has been coming down hard on managers who are seen as abrasive. (You note to yourself the irony with which your company's actions can be viewed. After all, didn't their emphasis on short-term results create problems like Roger to begin with?) Retention seems to be "in"; beating people over the head is "out." You review the results of your most recent survey of Roger's employees and peers. Here is what they tell you:

Roger is (in no particular order) . . .

- Ruthless

- Aggressive

- Demeaning to subordinates, he doesn't tolerate mistakes, and becomes very angry publicly when mistakes are made

- Someone who intends to get his way, regardless of the cost

Even more intriguing, his former boss told you, "Don't try to give him any advice. He already knows it all." (You again register a mild sense of irony. You had always thought that Roger's former manager knew it all or at least thought he did.)

Consider a few questions to get started with the task of assessing Roger's coach-ability:

1. On the basis of what you already know, do you think Roger is coach-able?

2. What role does the company's culture play in your thinking as you try to make this determination?

After asking yourself why this had to happen to you, you buckle down to the task of trying to do something with Roger. At this point, you might make some of the following inferences:

- You've known the Rogers of the world, and of this company, for a long time. There are plenty of them out there. They are usually so arrogant that they end up running into serious political problems as they move up the corporate ladder. Yes, they do get results, but through the use of brute force. They aren't necessarily bad people. They just don't take others' needs into consideration. They often offend people. Ultimately, they offend the wrong customer, senior manager, or product engineer, and suddenly, their careers go into a nosedive.

- You might blame the Rogers of the world for not being smarter and more skillful in their drive for results. After all, Roger has an MBA from a good school. Shouldn't he have known that you have to work effectively with people?

- You might blame his previous manager. You've attributed part of the problem to the fact that Roger's last manager was notorious for encouraging exactly the kind of behavior that Roger is now demonstrating. Certainly, his previous manager was not someone who would confront Roger about his interpersonal behavior.

- You might ultimately question the culture of your company. They hired and promoted Roger and his previous manager. Now they are suddenly saying that they want both results and a reasonable process for getting those results. They want people to feel valued and to learn. How can they expect the Rogers of the world to change their behavior overnight? Roger has been with the company for 5 years. He's learned a lot of bad habits. One of the habits he learned was to reject the coaching and advice of others. After all, those who couldn't solve their own problems were labeled by the previous management as "wimps."

After going through all the diagnostic possibilities in your mind, you're still confronted with the problem of figuring out how to deal with Roger. Should you try to coach him or not?

Part II: A Day in the Life of Roger

Perhaps out of the kindness of your heart, you decide to give coaching Roger a try. You see him sitting alone in the lunchroom. You grab a cup of coffee, walk over to him, and ask if he'd like some company. He is more than ready to tell you about himself and his problems.

Roger reports that he has had a rough day. Three of his direct reports "hinted" that they might be looking for work elsewhere. They also "hinted" that it was because of Roger. He knows this won't look good to the higher-ups. But hey, he's gotten the results. He deserves a shot at that next promotion. Sure, there are some whiners in his group, but they wouldn't be where they are today without Roger. Roger is pretty sure that his career has advanced because he's known who the right people are upstairs and made certain that they were happy, regardless. No one ever doubts whether or not he's going to make his numbers. That, after all, is the point of business. Having completed his monologue, he promptly gets up from the table, informs you that he has a very important meeting, and leaves the cafeteria.

If the story were to end here, you might again reflect on your own current challenges and come up with a few more inferences:

- This guy is even more arrogant than I thought! Perhaps he is beyond help. He didn't even ask me about how things were going in my new role.

- He doesn't want coaching. He just wants to complain about other people without really exploring anything of substance with me.

You might then ask yourself the following questions:

1. Is there any way to get through to him, to get him to open up about his own problems, and be open to some input from others?

2. If I try to coach him, how much of a drain is the effort going to be on my own time?

3. If I can't coach him, what am I going to do with him?

Part III: A Happier Ending?

Perhaps through a combination of techniques (some drawn from this book, we hope) and good luck, you actually get Roger to tell you a bit more about his management style and its origins. Would the following story, if Roger decided to share it with you, change your impression?

The next day, you and Roger again find yourselves talking over a cup of coffee in the cafeteria. Roger remembers that when he first came to work, he was a real idealist. He wanted to make sure that everyone was happy. He thought worker satisfaction was the key to productivity. He started bending over backward to help out his employees, but boy, did he get burned. Some took advantage of him. His own boss at the time threatened to fire him unless he got people in line. The company didn't want to hear anything about his dreams of high performance and happy workers. Roger had a family to support, and he decided he'd better do it "their way."

What inferences might you make now? Here are some possibilities:

- Roger has at least some ability to reflect on his behavior and its history.

- He had in fact learned some very bad habits. Those habits had unfortunately been rewarded financially and in other ways.

- Roger may have some ability to alter his style a bit. We actually don't yet know because no one has ever tried to help Roger improve his ability to work with others. There was a time, when he first started working here, that he might have gladly accepted coaching about his leadership style.

- It probably won't be easy for him to change. This set of habits has, unfortunately, been in place for some time.

Notice that the question of whether or not someone is coach-able is likely to involve the making of an inference or a whole series of inferences. (We talk about making inferences in detail when we talk about gathering performance data in a later chapter.) The reality is that the question of whether or not someone is coach-able is one you will probably have to resolve with incomplete data. Almost no one will tell you that they are not coach-able or that they don't want coaching. That stance is probably no longer politically tolerable in most organizations, even organizations that don't particularly care about the development of their people.

Most coaching managers we have interviewed or surveyed tell us that arrogance, as they see it, is likely to be the number one block to coaching. Yet as can be seen in the case of Roger, the appearance of arrogance can reflect a personality problem, but it can also reflect previous learning in an organizational culture that actually teaches and rewards arrogance.

You will probably find it easy to spot someone who is very coach-able, though we'll describe below the behavioral indicators of someone who is most prepared to take advantage of coaching. Identifying situations in which coaching is likely to be impossible is a more difficult problem. So what can we say to serve as a guide to you, to help you know how to predict when you aren't sure?

In General, People Do Want to Be Coached

The Gallup Organization, using more than 20 years of survey and interview data, has identified 12 "core elements" or needs of employees that are statistically linked to employee productivity, profitability, customer service, and the employee's interest in staying in his or her current group or company (Buckingham & Coffman, 1999). These core elements give us a clear picture of what workers want and what motivates them to make efforts that result in these organizationally desirable outcomes. The 12 core elements are are listed in Box 4.1.

Box 4.1

THE 12 GALLUP "CORE ELEMENTS"

1. I know what is expected of me at work.

2. I have the materials and equipment I need to do my work properly.

3.   At work, I have the opportunity to do what I do best every day.

4.   In the last 7 days, I have received recognition or praise for doing good work.

5.   My supervisor, or someone at work, seems to care about me as a person.

6.   There is someone at work who encourages my development.

7.   At work, my opinions seem to count.

8.   The mission/purpose of my company makes me feel my job is important.

9.   My coworkers are committed to doing quality work.

10.   I have a best friend at work.

11.   In the last 6 months, someone at work has talked to me about my progress.

12.   This last year, I have had opportunities to learn and grow.

SOURCE: Adapted from *First Break All the Rules*, p. 28, by
M. Buckingham & C. Coffman, 1999, New York: Simon &
Schuster.

Managers and management educators everywhere should be humbled by these findings, which drew on more than 20 years of interview and survey data from literally millions of workers. Interestingly, compensation is not one of the core elements. Some core elements are intuitively obvious. The first two reflect an employee's need for clear direction and logistical support. A review of the Gallup elements in general, however, gives the distinct impression that the relationship between the manager and the employee has the greatest impact.

What about coaching? The word isn't used in the study, but as we review these results, we suggest that almost every question relates to coaching, even if indirectly. Certainly, active coaching managers can be well aware of whether their employees' needs are being met. However, we can be more specific than that.

The following elements are directly related to coaching: having the opportunity to do what one does best, receiving recognition or praise, feeling cared about, knowing that someone is interested in one's development, discussing one's progress, and having the opportunity to learn and grow. Our interpretation of the results of the Gallup study is that there is powerful and quite specific evidence from business organizations showing the strength of employee interest in coaching that will lead to learning and personal or career development. This suggests that managers should assume, until proven otherwise, that people want to be coached, even if they don't show that behavior explicitly. We suspect that even Roger would like to learn. The question is whether or not he can allow himself to learn with his manager and other members of his team:

That is the real meaning of coach-ability. A review of the characteristics of coach-able learners sheds light on what it takes to learn with someone else.

Hallmarks of the Coach-Able Learner

What behaviors does the individual demonstrate who is capable of effectively engaging with a coaching manager? Despite the diversity of styles, personalities, and cultural backgrounds found in today's workforce, it is possible to make some useful generalizations. The hallmarks of coach-ability are listed in Box 4.2. Consider the degree to which Roger, the star of our case at the opening of this chapter, demonstrates such behaviors. The coaching manager should also consider the degree to which his or her behaviors demonstrate their own coach-ability. As we will see in Chapter 5, the manager's coach-ability can be an important step in creating a coaching friendly context that encourages employees to express their interest in being coached.

Box 4.2

HALLMARKS OF COACH-ABILITY

The most effective coachees show the following characteristics:

- They can reflect on their actions from a fairly objective point of view, without undermining their own self-esteem, and are able to accept their humanity.
- They are curious about their actions and the actions of others.
- They are able to accept that someone else may be more knowledgeable than they are.
- They are not bound by shame that inhibits their ability to share their self-observations with a coach.
- They are able to listen, particularly to balanced feedback, and deflect all feedback back to the coach.
- They are motivated by coaching and are anxious to keep trying to improve and to learn.

First of all, a coachee must be able to reflect on his or her behavior—to step back and examine it from a somewhat objective frame of reference. If you had a particularly troubling meeting with your team and you want to learn something from the event, you need to be able to describe to yourself and to someone else what happened. Furthermore, you need to be able to think about what you did differently this time in contrast to your previous efforts. You need to be able to see and accept that you did some things effectively and other things not so effectively.

This rather dispassionate stance is not always easy for an individual to take, particularly if his or her self-esteem is closely bound to his or her work effectiveness. If whether or not you see yourself as a good or worthwhile person depends on your success, it may be threatening to objectively observe yourself while you are in the process of learning something new. Things will likely not go as well as you might have hoped. The ability to reflect requires an acceptance of your mistakes and your humanity without a great sense of distress. Ideally, effective coachees are curious about their performance and the challenges of continuous improvement. The coachee is like a scientist, trying to understand the laws that govern his or her actions and the actions of others, and to exercise some control through that understanding.

As already implied, you, as the effective coachee, also need to be able to share your insights and observations with someone else, someone who can help you. This means that you will need to accept that someone else may have more knowledge or be more effective than you are. The emotion of shame, which accompanies a sense of being small or defective, makes us want to hide our hopes, concerns, or problems. Feelings of shame make an individual want to keep awareness of his or her mistakes from others, which can make coaching nearly impossible. Effective coachees are able to honestly raise their concerns with their coaching managers, rather than succumb to such inhibition. Ideally, effective coachees are sufficiently free from a sense of shame, which makes them able to proactively seek out coaching.

The effective coachee needs to be able to listen. He or she needs to be able to tolerate balanced feedback and consider the meaning of what the coach is trying to say. We have all had the experience of giving someone else feedback only to be met with a defensive attack in which each and every point of the feedback is rebutted ("Yes, but . . ."). Although the feedback is heard, it is not understood.

Finally, effective coachees are motivated by coaching. Having received feedback, considered its meaning, and considered what they might do differently next time, they are anxious to practice. They take full responsibility for change and want to exercise their responsibility so that the learning can continue and they can assess their progress.

Unfortunately, not every coachee will display these behaviors in the same way and to the same degree. The coaches we have interviewed are more likely to note that no one is coach-able all the time. Timing is important. Everyone has bad days, and on those occasions, the coachee might be particularly prone to defensiveness. The best coaching managers are good at spotting windows of time when coachees seem more available and ready to learn, the stress level isn't too high, and the coaches themselves have the time and energy to focus on the coachee.

We can see now that our subject, Roger, has trouble on several counts. He doesn't seem to be an effective observer of his own behavior. More important, even though he is facing some difficulties in his work, he appears reluctant to discuss them with his manager. At this point, he doesn't seem to want to be coached. We can't know that for sure, however, because he hasn't known his new manager very long. He may have important concerns about how he looks to his new boss. This concern with "looking good" goes beyond any sense of personal embarrassment or shame that Roger may experience. The need to "look good" has a political dimension as well.

The Problem of Impression Management

If we can accept the assumption that people want to learn, then why aren't more of them absolutely, even loudly, insisting that they get the kind of coaching they feel they deserve? Unfortunately, there is a cost to seeking out feedback. Susan Ashford (1986) and her colleagues have drawn our attention to the idea that feedback is actually a resource and as such, has a certain value. In particular, it can help us be more successful in our efforts to adapt to or master the world—or more specifically, our jobs. The effort to master our environment requires that we get to know and understand it. This requires exploration, interpretation, mapping, and organizing what we come to know about our context. Feedback, specifically coaching, can greatly aid in this process.

What has a value may also have a cost. If appearing to be self-assured is required for success in your job, there may seem to be a substantial cost associated with asking for helpful feedback. And the reality is that asking for explicit feedback is not essential in order to survive at work; there are other ways of learning. After all, opening yourself up for help is to admit your vulnerability. Viewed by one, albeit unrealistic, set of standards, admitting that you need help can represent a blow to your self-esteem: "You are not self-sufficient."

To avoid the problems associated with exposing one's vulnerabilities, we can watch others, read, overhear the conversations of others doing similar work, and engage in trial and error learning, among other strategies. These "implicit" strategies of learning have a much lower cost, at least in some environments. It must be noted, however, that trial and error learning by itself is very inefficient. Implicit learning strategies in general are likely to be less effective in the absence of some opportunity to reflect, with someone else, on what one believes he or she is seeing and interpreting. Of course, implicit learning strategies may also be feedback-poor.

Nevertheless, implicit strategies of learning allow us to have greater control over the impression we believe we are creating in the minds of others: "If I look like I know what I am doing, then I'll probably be able to make it here." This concept is accurately captured in the notion of "heroic leadership" (Bradford & Cohen, 1999) and the idea that success comes to those who have all the right answers.

The ultimate point of this perspective is as follows: People probably won't appear to want coaching unless the cost of seeking it is less than its perceived value. Creating a coaching friendly context in part requires the manager to make sure that there are few, if any, costs to an employee who seeks out coaching. However, we encourage you to make the assumption that many, if not most, of your employees are consciously managing the impression they want to project to you. You need to ask yourself, "Am I signaling to them in any way that I don't want them to ask for coaching?" Roger has been in his firm for 5 years. There is at least some evidence that he learned the importance of impression management early in his career with the firm. He somehow got the impression that only "wimps" asked for coaching. If that is the only real barrier to his coach-ability, his stance may change over time.

Barriers to Coaching: What Does a Lack of Coach-Ability Look Like?

Once again, we issue the cautionary note that that most people are coach-able, except for a few. Here, we'll look at the exceptions. On the basis of our interviews and a review of the management literature, six potential barriers stand out as being very likely to be confronted by the coaching manager. The first four reflect characteristics of the individual employee. The final two reflect a mismatch between employee and manager.

- The already-mentioned problem of arrogance ("I don't need any help") coupled with a lack of insight
- A lack of interest in learning what the manager has to offer
- Lack of personal resilience or self-esteem
- The employee who is burdened with too much stress, particularly personal or family stress
- A significant cultural barrier between the coaching manager and his or her employee
- A mismatch between the career stage and needs of the employee and the career stage and needs of the manager

ARROGANCE: THE OVERESTIMATOR

As one of our coaches put it, "Arrogance, you know, they've got all the answers. Doesn't seem to matter whether or not they actually do have all the answers, they just think they do. They don't really want to talk with you at that point." This particular coaching manager doesn't give up on people who display such arrogance. Rather, he waits and chooses the right time to address this most difficult of coach-ability issues. He admits that coaching the arrogant employee can be more than a bit stressful.

The word *arrogance* summons up a great deal of emotion. Just the thought of dealing with an arrogant individual can be annoying and even intimidating. It brings up memories of meetings dominated by a team member who was sure of his or her perspective, regardless of the input of others; memories of discussions that went nowhere; memories of a tyrannical pursuit of results, no matter who got hurt; or memories of the sense of intimidation one experienced while trying to address a problem with an arrogant person. Arrogant people have a destructive impact on those around them. (In the interest of fairness, we should add that not everyone feels this way. Some people admire the extremely confident, even cocky, individual who "says it like it is, even if you don't want to know." In fact, one could argue that there is a place for such behavior under certain circumstances.)

However, personal style or method of presentation isn't at issue here. The issue here is whether or not the arrogant individual can engage in a learning relationship and benefit from coaching. The research to date is not promising. First, we should define more specifically what we mean by arrogant in this regard.

Rather than use an emotionally loaded approach, it is more useful to think about the cognitive framework that underlies what appears as arrogance on the surface. The problem is one of self-assessment versus the assessment of others. Researchers now have many years of experience in the use of multi-rater feedback instruments. *Multi-rater feedback,* or 360-degree assessment, as it is also known, allows an individual to receive feedback from not only the boss but also peers, subordinates, and other key stakeholders in relation to his or her effectiveness. Raters are usually chosen by the individual who is the subject of the assessment but are sometimes chosen by his or her manager; they rate the individual in relation to both outcome and process measures, such as interpersonal savvy or the ability to build an effective team.

The subject of the assessment is also asked to rate his or her own effectiveness. Self- and other-ratings can then be compared. Researchers can also compare the relationship between these two sets of ratings with other data in an effort to understand the meaning of gaps between self-assessment and other-assessment.

Table 4.1   Self/Other Ratings

Type	Ratings	Likely Outcomes
Overestimator	Self-ratings higher than other-ratings	Very negative; the employee is unaware of weaknesses
In agreement/Good	High self-ratings similar to high other-ratings	Very positive
In agreement/Bad	Low self-ratings similar to low other-ratings	Negative
Underestimator	Self-ratings less than other-ratings, which are high	Mixed, because the employee may not recognize skills and talents that could help him or her take on greater challenges

SOURCE: Adapted from "Do Managers See Themselves as Others See Them? Implications of Self-Other Rating Agreement for Human Resources Management," by F. Yammarino and L. Atwater, 1997, *Organizational Dynamics, 25*(4), p. 40.

Yammarino and Atwater (1997) describe four different relationships between self- and other-ratings that are useful for any manager to consider while coaching. These relationships are presented in Table 4.1. When an individual sees himself or herself as effective, and others agree, that individual is very likely to be successful and help the organization. Individuals who have negative self-assessments with which others agree will probably be neither successful nor helpful. However, they may have insight into the problem and can work on changing their roles.

The individual who has a negative self-assessment with which others don't agree, the underestimator, presents an interesting problem that we will discuss further. The most negative outcomes for both the individual and the organization, however, are observed when an individual's self-assessment is consistently higher than the assessment of others.

Most of us overestimate our effectiveness in a few areas of activity. That is simply human nature. However, individuals who generally overestimate their performance are likely to be unconsciously engaged in denial. Their self-concepts do not allow them to take in or effectively work with information, probably readily available from the environment, which suggests that their performance is poor. The manager will almost certainly have to address the problem but will find the employee uncooperative, or worse.

Truly arrogant individuals are people, in the eyes of our coaching managers, who don't realize they are arrogant. They are intimidating to others but have no insight into the magnitude of their intimidation. The combination of problematic behavior, a rigid self-perception, and a lack of insight create a very difficult circumstance for the coaching manager in such a situation. By way of contrast, we all know people who are perhaps generally overconfident, but who, under the right circumstances, will own up to a fault or two. Gentle confrontation of their arrogance can lead to a self-deprecating confession and sometimes even a genuine effort to respond. The coaching friendly context, to be discussed in detail in the next chapter, can aid in such self-acknowledgment.

What can a coaching manager do with an overestimator? The managers we've interviewed typically don't give up on such an individual, particularly if he or she still has some overlapping goals with the business. In addition, it is often the case that the origin of the individual's inflated self-assessment stems from the presence of an ability that the individual has actually been able to demonstrate to a successful end (Kaplan, Drath, & Kofodimos, 1991). In fact, it is difficult to be arrogant in the complete absence of talent. If the overestimator does have some special gift, he or she is very likely to feel like a victim when confronted. Ultimately, the decision as to whether or not to keep trying belongs to the coaching manager.

Our coaches have told us that in working with the overestimator, timing is everything. They have to look for a moment to deliver powerful and credible feedback to the individual. Yelling angrily at the overestimator is not a powerful intervention—just the opposite. The overestimator would then have reason to discount whatever content and data are in the message and feel even more misunderstood.

Every coaching manager should view his or her efforts to coach as an experiment. While conducting an experiment, one looks for results. If the desired results are not forthcoming in a reasonable period of time, another intervention may be called for. We encourage the coaching manager not to spend all his or her time trying to get through to every employee. Arrogant, chronic overestimators are actually fairly rare and often come to the attention of coaching mangers when they find themselves spending an inordinate amount of time putting out the fires started by such individuals.

AN APPARENT LACK OF INTEREST IN LEARNING

A number of the managers we've talked to believe that some of their biggest coaching successes occurred when they accepted that an individual was in a job for which he or she was not suited—and worse, did not like. The successful outcome involved helping the employee remove him- or herself from the job or the organization in a positive way.

In an era in which a focus on retention of employees seems all-important, such "successful" outcomes may seem counterintuitive. However, once the amount of time, energy, and stress required to try to help someone change his or her mind about a job are totaled up, the logic becomes clear. Many managers would be better off with no one in the job than with someone who was unhappy and was not going to get any happier, regardless of what anyone did.

We have stressed several times so far the importance of being careful about who you hire. Unfortunately, the reality is that most managers are likely to take over a group built by someone else, perhaps even for another task (the "inheritance tax"). Given the rate of change in most businesses today, the work that was once of interest to a particular employee may permanently disappear.

When the task of a group changes radically, all employees will react with anxiety and some, with a sense of loss. It will take time and managerial support to help employees adapt to such change. Most will. Those who find new work today that is consistent with their pattern of interests will probably make such an adjustment while working under a reasonably effective manager. However, some may not.

Once the manager has been able to determine that most employees have adapted and are moving ahead with new work tasks and processes but that some individuals have not, interventions in addition to developmental coaching per se may be called for. Interest patterns are rather stable and tend not to change over the course of our lives, even though the work we do to satisfy those interest patterns may change dramatically (Holland, 1992). Contrary to what many managers believe, we cannot make ourselves like something we don't like. For example, a manager who, as a supervisor, loves hands-on contact with her employees may find the political demands brought on by the growth of her unit and her de facto rise to upper-middle management to be both boring and stressful. The computer scientist who loves interfacing with customers may find the work of sitting at a terminal writing code to be abjectly uninspiring. As the old saying goes, promote your best salesperson to sales manager, and you lose a good salesperson and gain a lousy sales manager.

Failure to confront and accept an individual employee's lack of interest in a particular job can lead to hard feelings, declining morale, and poor performance. Managers can become increasingly frustrated by the failure of their attempts to help individuals change. Employees may display a variety of reactions, including anger at their managers, as well as anger at themselves about their inability to "get onboard." Both would be better off considering the possibility of helping an employee find stimulating work inside or outside the immediate coaching manager's business unit, as appropriate.

Managers should also be aware that many employees don't know how to manage their own careers. Even the brightest people in your organization may not understand the importance of thinking about what they really want out of life. Secondary and higher educational institutions in the western world don't always help, either. Take it as a given that some of your people will be in the wrong place at the wrong time and not really know it. This may represent the most common barrier to coach-ability.

PERSONAL RESILIENCE AND SELF-ESTEEM: WHAT ABOUT THE UNDERESTIMATOR?

Underestimators have their problems as well. Although they can be successful, they may misdiagnose their strengths and, as a result, make poor career or leadership decisions. They may lower goals in line with their assessment of what is possible. They may display low self-esteem and the emotional swings that accompany a more fragile self-concept. Most tragically of all, they may not pursue opportunities in which they are interested because they are convinced that failure would result.

Luckily, such individuals may respond very well to the coaching strategy we describe in this book. It is true that people with low self-esteem are not likely to respond to gratuitous compliments; the underestimator can discount such compliments. Worse yet, gratuitous compliments perceived to be offered out of sympathy may even further lower the self-confidence of underestimators. They may come to believe that you, the coaching manager, don't think they are up to the task of facing reality. However, when individuals who underestimate their performances are asked to reflect on those performances and are given robust feedback about what went right and what went wrong, the data of self- and other-assessment can be scrutinized side by side. This process may allow the underestimator to see the cognitive error he or she is making and consider the impact of that error.

Unfortunately, it is not always possible for such a strategy to help the underestimator. To make use of feedback, it helps to believe that there is something you can do about whatever it is you are trying to change. This has been described more generally as the individual's *locus of control*. The degree to which an individual believes that he or she is more or less in charge of his or her own destiny is related to both the situation and the individual. If the employee truly has no options and must simply accept whatever the situation dictates, coaching can be an aid to learning from what has transpired.

However, if the individual's lack of an inner sense of being able to have an impact on his environment is largely a function of his or her personality, that individual may not respond to the coaching manager's best efforts. There is evidence that people who have a greater sense of control in their lives are more able to tolerate critical feedback (London, 1997). Those whose sense of a lack of personal control is chronically low may be unable to tolerate the feedback give-and-take required of an effective coaching relationship. Such individuals may unconsciously feel a need to engage in defensive routines that serve to protect their highly vulnerable sense of self. As frustrating as this may be for the coaching manager, it is important to realize that there are limitations to what coaching can do. Coaching by a manager is no substitute for therapy.

We do not want to leave the reader with the impression that unless your employee has low self-esteem, you can get away with being extremely negative. Critical feedback should always be used sparingly and even then, only with the intent of being helpful. Feedback that is not given with the intent of being helpful can be destructive. We have talked with a number of managers who might be labeled as "tough" who have described how hurt they have been at the hands of an excessively negative executive coach or CEO. The coaching manager needs to maintain a helpful attitude with everyone, those with low and high self-esteem.

THE IMPACT OF PERSONAL STRESS

When an individual, even a great employee, is caught up in a significant personal or family dilemma, he or she may be far less able to engage in learning activities at work. One of our coaching managers described the importance of "paying attention to the whole person." It may be important to understand the basic problems associated with having too many stressors in one's life. We discuss this problem in much greater detail in Chapter 13. Here, we offer a few important points.

People actually need a certain level of stress in order to function effectively. Stress is the natural outgrowth of our efforts to adapt and master the challenges in life. You can think of each of us as having a kind of "set point" at which we are at our best. We may feel anxious, but we feel challenged as well. We're in a good fight, but we think we have a chance of winning.

Confrontation with additional stressors when we are already at the set point can take us to a state of distress that impairs our ability to function. The more threatening the stressor, the more distress is added to the individual's burden. Illness, child care issues, divorce, problems with an elderly parent, alcoholism or drug use, and emotional crises are just a few of the problems that can bring with them an acute level of distress. Coaching managers should be aware that the percentage of individuals in the workforce who are experiencing such levels of personal stress could be higher than they might expect. Some researchers estimate that as many as 25% of workers suffer from stress-related disorders (Sperry, 1993).

The coaching manager's approach to the individual who is experiencing a stress-related problem might be somewhat different from that of trying to engage the individual with low self-esteem, the underestimator. The matter may be one of timing. The stress-related problems may be transient. An employee with family problems may respond well to a solution, such as moving to a part-time status, which has been negotiated between the employee and his or her coaching manager. Such a solution may involve providing support or time off to the employee while the impact of the stress is being felt.

In both instances, we recommend that coaching managers be prepared to call their company's employee assistance program, human resource staff, or company medical consultants support. Trying to work with an employee who is engrossed in a serious stress-related or self-esteem-based problem can be very stressful in and of itself. The manager needs focused support from someone knowledgeable about the role that personal stress can play on learning and performance.

WHEN DIVERSITY BECOMES A BARRIER

Given the diversity of the workplace, it is likely that coaching managers will find themselves coaching people from a different gender, age group, race, ethnic group, cultural group, sexual orientation, or country of origin. The question we now confront is, to what degree is diversity between coach and employee a potential barrier to their ability to build an effective coaching relationship? In discussing this challenge with our coaches, we hear near unanimity in the belief that diversity represents a challenge but should not be seen as representing an insurmountable barrier. It is essential that the coach, and if possible, the coachee, be vigilant regarding the potential impact of diversity of experience, background, outlook, and even personal style. Diversity represents a potential challenge to the coaching relationship in several ways.

First, diversity can make effective communication more difficult. Coach and coachee may not understand what the other means. The word *leadership,* for example, can have very different meanings when viewed through a cultural lens. Some think of the leader as facilitator, whereas others think of the leader as director. Making sure there is agreement on the meaning of important words is essential in defining and interpreting performance processes, goals, and outcomes.

Diversity also represents a challenge to empathy, the ability to put oneself in the position of others and see the world through their eyes. Most of our coaches have told us that empathy is possible once the impact of diversity is understood and mutually explored. While talking about leadership, sales, or other interpersonal activities, coaching managers will often ask questions such as "How might you address this back home?" Hearing how the coachee sees the situation, which may be quite different from the perspective of the coaching manager, helps the coaching manager step into the coachee's point of view. The coach needs to ask the help of the coachee to make this leap of understanding. If the coach ignores the notion, for instance, that it might be difficult to be the only person of color on a new team, he or she may be missing a very important influence on that individual's development.

For this reason, some scholars have suggested that the greater the level of similarity between coach/mentor and coachee/protégé, the more likely the coaching or mentoring relationship is to be successful (Kram & Bragar, 1992). Similarity of race, age, gender, or culture of origin between manager and employee, however, is no longer possible in every case, nor is it always desirable, for a variety of reasons. It may be important for both coach and coachee to learn how to work cross-culturally in order to do their jobs. The coaching relationship then offers a vehicle for growth for both parties. At the same time, there may be a limit to how far even the best coaching manager and coachee can go toward closing the diversity gap. The coaching manager can't be all things to all people and neither can the coachee. The reality is that we all probably need a bit of support from someone who has personally experienced and understands our culture, as well as support from people who are quite different from ourselves.

Gail McGuire (1999), in her study of a large financial services firm in the United States, found that white women and women and men of color were able to access coaching or mentoring help with a frequency approximately equal to that of white men; this suggests that the barriers of diversity do not inhibit the building of coaching connections. However, she did find that what was discussed in the coaching relationship was influenced by the gender and race of both the coach and coachee.

McGuire (1999) also found that similarity seemed to have an impact on the degree to which emotional closeness developed between coach and coachee. Role modeling and friendships were less likely to develop in the absence of similarity of background. However, it was not clear whether similarity of gender or race had an impact on the degree to which coach and coachee addressed more career-related concerns, such as performance coaching, feedback, and assignment of challenging work.

As we have stressed, coaching and mentoring are not the same. Coaching is more focused on the work and is less likely to involve the kind of emotional closeness found in mentor relationships. As such, coaching might be particularly well suited to a diverse workforce and a diverse world. Expectations of coaches are different from those of mentors. Although much research remains to be done on this critically important area, we can only conclude at this time that dissimilarity of backgrounds can be a barrier to coach-ability, but it doesn't have to be. The challenge is for the coach and coachee to move beyond dissimilarity and create an effective enough coaching relationship so that learning can continue.

Table 4.2   Career Stages and Coaching

Career Stage	Personal Need
Establishment	The new employee probably has the greatest need for coaching.
Early career	Continued need for coaching and support, though the employee is increasingly able to work autonomously. May need more career guidance as part of coaching.
Advancement	Exposure to senior management and challenging work. Sponsorship and support for taking on new challenges.
Maintenance	Autonomy in his or her work. Opportunities to help others develop.
Exit	Consultative roles that still have an impact.
SOURCE:	From "Career Dynamics: Managing the Superior/Subordinate Relationship," by L. Baird and K. Kram, 1984, *Organizational Dynamics, 12*(4), p. 54.

A MISMATCH BETWEEN THE CAREER STAGE OF THE EMPLOYEE AND THE CAREER STAGE OF THE MANAGER

Many of our coaching managers have told us that they may vary their approaches to coaching in response to, among other things, the career stage of the employee. Some report that they tend to coach newer employees more frequently. Some report that they coach senior-level employees less. Some coach highly experienced employees only when directly asked. In working with senior-level employees, they focus on making sure that they get very challenging assignments and have the right resources to address them.

This finding is consistent with the findings of management researchers Lloyd Baird and Kathy Kram (1984). They came to the intuitively appealing conclusion that at different career stages, people have different needs. They described five distinct career stages, all of which are relevant to coaching. Those stages and the associated needs that are paramount at each stage are listed in Table 4.2. The five stages are establishment (just getting started), early career, advancement, maintenance, and exit.

Early in an employee's career, during the establishment stage and just beyond, there is an acute need for coaching and feedback because the employee may know very little about how to survive and be productive in the new career and organization. Employees in the establishment and early career stages have the most to learn in the shortest possible time.

In the advancement phase, individuals need to take on more work independently and show what they can do. In essence, they become progressively more capable of thinking through and solving problems on their own or with their teams, and they need less basic guidance. The individual in the advancement stage may be strongly focused on his or her own career and have less interest or energy for helping others.

In the maintenance phase, particularly if the individual has been successful, he or she is expected to coach. The employee, now often a manager, has significant responsibilities for taking autonomous action and feels less of a need to "prove" something to others. They may have more interest in building an organization and in the development of others.

Finally, in the exit stage, the employee's upward mobility is limited. He or she has already contributed to the firm and/or the profession but still wants to have an impact. Many employees at this stage find the opportunity to help others develop to represent a very meaningful contribution, a dignified and helpful way to close out a career.

The potential barrier for coach and coachee emerges when each has expectations of the other that are "out of sync" with their career stages. If the coaching manager tries to coach a senior-level employee in the same way that he or she coaches a junior-level employee, the senior employee may feel infantilized and rebel. Coaching and feedback become destructive rather than constructive.

A more senior employee will probably not wish to have his or her technical judgement questioned but may be open to coaching on strategic and political issues. Unfortunately, a younger coaching manager may have much less to offer in this regard. Likewise, the very new employee may have a great need for coaching. However, a manager caught up in the advancement stage may perceive that he or she has less time and energy for coaching than the new employee would like.

We caution against the view that lack of synchrony between the career stage of managers and employees has to be an overriding barrier. We have known many good coaching managers who are still early in their careers. As long they are as skilled at coaching and don't claim to be expert in areas or ways they are not, their effectiveness will not be undermined by their age or career stage. Likewise, we would argue to managers in the advancement stage of their careers that coaching could help them advance even more rapidly. We have also seen many senior-level employees make good use of rich coaching relationships that address their real needs. This makes sense given the nature of today's work.

The concept of the career stages we have just outlined may in fact be changing in the new economy; organizations have shorter life spans, and those that do survive have to adapt to very rapid change. (Some readers who look at our list of career stages may wonder whether anyone makes it to the maintenance stage at this point!) Yet senior-level employees who accept that they may have to start their careers over from time to time, to keep up with such rapid change, may find the opportunity to engage in the give-and-take of coaching to be very useful.

An experienced a manager as Jack Welch, former CEO of General Electric (GE), has taken advantage of (and insisted that his peers at GE do so as well) a "reverse" mentoring program. Executives needed a hands-on knowledge of the World Wide Web to guide the firm into the era of e-commerce. The best way to learn was to tap the younger, Web-savvy generation of GE workers for help. Junior employees, chosen to serve as technology coaches to senior executives, met regularly with their "coachees" to help them learn how to "surf the Web" (Schlender, 2000). Such a coaching model can work, even though the career stages of both coach and coachee may clearly seem "upside down."

Coaching managers who tell us that they coach more experienced workers just as much as newer workers say that coaching focuses on more sophisticated issues. Strategy, leadership, and client relationships are examples. This group of coaching managers believe that coaching needs to continue as part of succession planning within their business units.

Finally, we should stress again that coaching is not just for the coachee. Coaching promotes organizational learning and learning on the part of the manager. In that sense, it is the coachee's obligation to engage in coaching, at least to a degree, regardless of career stage.

Coach-Ability: Treat Each Employee as an Individual

This exploration of the factors that promote or inhibit an individual's ability to engage with a manager in a coaching relationship may have raised more questions than answers for the reader. Although we can describe the factors that suggest a high degree of coach-ability, and we can describe some commonly seen barriers to coach-ability, ultimately, the best coaching managers don't use a formula or cookbook. They treat each employee as an individual. They are likely to try a variety of approaches to an employee's development before concluding that an employee is beyond help or is in the wrong job.

So is Roger coach-able? We actually think he might be.

5

Creating a Coaching
Friendly Context

IN THIS CHAPTER, WE DESCRIBE THE FOLLOWING:

- What a coaching friendly context is like
- How individual managers can create a coaching friendly context, regardless of their larger organizational surroundings

Learning requires a level of openness that some managers and employees find threatening. We believe, however, that once they are used to such a level of openness, employees and managers will find it helpful and even stimulating. In this chapter, we describe what both can do to overcome that threat.

Both the manager and the employee—really, all the employees in any given work group—must create a context that makes learning possible. They must feel comfortable discussing issues openly and freely, with an eye toward learning. This is what we mean by a *coaching friendly context*. The coaching friendly context, when fully developed, allows a market for coaching and learning to emerge. At that point, the coaching manager may even spend less time formally coaching because coaching is going on almost everywhere, most of the time. The coaching manager coaches team members. Team members coach each other and they also probably coach the manager.

Most employees do not experience their context, the workplace, in that way. For most of us, when we use the term *context*, it is easier to think about contexts that interfere with learning, rather than promote it. Does the situation we describe in the following case sound familiar?

Case 5.1: Financial Co.—A Learning Context?

Times are tough at Financial Co. (the name and industry have been disguised). Born of a set of companies that were strung together through difficult-to-fathom merger and acquisition activities, Financial Co. was grasping, unsuccessfully it seemed, for some sense of purpose or vision. Many of its product lines were in very bad shape. Mismanagement over the years had turned cash cows into obsolete bureaucracies. Competition had successfully encroached from all sides.

Employee turnover was high, in part driven by the (accurate) perception that senior management was ruthless in its focus on the bottom line. The stock price had dropped so low that with any further decline, delisting of the stock from the exchange would become a very real possibility. Managers were expected to hit their financial targets by any means necessary. "If you can't get it done immediately, we'll find someone else who can, and you're out!" was the explicit message from the CEO. Fear and mistrust were rampant. Mistakes were not to be tolerated.

New hires were told that they needed to be able to "hit the ground running." You had to be really good at what you were hired to do. There was no time to develop new talent. (Of course, this begs the question of why anyone who was "really good" would want to work for such a company.) Many managers expressed open disdain for the corporation, when they had the time to think.

Is coaching, the development of others, possible in such an organization? Isn't it true that this type of short-term focus is anathema to thinking about employee development? If managers receive no reward—indeed, run the risk of being punished for spending time coaching employees— won't all such activities cease?

What do you think? Could you imagine trying to help the people who work for you develop while you are working under the weight of such intense pressure? Taking this from an action-planning point of view, if you wanted to try and help your employees develop, what would you need to do?

We suggest that you start by making sure that you and the members of your group take a bit of time to reflect on your work and what is going on around you. When surrounded by a sense of panic, people rarely feel as though they have the time to reflect. They feel the urge to just *act*. Of course, as we discussed in Chapter 1, the tendency to act without reflection probably leads to doing more of the same, which ultimately wouldn't help Financial Co.

After creating some pockets of time for people to reflect on their work, you would then have to make them feel that it was safe to do so. Would they trust you enough to talk openly about their work, rather than feeling as though they needed to stay out of the way and "keep their heads down"? Even if they did trust you, would they trust that you could protect them? After all, to learn from their performance and their mistakes, they would have to talk about them with you. Perhaps you would be forced to talk about these kinds of problems with your own boss. Perhaps one of their peers on the team would let it be known that this was a group with problems. Word would get out, and some careers at Financial Co. would be over. Obviously, such an environment discourages any kind of developmental work. It is easier to develop leaders, for example, at companies such as General Electric (GE), where former CEO Jack Welch set the standard by spending as much as half his time on such "people issues."

Nevertheless, we have repeatedly seen that even under such harsh conditions, coaching can and will take place. *The only person who can really have an impact on whether or not coaching will take place in any given setting is the individual manager.* Coaching is not completely dependent on the larger organizational context in most cases. In our experience, managers who want to take active roles in shaping positive developmental opportunities for their employees will find a way to make it happen. They protect their employees from a toxic environment and in the process, create a coaching friendly context.

We were fortunate to have a manager from Financial Co. attend one of our coach training programs. He was there because of his capacity as a team leader. His team was involved in an innovative project at Financial Co. that even the CEO hoped would help improve the firm's business situation. The task of the team leader and his group in bringing this project to completion was extraordinarily risky, however. If they failed, they would quite likely all lose their jobs.

The team leader reasoned that the only way he could get some of the best minds in the company to work on the project was to make sure that they would learn a lot from their experience. He also felt that he had to play an active role in helping them integrate the experience with their own career plans. A "natural" coach, he was given no support from corporate but was simply determined to make it possible for his people to develop, even under such difficult circumstances. He managed to create a coaching friendly context under bitterly harsh conditions. He was coaching, and his employees responded very positively to his efforts.

Evidence from other researchers supports this rather provocative contention: In most cases, the manager can create a coaching friendly context even if the larger environment is hostile. Amy Edmondson (1996) studied team learning in hospital-based nursing units. Nurses work under very difficult circumstances. Their work is highly technical, demanding, tedious at times, and very highly regulated. When a nurse makes an error, people can be hurt. Doctors, hospitals, and nurses can be sued. Such incidents can make the front pages of the newspapers. Politicians get involved, and so it goes. Is this a coaching friendly context? Wouldn't such conditions create an absolute intolerance of mistakes that would make it practically impossible for people to talk about their performance? Not necessarily.

Studying different nursing units within the same hospital, Edmondson (1996) found statistically significant differences from group to group in nurses' willingness to talk about medication errors. In some groups, to talk about a medication error was a tacit admission of guilt and responsibility, and one's career could immediately be threatened. In other groups, medication errors were considered too important not to talk about. In those teams, nurses expressed the view that they needed to learn more about what went wrong and what could be done to improve their accuracy.

The more open groups did report more medication errors than the more closed groups. (When you make it possible to really talk about the work your team is doing, you may not always like what you hear. Be prepared for that.) Digging deeper into the problem, Edmondson (1996) found independent evidence that strongly suggested that the rate of errors was actually not higher in the open groups. Rather, individuals in the more closed groups were actively suppressing discussion of errors. They were covering up to protect themselves from punishment. The nurse manager's actions and behavior played a signif- icant role in determining whether or not those who worked in such units believed that it was acceptable to learn from their performance and their errors. (If you were sick, in which kind of unit would you like to be hospitalized?)

This is the challenge our coaching managers put before you. If you are lucky enough to be working for a supportive and open company, such as Southwest Airlines, or you are part of an enlightened entrepreneurial start-up or a family business that places a high value on employee development, go ahead and coach. You are probably in a coaching friendly context already. Your employees may even be expecting you to coach, so you'd better do it. Look around you and watch how other managers in your firm coach and create learning oppor- tunities. Borrow what you see that is consistent with your own leadership style (assuming that you want to incorporate coaching into your leadership style).

If your own context is not quite so supportive, or even downright harsh, we believe that you will need to intentionally shape the immediate context around and within your work group to make your efforts at coaching and learning productive. You will also need to consider intentionally creating a coaching friendly context for new members of your group, as well as when you take over a new group, regardless of the culture of the larger organization. To do so, you will have to manage yourself and your relationships with the other members of

Table 5.1   Organizational Values and a Coaching Friendly Context

Supporting Values	Inhibiting Values
Trust and openness	Mistrust and fear
Tolerance of mistakes, learning from them	Intolerance of mistakes, blaming of the perpetrator
Careful attention to hiring the right people	Lack of careful attention to hiring, credibility of members
Learning for the long term is important	We should focus single-mindedly on evaluating today's performance
Reward systems shouldn't punish time spent developing people	Reward systems focus only on short-term results
People should feel valued as individuals	People are a "means to an end"

your group. In certain circumstances, you may also need to manage the relationship between your group and the larger organizational context. However, before describing actions that can help you create a coaching friendly context, we'll describe the look and feel of one in more detail. (Please note that this description of a coaching friendly context is also relevant to CEOs or entrepreneurs who are seeking to build or shape a company culture.)

The Coaching Friendly Context, Defined

In the coaching friendly context, learning is taken for granted to be an important, if not always directly discussed, ingredient of both personal development and business performance. People in a coaching friendly context naturally and informally reflect on their actions, discuss their problems and goals, and ask for feedback and advice. The values and beliefs that serve as a foundation for such a coaching friendly context, along with those that don't support a coaching friendly context, are listed in Table 5.1. Where appropriate, we use examples from one of the more coaching friendly contexts we've run across, the After Action Review Program (AAR) of the U.S. Army, to illustrate what one organization has done to promote learning and reflection (Garvin, 2000).

TRUST AND A LARGE MEASURE OF OPENNESS

As is the case with much of leadership, trust in the relationship between manager and employee is probably the most important element of a coaching friendly context. The employee must believe that he or she can be open with the manager without fear of punishment. The manager must consistently behave in a fashion that reinforces such trust. The manager must act with integrity in this regard. Trust of this kind between manager and employee makes it possible for employees to support their managers even when times are tough. Such trust is based on (a) an explicit awareness of what is important to each individual in the relationship and (b) the knowledge that they will make sincere efforts to help each other meet their goals. We can't emphasize this latter point enough: Trust is built between individuals. The coaching leader must have a relationship with each individual on his or her team to successfully help them learn through coaching.

MISTAKES TOLERATED BECAUSE THEY ARE USEFUL FOR LEARNING

Mistakes are not usually viewed from an evaluative perspective in a coaching friendly context. Yes, mistakes do create problems for any business. Certainly, some mistakes are intolerable. On balance, however, in a coaching friendly context, mistakes are viewed as opportunities for learning. A famous coaching story from the early days of IBM illustrates the point. An executive responsible for a particularly important and expensive project came to Thomas Watson Sr., the founder, to report that he had failed. The executive then offered his resignation to Watson. At this point, Watson supposedly responded, "Why would I want to lose you? I've just invested a lot of money in you." The considerable financial costs of a failed project were important, but Watson felt that in the process, the executive had learned something even more valuable.

The After Action Review (AAR), described briefly in Chapter 1, offers an example of how trust and an officer's tolerance for mistakes are intertwined as a vehicle for learning. The official policy of the AAR program holds that whatever is said in the AAR will not come back to injure a soldier's career. Inclusion of a soldier's input from an AAR into his or her personnel record is explicitly forbidden. However, policy by itself is not enough to ensure trust. Policies are carried out by individual managers. Our interviews with servicemen and -women who have been through AARs indicate to us that the perceived value of the exercise was very much dependent on the integrity with which the officers involved stuck to a focus on learning. If information about mistakes made were to somehow "leak" out, and the careers of individuals who participated in an AAR were injured because those individuals had been candid, even the army's AAR policies wouldn't be enough to ensure a coaching friendly context. The policy can help because it backs up the manager, but the integrity of the manager is the factor that determines the real value of the AAR.

ATTENTION TO HIRING THE RIGHT PEOPLE

It is important to look at the issues of trust and tolerance for mistakes in more depth. Obviously, no organization has an infinite capacity for error. We would never suggest that a manager tolerate an inordinately high level of error. The answer to this seeming paradox can be found in research on "psychological safety" and learning in high-performance teams. Edmondson (1999) found that psychological safety on a work team represented a shared sense of trust, a caring for one another as people, and respect for each other's competence. Those three factors created a context for team learning that resulted in improved group performance. We draw your attention to the last of the three factors, respect for each other's competence.

It is easier to trust people, even to allow them to make mistakes, if you see them as fundamentally in the right job and being able to perform that job to at least a minimal degree. This means that they can make a credible claim to being up to the basic tasks of the job, though they may still need to learn more. If those aspects aren't present, a mistake understandably becomes much more threatening. One condition for a coaching friendly context, then, is that the team or the organization has been relatively successful at getting competent people in the right jobs. This requires paying attention to competence and not just gut reaction in the selection process, as well as hiring people who are open to learning. It is much easier to coach good or adequate performers than performers who are failing. It is simply easier to trust that they will, on balance, do an acceptable job and responsibly try to learn from their mistakes. In our view, effective hiring is an essential foundation for effective coaching. Mutual respect as an outcome of an effective hiring process provides the foundation for trust.

AN INTEREST IN LEARNING,
NOT JUST IN TODAY'S PERFORMANCE

Financial Co. runs the risk of consuming its own feedstock. Although today's business performance is important, a company's long-term competitiveness is rooted in the ability of its people to learn and adapt. Even during the worst of times, attention to learning is visible, for instance, when the firm doesn't eliminate its training budget, uses downtime for strategic or important projects that will help the business, creates opportunities for personal learning on the part of employees, and demonstrates a recognition of the priority placed on learning. Attention to learning, which ultimately validates a manager's efforts to coach, signals to everyone that the group exists for both today and tomorrow.

One might expect that the U.S. Army would have a rather short-term, performance-oriented focus. After all, when the battle is over, army personnel are undoubtedly glad to be finished. Yet the senior commanders have explicitly and forcefully committed themselves to the idea that personal and organizational learning are essential for *tomorrow's* effective performance. This commitment is communicated through the army's insistence on the regular use of AARs. They are not considered optional. The learning that emerges from the AAR is, then, used as part of the army's knowledge management system.

REWARD SYSTEMS THAT ENCOURAGE MANAGERS TO SPEND TIME COACHING

Closely related to a value on learning are reward systems that create tangible positive outcomes for managers who are effective at employee development. If managers are paid solely for today's results, that is what many managers may focus on. Our point here is to watch out for pay systems that actively discourage coaching. However, we issue a cautionary note about the use of pay for performance as a vehicle for changing managerial behavior when it comes to encouraging coaching (and almost anything else). There is a growing body of evidence suggesting that external rewards (pay) undermine intrinsic motivation (performing because it fits with your personal need or motivation). Jeffrey Pfeffer (1998) is one of a number of management researchers who have shown that pay for performance serves to make people feel controlled and make them do what the controllers (those with the money) want, rather than exercise personal judgment.

Managers who coach "for the money" are not necessarily operating with the motive of trying to be helpful (see Chapter 3). For instance, a small number of lawyers, consultants, and psychotherapists who have appeared to be profoundly greedy in the conduct of their business affairs have made the practice of their professions suspect to many others in the larger population. Employees need to trust that they will get their manager's attention for reasons that go beyond the paycheck. Certainly, compensation systems should reward a manager's work in the development of employees. The reality is that coaching managers are often not compensated directly for such efforts but keep coaching anyway. (They would argue that even though they are not directly compensated for coaching in most cases, coaching helps them reach their business goals, so the reward in indirect.)

This is not a book about the latest debates over appropriate compensation practices. However, we encourage organizational designers and human resource executives to consider whether the reward systems in play in their firms support coaching or inhibit it. Reward systems that place an enormous amount of a manager's pay at risk on the basis of the quarter's business results can get the attention of even the most dedicated and gifted coaching manager.

You may be willing to coach your employees for strategic or personal reasons even if the payoff is not fully tangible in the short term. However, you probably won't want to coach if it will cost you and your family a substantial amount of money.

The U.S. Army doesn't use a compensation system to encourage unit commanders to hold an AAR. It is an expected part of their jobs. A failure to do so would be considered a performance problem of the highest order.

PEOPLE VALUED FOR THEMSELVES, NOT JUST AS A MEANS TO AN END

The last value that promotes the emergence of a coaching friendly context is perhaps the least tangible, yet it serves as a foundation for much of what has already been discussed. A coaching manager says to himself, "George (an employee) is under way too much stress at home to deal with all this. I need to lighten his load for a little while." Such a manager has put himself in the position of the employee and thought about the needs of the whole person. Employees are people, who learn and perform. The process is not mechanistic. Significant status differences between managers and employees can undermine organizational performance (Pfeffer, 1998). Status differences make individuals feel undervalued. People who feel valued are much more likely to want to learn. They feel that there is a more genuine overlap between the organization's goals and their own personal goals. Likewise, people who are overwhelmed and burdened by stress may be in no condition to learn. We'll talk about the timing issues that arise while trying to create a coaching moment; suffice it to say that being sensitive to the needs of others is critical to the coaching and learning process.

Although soldiers are ultimately a "means to an end" in the sense that they serve a purpose that is higher than their own self-interests, officers have for centuries known that the personal relationship between commander and soldier is an essential part of the bonding that holds a unit together. When the commander listens to a soldier in an AAR, respects his or her opinion, and takes his or her feedback seriously, the soldier feels valued.

The Coaching Friendly Context and the High-Performance Organization

Note that the six values that we believe support a coaching friendly context also characterize many high-performing work organizations (Pfeffer, 1998, 2000).

High-performance work organizations significantly outperform their competitors and view the workforce as a crucial competitive weapon. These six values are also consistent with the Gallup 12 questions, already discussed and shown to be linked to profitability, customer service, and employee retention (Buckingham & Coffman, 1999). Yet these are the values cited by our sample of coaching managers. For this reason, we have become absolutely convinced that there is no contradiction between developmental coaching and business success. Indeed, the evidence suggests just the opposite.

Alas, however, we have lost this argument with a few entrepreneurs and general managers who felt otherwise. We began this chapter by insisting that managers can determine whether or not coaching can effectively take place in their own units. What, then, should managers try to do to create coaching friendly subcultures in their own business units?

Creating a Coaching Friendly Context in Your Business Unit

The actions listed in Box 5.1 can help you create a coaching friendly context in your organization. As much as any suggestions in this book, they are based on the input of our coaches. The goal of these actions is for you and the employees in your business unit to be as comfortable as possible with the way you behave as a coaching manager. These actions also serve as signals to your employees, some direct and some implicit, regarding how they can participate in the coaching process.

Box 5.1

CHECKLIST FOR A COACHING FRIENDLY CONTEXT

Here is a checklist of actions you can take to build a coaching friendly context in your own unit:

1. Have you explained your management philosophy, including your approach toward mistakes,

    - To your group?
    - To new members?

2. Are you able to "walk the talk" and be true to your management philosophy?

3. Are you accessible? Do you make it clear that you do want to know:
   - When people have questions?
   - When people think they need help?
   - When things are not going well?

4. Do you convey in words and actions an interest in your employees when they ask to speak with you?

5. Are you clear in your own mind about the distinction between coaching and evaluation?
   - Have you communicated this distinction to others?
   - Do your coaching efforts support or conflict with your performance appraisal program?

6. Do you demonstrate through your actions that you want others to coach you?
   - Do you listen to feedback without retaliating?

7. Do you help the members of your group deal with threats of punishment from outside the group?

EXPLAINING OR SIGNALING YOUR INTENT TO COACH

We advocate that coaching managers explicitly inform the members of their group that they will use coaching as part of their day-to-day approach to leading the group. In addition, we suggest that coaching managers clarify how they will react to questions from their employees, performance problems, and mistakes that employees make. This is particularly important when the manager is taking over a new group or orienting new employees in an existing group. We say this with some trepidation because we have also been told by some very assertive businesspeople that managers shouldn't make a "big deal" out of the fact that they coach. This approach is rarer, however. Most of the managers we talk with indicate that it pays to be explicit about what you are doing as a coaching manager if for no other reason than that most employees are simply not used to it.

One of our coaching managers has a series of in-depth meetings with each new group member. She gets to know them as individuals but also tries to help them get to know her. As part of this process, she explains how she hopes the new employee will make use of their twice-monthly individual meetings and weekly staff meetings. She explains that the new hire can bring up anything he or she wants to discuss: career issues, work problems, good ideas. She'll probably listen and ask questions because that is her style. She also tells new hires that it is okay to come into her office and ventilate their feelings: "Better they do it with me than with a client."

We aren't suggesting that managers exaggerate their emphasis on coaching. However, we are concerned that unless managers are explicit about their intent to coach and what they expect of people who work for them, some, perhaps many, of their employees won't know how to effectively participate in the learning process. We've asked our coaching managers whether or not new employees are surprised that coaching is a normal part of business activity. They answer "yes," many are, unless they've had a mentor or coaching manager before (which most haven't). Consider the assumptions that many employees hold on the basis of previous experience:

- How many of us have heard, "Don't come to me with problems, come to me with solutions." Although we can understand the harried executive making such a statement, this advice has reached the status of folklore in the American business culture. This statement, probably the most anticoaching statement we've heard, is, ironically, derived from a command-and-control model of leadership. The leader is too busy to talk things over with others because he or she is making all the really important decisions. In a coaching friendly context, the leader delegates work to others. The leader then helps people doing the work by providing consultation and other resources. The leader has to be available for meaningful consultation under such circumstances. Consider the alternative statement used by one of our coaches: "Don't come to me with a problem until you've spent a little bit of time thinking about it and have thought of at least one possible solution. It doesn't have to be the right one; it can even be a crazy one. I just want you to do some thinking before I jump in to help." The meaning of this message is very different. This statement doesn't convey "Don't bother me." It conveys "You need to take some responsibility for this, but I'll help."

- Most employees expect to be evaluated, not coached. Remember that this is the experience of almost everyone in business today. They may have never been coached. If you start trying to coach them before you've set the stage by explaining your actions, they make think you are laying a trap.

- Many employees are told what to learn. "Get *your* job right before you go thinking about mine" is the control-oriented manager's dictum on learning. When employees are told not to think, they no longer find value in learning.

It is worthy of note that the army does make a "big deal" out of coaching. We suspect that such an effort has been necessary because the previous environment was so toxic to the kinds of interactions required for learning. We suggest that if you find yourself taking over such a group, you may need to work very hard to communicate your own focus on learning to others and how you expect them to participate in that effort. The "big deal" may be quite warranted.

MAKING YOURSELF ACCESSIBLE

Having explained your management philosophy and your approach to coaching to your employees, follow-through on your part is critical to sustaining your credibility. Your interest in following through is communicated by your attention in words and with body language when a coaching opportunity occurs. Consider the following example:

Case 5.2: Fred, the Coach

(The following is a true story. The names are disguised.) Have you ever "been there"?

Samantha was a group manager in a well-respected consulting firm, one known for its interest in the development of its employees. She had just returned from an unsettling client engagement. One of the senior managers in the client firm accused her of not being committed to the project and felt she was not sufficiently available to the client team. This information was in direct contrast to the verbal and written feedback she had received in the client review meeting 2 days earlier. Sitting in her office with the door closed, she felt deeply discouraged about her performance and her career. She wasn't even sure what she had done wrong.

Feeling an overwhelming need to talk, she was relieved when she heard the familiar sound of keys in the door to the office next to hers. Her director, Fred, was coming in from the field as well. Though she didn't normally talk about her own doubts or her failures with others in the firm, let alone her boss, she felt as though she had no choice. She needed to talk and to figure out what had gone wrong. Also, Fred spent a lot of time "preaching" about the merits of coaching and prided himself on being an avid practitioner of the latest management development techniques. Samantha felt it might be safe to talk with Fred.

When she knocked on Fred's door, she heard, "Come in," in his usual, somewhat stuffy manner. After an exchange of small talk while Fred was unpacking his briefcase, Samantha began to explain what had happened with the client earlier in the day. Fred kept unpacking, never looking at

Samantha. Samantha continued to describe the problem, obviously in distress. Fred began to read his e-mails while offering a perfunctory "Too bad." Samantha knew he wasn't listening. And why should he? This problem won't affect his bonus, let alone his career, she thought to herself. But she continued to feel a powerful need to talk. She kept trying, to no avail.

All at once, Fred began to complain to her about the e-mail he had just received from the company's CFO. Samantha could tell that everything she had said about herself, her worries, and the client had never been heard. Fred had gone on to *his* next issue. As he continued to rant about the CFO and the finance department, Samantha eased herself out of the room, saying, "Excuse me, I think I heard my phone." She left feeling very much like a nonperson and wondered why she had even bothered going to her boss in the first place.

Obviously, Fred communicated in words and body language that, at this particular time at least, he wasn't interested in coaching Samantha. This is one example in time and may not represent Fred's typical behavior. However, it will not take many such instances for Fred to undermine his efforts at creating a coaching friendly context.

Fred preaches coaching but isn't accessible. He doesn't listen to Samantha. He doesn't ask appropriate questions (see Chapter 6). He turns away from her and starts reading his e-mail. Finally, he changes the subject from her concerns to his own. The message to Samantha is twofold. First, Fred doesn't help Samantha figure out what went wrong, which is one of the most basic responsibilities of the coaching manager. Second, Fred doesn't care about Samantha. In Fred's defense, he may have been busy or tired himself. He may have been in no mood to coach Samantha. If that were the case, and he wanted to maintain a coaching friendly context for the long term, he might have said to Samantha, "This sounds very bad. I'm afraid that that I'm just exhausted. Let me catch my breath and then let's talk, say at 4 p.m. today." Fred delays the coaching dialogue but stays true to the ideal that coaching is important. He also communicates to Samantha that he does care about her and wants to help.

Fred's actual behavior suggests that he doesn't want to deal with or can't handle problems—for example, his reaction to the CFO's e-mail. Though it may or may not be true, his behavior signals that he wants to hear only about things that are going well.

Contrast Fred's behavior with the report from another coaching manager. Jack coaches a global marketing team. He coaches by telephone. He prefers to talk with his team members from a conference room rather than from his own office. "I know myself. I'll look at the e-mails or start glancing at whatever is on my desk. People can tell when you aren't really focused on what they are saying, you know. I have to put myself somewhere I can really focus. I want to encourage them to pick up the phone and call me when something's going on."

Accessibility involves open-door management. One coaching manager rearranged his office rather than have people see his back as they entered the room. Another coaching manager gives group members his home telephone number and encourages them to use it. Most coaching managers practice management by walking around. They'll stop in at an employee's cubicle or office and chat, sending out a clear message: "I'm here, let's talk."

CLARIFYING AND COMMUNICATING THE DISTINCTION BETWEEN COACHING AND EVALUATION

Ultimately, as a manager in most organizations, you will also have to evaluate your employees. You will have to make decisions that will influence your employees' pay. You may have to terminate an employee for nonperformance. Don't these responsibilities make it more difficult to create a coaching friendly context? We say that they can, but they don't have to. Coaching can actually support the process of evaluation when the two are kept distinct.

To coach effectively, you must first of all be clear in your own mind as to when you are evaluating and when you are coaching. Organizations that both coach and evaluate tend to use a variety of rituals that help them punctuate the transitions from coaching to evaluation. Many now explicitly separate performance management and coaching feedback.

Regardless of the timing, the conflict between performance appraisal and developmental coaching is most likely to occur when the manager has not done enough developmental coaching. One of our coaching managers resisted the notion that there was a conflict between the two. "I coach all the time, so when performance appraisals are given, no one is ever surprised. The data are already clear. They know I have tried to help. The performance appraisal is when we tally the score."

While coaching, you may not formally tally the score—the coaching manager focuses on learning from a particular situation. Ultimately, though, the manager has to tally the score if the learning in question is critical to the success of the employee and the business unit. If the manager has done a great deal of coaching around an important developmental goal, the process of evaluation has actually already taken place, implicitly and informally. Employees know that their manager will ultimately formally evaluate them. The question is: Will it be done in a just fashion? If the employee has not been coached, when the appraisal and evaluation does occur, it will have a much greater sting.

In our view, the problem with evaluation has as much to do with day-to-day behavior as it is does with formal performance appraisals. Looks of disapproval, undue or humiliating criticisms, a withdrawal of friendliness, and other behaviors following a problem, though implicit, are powerful signals to the employee that say, "You screwed up!" As one of our coaching managers put it, "If I say, 'Don't worry about it' and don't back that up, walk the talk, then I'm going to blow it with that employee. I can't say 'Don't worry about it' and then keep bringing it up in a critical way. I have to grit my teeth and let it go."

We all want to feel that we're okay in the eyes of others who are important to us. This is a particularly powerful dynamic between leaders and followers. The leader's verbal and nonverbal cues to group members are probably more powerful messages than losing 1% of a raise. Another coaching manager told us, in that regard, "You have to hold your temper. If you get angry, sometimes just once, you may make it impossible for that employee to really come back and tell you the truth." This statement sets a high standard. After all, we're only human. Nevertheless, we draw your attention to the importance of managing your own emotions as a key success factor while trying to create a coaching friendly context.

ENCOURAGING EMPLOYEES TO COACH YOU

We have been told, repeatedly, that one of the best ways to encourage a coaching friendly context is to encourage people in your unit to coach you. The reasons are probably obvious. The manager models openness, how to take feedback, an interest in improving his or her performance, and an interest in learning. The manager shows others in the group how to receive coaching in the process. This is important because, as we've stated repeatedly, most employees haven't been coached and as a result, don't know how to use it.

Many coaching managers have also told us that they discuss their interest in being coached with new hires. They explicitly encourage upward feedback. An important payoff to encouraging employees to coach is that they can learn coaching skills as well. Most of the coaching managers we have talked to report that they do rely on peer-to-peer coaching within their work groups.

HELPING THE MEMBERS OF YOUR WORK
GROUP DEAL WITH THREATS FROM OUTSIDE YOUR GROUP

The following quotation from a division vice president in one of our training programs says it all: "If someone is trying to do 10 things, does 7 right, and 3 wrong, that's okay with me. We'll talk about it and try to figure out what went wrong with the other 3. I just have to make sure that corporate doesn't find out.

They somehow don't believe that a batting average of .700 is adequate." (For those who don't know the game of baseball, a batting average of .700 means that a batter has gotten a hit in 7 out of 10 trials. No one in history has ever come even close to such a batting average. Averages of .290 to .350 are considered very good.)

This challenge represents, we believe, one of the most difficult tasks facing the coaching manager whose larger organizational context is not coaching friendly. In addition to the politics of trying to protect your team, this issue has an ethical dimension as well. In some industries, there may be a legal problem in withholding information about an employee's difficulties from your own manager. Auditing firms, energy companies, and health care institutions, just to name a few, must follow very strict legal guidelines or risk running afoul of a variety of governmental regulations.

Having stated that this is a tough challenge with an ethical component, however, we don't mean to say that the dilemma is without creative resolution. Trust in most businesses isn't total and doesn't have to be. Trust does have to be credible, however. Employees working for a coaching manager must trust that, on balance, he or she will support them. This doesn't mean that managers will cover up for serious mistakes, but they will help employees deal with these issues when they come to light. Managers lose a significant level of credibility when they don't represent their employees to the outside world. Sometimes, that representation must be personal and assertive.

Protecting a Coaching Friendly Context Over Time

As you look at the list of questions back in Box 5.1, you might consider how well you've done in creating a coaching friendly context in your business unit. You may feel good that you can answer most of the questions in the affirmative. Unfortunately, we have bad news: You should not rest on your accomplishments to date. A coaching friendly context represents a dynamic environment within a larger dynamic environment. It is subject to change. It needs to be constantly nurtured if it is to survive, particularly in difficult times. One of our favorite companies, an extremely innovative family-owned manufacturing firm, created enormous excitement in its highly unionized workforce by creating an environment that promoted collaboration and learning. After 5 years, the firm and its employees had made enormous gains.

After 10 years, even though there was no change in leadership, the firm had slipped back a bit. Coaching had taken a backseat to other more pressing activities. There was a renewed sense of suspicion between labor and management.

Quality (the business rationale for coaching in the first place) began to decline. The CEO told us, "I think we became overconfident, didn't pay attention to what was really important to us all. We just got caught up in the day-to-day." With this renewed awareness, the firm was able to recapture some of its energy for learning. Coaching activities and other learning-oriented initiatives resumed.

This small but dynamic firm had started to look more and more like Financial Co. We suggest that if a leader strongly embraces the ideas of coaching for learning, he or she should do so because of the belief that coaching and learning are essential for business success. If that is the case, then safeguarding that effort for the long term is critically necessary. Note that the CEO of the firm didn't say, "We didn't have time for coaching." In fact, he readily admits that that wasn't the problem. Coaching doesn't take a lot of time. They'd simply stopped paying attention.

6

Stopping the Action and Starting a Coaching Dialogue

IN THIS CHAPTER, WE DESCRIBE THE FOLLOWING:

- How coaching managers help employees seize valuable learning opportunities
- Techniques for stopping the action and starting a coaching dialogue that results in the employee taking ownership for learning

Your efforts to create a coaching friendly context by talking about coaching and being open to feedback yourself can help create a coaching friendly context, but it is coaching itself that has the greatest impact. In the coaching friendly context, people seize learning and coaching opportunities both formally and informally, whenever they can. Most likely, your work is fast-paced, and your business unit is filled with people who incessantly focus on action. They need to get it done, *now*. Somehow, you have to find a way to stop that action, if only briefly, and engage potential coachees in a useful coaching dialogue.

We list the steps in the process in Box 6.1 and will review them here. Some coaching managers follow the steps in a fairly linear way. They may stop the action by holding a scheduled coaching session. Planned meetings are particularly useful for employees who would like to bring up a historical issue (for example, an issue from this morning, or last year). Planned meetings are also important for those who travel or whose schedules are so frantic that if they don't create a structure to protect a few minutes of their day, it won't happen.

Box 6.1

STOPPING THE ACTION AND STARTING THE DIALOGUE

1. Maintain a coaching mind-set.

   - Make sure you are ready to coach, not evaluate or appraise performance.

2. Look for useful coaching opportunities before, after, and at natural stopping points during an activity.

   - What is the learning potential?

     - Does the situation involve a challenge for the employee?
     - Is it important to the employee?
     - Is it important to the company?

3. Assess the timing.

   - Is the employee able to engage with you now about this issue or topic?

     - Can you and the employee make adequate time for the dialogue?
     - Is the employee in a receptive frame of mind or emotional state?

4. Take a minute to establish rapport.

5. Ask reflective questions, listen, and probe for understanding.

   - When appropriate, ask follow-up questions.

     - While being empathic, help employees think about their roles, their intent, and their actions.
     - Try to help the employee avoid blaming others.

6. Help the employee define and take ownership of the real issue, challenge, or problem about which the employee needs to learn more.

   - Avoid providing premature or gratuitous feedback.
   - Avoid giving advice or jumping in with the solution.

7. Ask the employee what he or she would find useful as a next step, unless you feel that, on the basis of the issue or the potential costs of failure, you need to direct the employee to a next step.

   - The employee may be ready, on the basis of self-reflection only, to try out a new approach or idea.
   - The employee might find it useful for you to provide feedback on the spot.
   - The employee might find it helpful to get more data about his or her performance or the issue at hand.

> • The employee might find targeted advice useful. However, be wary of giving advice prematurely.
>   - Make sure that the employee has done a thorough job of independently thinking it through.
>   - Make sure that the employee owns the solution.

The reality is that most managers don't physically spend a lot of time in the same space as their employees, even those who practice "management by walking around" (MBWA). Some managers, such as those supervising employees at some distance, may spend very little time indeed. As we discussed in Chapter 5, making yourself accessible invites employees to bring learning issues to you. Most of our coaching managers report that they do create some formal structured time for coaching to create accessibility. This usually takes place in person, though for some managers, routine scheduled coaching sessions take place by phone.

However, even managers who coach in a scheduled way tell us that they also look for impromptu coaching opportunities, the timing of which may not always fit the schedule. Developing effectiveness at spotting and working with good coaching opportunities can take some practice. Given that most managers have very little time, we believe that the ability to take advantage of impromptu and immediate coaching opportunities can be of enormous help to both you and your employees.

When you are able to spot and make use of naturally occurring learning opportunities, the learning can potentially be immediately integrated with the work at hand. The employee can go out and test new ideas in a very timely fashion. Stopping the action and starting the dialogue represent two closely intertwined steps in the developmental coaching model. The coaching dialogue we describe in this chapter can be used to help extract learning from such spontaneous coaching opportunities, or it can be used in scheduled coaching meetings. The coaching dialogue, whether impromptu or formal, should also result in the employee's defining what he or she wants or needs to work on so that the employee takes psychological ownership for the learning process.

We'll walk through the steps involved in stopping the action and creating a coaching dialogue by seeing how they could be helpful in the case of George. At the end of the chapter, we will present two other case examples and discuss what our approach to stopping the action and creating a dialogue might be in those situations as well.

Case 6.1: George, the Struggling Team Leader

George has been a team leader at the company for the past 3 months. He is very good technically, but his interpersonal skills leave a great deal to be desired. Historically, George has been quick to anger, and when he was angry, he would be publicly critical toward the target of his annoyance. Even in the very recent past, his anger (always verbally expressed and without profanity) could be so emotionally intense that his fellow team members would find him intimidating. His manager has discussed this with George several times. George recognized that this was a problem and has been trying hard to control his anger.

The feedback his manager has received more recently from the rest of his group members suggests that George is really trying to work on the problem but his solution isn't necessarily making things better. (It isn't unusual for people to "overcorrect" while trying to change their behavior.) Now, instead of flaring out at others when he's upset, he becomes silent. He has been trying to follow the old adage "If you can't say something nice, don't say anything at all." Unfortunately, his new style confuses people. George is generally somewhat quiet. Now, people don't know when he is being quiet because he is upset and when he is just being himself. The net result of all this is that people sometimes still find him to be intimidating, even if less hostile.

However, George is a well-intended, highly motivated individual. When he's not under stress, he handles himself well and genuinely tries to do the right thing. He wants his manager to help because his aspiration is to use his current assignment to prepare himself for possible promotion to a director level position. Aware of George's motivation and strengths, his manager feels inclined to help.

His manager came to George's team meeting to do a brief presentation on a high-level strategy issue. The manager chose to stay at the team meeting after he finished his presentation because he knew it would give him a chance to watch George in action. When a difficult issue involving another group came up for discussion, George's body language and nonresponsiveness made the manager very uncomfortable. When one team member spoke to George, he didn't really respond, he just wrote down the team member's comments and went on to the next subject. Similar interactions occurred throughout the meeting. Team members didn't follow up on one another's comments. There was no debate. Few new ideas were generated. They also didn't seem to be having any fun. It seemed clear to the manager that George's meeting wasn't that productive. (The manager didn't believe that the team was being particularly quiet in response to his presence. He knew them all fairly well and knew that they were comfortable with him.)

After the meeting broke up, George walked toward his manager and said (so that no one else could hear), "See what I mean, I can't get anything out of these people." He seemed frustrated and started to walk back to his office.

Seizing a Coaching Opportunity With a Coaching Mind-Set

Several factors should be considered when assessing whether or not a good coaching opportunity is at hand. First of all, is the coaching manager thinking about the potential for learning that is inherent in the situation? Let's say that most of the people on George's team were about to go on vacation. This could readily explain their lack of involvement in the meeting and obscure the issue of whether or not George played a role in their behavior. In this case, however, there were no such extraneous forces at play. George was caught up in the action and didn't realize how he was coming across. Though there was no emotional outburst, the manager is concerned about George's new, more passive approach to dealing with stressful discussions, knowing that George is still having trouble dealing with team discussions that become tense. He knows that George is working on the problem, but he also knows that there may be more work to be done. To spot such situations, the manager needs to maintain a *coaching mind-set* on a fairly regular basis.

BEING VIGILANT FOR LEARNING OPPORTUNITIES

In addition to an attitude of helpfulness, as we discussed in Chapter 3, the coaching mind-set also involves being vigilant for learning opportunities, being able to quickly relate them to the employee's needs, and then having some idea how you might intervene. Coaching doesn't have to take a lot of time if the manager is mentally prepared.

As part of this vigilance, coaching managers also have to be vigilant about their own agendas. Are they ready to coach, or are they ready to slip into the appraisal of performance for the purposes of evaluation? Let's say that in this case, the manager is increasingly concerned about members of George's team leaving the company. These are highly valued employees. The manager sees George behaving in a way that could cause the employees to disengage even more. The manager might feel a sudden surge of anger directed at George because of his behavior. The manager has told George a dozen times to be more responsive to his people. Perhaps this time, the manager feels as though his patience has run out and comes to believe that George isn't going to "get it," no matter what anyone says. The next stop for George might then be a formal performance improvement plan.

The coaching mind-set requires that a decision be made at that point. What direction should the manager take? He may be justified in treating George's behavior as a serious performance problem and begin a disciplinary action. If, indeed, the manager has tried to coach him on this kind of behavior a dozen times, that may be the proper direction to take. It may be helpful, if emotions are running high, for the coaching manager to do nothing immediately but reflect on what he sees and perhaps consult with others as well.

ASSESSING THE IMPORTANCE OF THE OPPORTUNITY

Let's assume that the manager decided that George was coach-able and that the situation did not warrant the use of a more evaluative management tool, such as a performance improvement plan. How should the manager assess such opportunities to help George become a more effective team leader? Learning opportunities can come along at any time, but they predictably emerge at "punctuation points" of life: (a) at the beginning of an activity or a new job, (b) when a result occurs that allows for the assessment of whether or not things are going in the right direction, (c) when something novel is interjected into a situation, and (d) on completion of a task or a logical unit of work, even though the larger task may not have been completed. When the work is moving along and the task involves maintenance of a well-understood process, there may be fewer important learning opportunities. Related to this, the potential for learning is likely to be greater in a situation that is challenging and takes the individual to the limits of his or her current knowledge and capabilities (Hicks & Peterson, 1997).

However, assessing the importance and therefore the learning potential of even a challenging situation also involves consideration of the level of interest the employee has in learning from that situation. The degree varies to which an individual is invested in learning a particular concept or skills. Alan Clardy (2000) described three different types of "learner-directed" learning projects, described as follows.

In the *induced* learning project, the individual employee has to deal with an organizationally imposed challenge and must learn to adapt to that challenge. The context provides the opportunity for learning, but the individual employee may be more interested in compliance. Simple direction rather than developmental coaching may be the most appropriate guidance from the manager in such a situation: "This is the way you have to fill out your expense forms, we all have to do it this way, so let's get onboard and do it right."

In a *voluntary* learning project, the individual employee, curious about something, digs into a problem with no organizational prodding. The employee's motivation to learn is probably high, though there may or may not be a payoff for the organization. Entrepreneurial employees in particular may stumble on an interesting idea and spend a great deal of time on it, sometimes annoying their managers in the process. The reality is that a manager can't necessarily be expected to respond to every employee idea, particularly if those ideas are tangential to the work of his or her team.

Probably the greatest learning potential exists when the individual's motivation meets the organizational needs head-on. The individual employee wants to learn how to be successful in a job that the organization needs him or her to do. In such a *synergistic* learning project, maximum challenge meets maximum motivation. This is an important situation from the employee's perspective. It is also an important situation from the organization's perspective. The learning potential is enormous.

Note two points with regard to learning potential. We state again that if you have been relatively careful in hiring, employees are more likely to want to take on the challenge with which the organization needs them to engage, making synergistic learning projects more likely to occur. However, the employee also has to know what that challenge is! Consider again the Gallup study of 12 core elements linked to productivity, profitability, and retention (Buckingham & Coffman, 1999). Core element number one is knowledge of "what is expected of me." Employees need to know, at least generally, what they need to learn. In Chapter 7, we discuss this problem in some detail. For now, a simple example will suffice. If employees know that the firm has determined that sales associates need to become more adept at showing how the firm's products can integrate with those of its competitors, they will likely be motivated to learn about the technical issues that must be addressed in such an integration. If employees don't know what the firm wants, it will be harder for them to look for appropriate learning opportunities on their own.

One of the concerns that managers have when they begin to coach is that they will be perceived as "micromanaging" their employees. We have rarely heard this complaint from employees when the manager focuses his or her coaching efforts on important aspects of the employee's actions or behavior. If the manager has a sense of what the employee is trying to achieve and the challenges the employee faces, he or she will be much better positioned to intervene with coaching in important situations.

This situation seems to have a great deal of learning potential for George. From his perspective, it is synergistic. He wants to learn, and it is important to the organization that he be successful. The situation also seems to represent a significant challenge for George because it calls on him to develop new inter-personal skills—not an easy thing to do. This situation is important, then, and worthy of intervention.

IS THE TIMING RIGHT?

Just because the situation has a high learning potential doesn't mean that a focus on learning will necessarily be appropriate. The dictum to stop the action and seize the opportunity suggests that George's manager would do well to ask George to talk right after the meeting. His manager could immediately begin the process of trying to establish a coaching dialogue.

However, let's say that George is ill that day. He may not feel up to talking about what just happened. Perhaps he has no time because he must hurry off to a meeting with the CEO. If so, he may be so anxious about the next meeting that he won't be able to concentrate on learning from the most recent one. Immediacy is important. If you wait too long to intervene, you can lose the benefits of immediacy: good data about what just happened, clear recall of that data, and the helpful residue of emotions that go along with the sense of being challenged. If George is stressed about other things, his manager's interest in discussing the matter with him right away may come across as a criticism. Immediacy isn't always possible.

In this case, George is annoyed, but this doesn't seem to be a major problem. He doesn't seem to have anything else pressing, and his manager has the time. Because he and George had talked about this issue previously, the manager anti-cipates that it would take about 15 minutes to talk with George about what had transpired. If the discussion is going to be difficult or complex, they may need to talk for 30 minutes or an hour. In any case, the coaching manager needs to make a rough estimate of how much time the discussion might take (you'll never know for sure) and whether or not that is realistic for both parties. If the manager and/or the employee don't have the time now, at least they can schedule a follow-up meeting. If the follow-up meeting is scheduled right away, even though it may not take place for several days, both parties know the issues and may still be able to use their experiences from the meeting to draw on for learning.

ESTABLISH OR REESTABLISH RAPPORT

If the coaching manager and employee haven't done so already, they could make good use of a few minutes of small talk, just to establish rapport and comfort. The degree to which the manager needs to attend to rapport has to do with the nature of his or her relationship with the employee. If the relationship is solid, particularly if the two have been working on a particular issue already, as is the case with George and his manager, it may feel right to jump in and start the coaching dialogue right away. However, we suggest that the coaching manager make it clear that he or she would like to talk about what has just happened (or that recent situation, etc.) if this has not already been established. If the employee is expecting social chat, the manager may need to signal that he or she would like to talk about something important.

In this case, George's manager said: "Thanks for inviting me to the meeting, George, it saved me a lot of time, not having to pursue everyone on your team to talk about this new strategy. It was also good for me to get a sense of how you and the team are doing, since we've been talking about that in our meetings. Do you have a few minutes to debrief?" George responded in the affirmative out of his frustration with the team, his wish that he could do something to improve their ability to communicate with one another, and the knowledge that his ability to manage the team is important to his career. We can guess that he was also a bit nervous having his boss in the room and wanted to appear cooperative (note that even when people want to learn, impression management is still a concern).

George's manager, then, actually asked permission to stop the action. Granted, it might have been hard for George to say "no" at that point, but his manager was purposefully respectful of George and his time. His tone of voice also signaled that he recognized that this was a tough issue for George and that he wanted to help. In asking for permission, however, he also asked George for his active participation in what George had come to understand was a coaching or learning discussion. If George had been ill, had another major challenge coming up in the next few minutes, or was so angry he couldn't talk about it, he would have had an out.

ASK REFLECTIVE QUESTIONS, LISTEN FOR UNDERSTANDING

Coaching, particularly developmental coaching, is not just feedback! We can't emphasize this enough. From our consultation and training experiences, we have come to understand that many well-meaning managers believe that when they give feedback, they are coaching. Certainly feedback is an important part of coaching. Furthermore, managers who provide carefully thought-through feedback do a lot better by their employees than those who don't. Nevertheless, feedback by itself, no matter how immediate, sometimes backfires. A story from one of our managers illustrates the point.

She was working with a high-potential employee who had a habit of over-committing. The employee, a very talented but somewhat scattered young man, was highly motivated to do the right thing for his company and his own career. However, he seemed to have a characterological tendency to say "yes" when he should have said "no." Whenever the manager caught him doing that, she would try immediately to give him balanced feedback about his having taken on yet another commitment that he might not be able to honor.

The problem is, the employee's role involved highly visible customer services tasks. He thought that he probably shouldn't be saying "no" too often and quickly defended his position. His manager ended up feeling as though "he just wasn't listening, he was just defending his actions," which was true. However, the employee felt that he should defend his actions. He hadn't stopped to think for himself about decision-making rules that might govern when to say "yes" and when to say "no." He hadn't really thought through the impact of his behavior. Perhaps most important, he took no ownership for the issue. He felt that his boss was wrong, didn't understand his point of view, and ultimately, that he was being micromanaged. His manager had taken ownership of the problem. Two highly motivated individuals had created a non–coaching friendly context in their relationship. Advocacy of one's position, no matter how carefully thought out and how caringly delivered, doesn't necessarily create learning. Feedback in advance of an initial self-reflection on the part of the learner is advocacy. A dialogue is something quite different.

As a coaching manager, there is a power differential between you and your employees. To a surprising degree, they want to please you or at least stay out of harm's way in their relationship with you. If you signal that you have the right answer, the employee's natural response may be to acquiesce to your point of view. After all, you seem wiser, have a position of authority, and may even be older. To understand this problem more thoroughly, it is useful to consider the definition of the word *dialogue*.

Drawing on the work of David Bohm, Peter Senge (1990) calls our attention to the distinction between a discussion and a dialogue. In a *discussion*, the participants are trying to persuade one another of the correctness of their point of view. Discussion represents the most common form of interaction for most of us when we talk about issues of importance. George's manager could have started the coaching session by pointing out to George that his body language tends to be intimidating and that the impact of his intimidating style is that his team is unwilling to risk being open with him. A cursory reading of the case would suggest such a scenario.

How might one expect George to respond if confronted with that kind of feedback? He might well become defensive. He might talk about how much pressure he's under to achieve results and insist that his team should start acting like adults and tell him whether he's coming across inappropriately. We can guess where such a discussion might lead. George's manager might come back with a more direct confrontation, perhaps offering several examples. George, being human, might tend to feel the need to deflect each example. George has a point of view, which in fact is quite valid. Likewise, George's boss has some useful insight as to the dynamics taking place between George and his team.

In a *dialogue*, however, the parties attempt to engage in an interaction that can help raise the underlying assumptions or perceptions that serve to support whatever behavior is taking place on the surface. The first task of the coaching manager, then, is to encourage the coachee to explore his or her own perceptions of or assumptions about what has transpired. If George can be honest with himself (and in a coaching friendly context, one hopes this is possible), then he can explore his own behavior and the factors that drive the behavior. We illustrate this below.

The coaching managers in our research report that the easiest way to create a dialogue is to ask questions while withholding criticism, feedback, or advice. A properly phrased question can encourage both parties to think about what has happened without making either feel defensive. "George, how did it go for you in the meeting?"

Some managers are reluctant to ask questions. They may not believe that an employee will honestly or accurately appraise what they have done or be open about the assumptions that guided their actions. Of course, if the employee has reason to be defensive—if the context is not coaching friendly—this is likely to be the case. If the context is coaching friendly, a question can offer a powerful invitation to reflect on what has happened, why, and what might be done differently next time.

Given that most interactions in business are probably more aptly characterized as discussions (the advocacy of a position), we accept that asking questions instead of telling others what to do may be quite a change for the average manager. Nevertheless, the feedback we have received is that a good question is often far more powerful than a great directive. Indeed, recent research strongly suggests that the behavior of managers who are seen by others as creating the most learning in their organizations includes the frequent use of questions that encourage employees to think for themselves about the issues at hand (Ellinger, Watkins, & Bostrom, 1999).

Examples of useful dialogue-building questions can be found in Box 6.2. These questions are all intended to encourage individuals (or a team, as the case may be) to think about what just happened and about the role they played in it. Although employees may need to talk about their context or the other people involved, they fundamentally have little control over others. They can learn the most from reflecting on themselves, their actions, their assumptions, their goals, and the outcomes that occurred in response.

Box 6.2

BASIC INTRODUCTORY QUESTIONS USEFUL FOR CREATING
A COACHING DIALOGUE

How did it go for you today?

- Follow-up probes: Tell me about it. What happened then? Let's go over the details.

What did you see taking place?

- This question is more specific than the previous question and encourages employees to focus specifically on their own observations, not the manager's. It offers an implicit validation that the employee's point of view is important.

What were you trying to accomplish?

- This question encourages employees to reflect on their intent in a given situation.
- Follow-up probes: Did it work? Did you succeed?
  - If yes, why? If no, why not?
  - The follow-up questions ask employees to consider whether or not what they hoped to achieve was achieved and what role they played in the outcome.
- Questions about intent can be very useful for well-motivated or assertive learners.

A debriefing series for use in helping an employee think about a process:

- What do you think you need to keep doing?
- What do you think you need to start doing?
- What do you think you need to stop doing?

A debriefing series for use after a project:[a]

- What did we set out to do?
- What did we actually do?
- Why was there a difference?

Questions to avoid:

- Questions that suggest blame.
- Questions that encourage the learner to dig into the "why" before you both have a clear picture of what happened.

a. Courtesy of U.S. Army's After Action Review (Garvin, 2000).

George's manager posed the simple question "How did it go for you in there?" Because the two of them had been working on George's team leadership skills, George was ready to respond with his own perceptions of what had taken place. He talked of his frustration and how the team didn't seem to be responding to his efforts. His manager then followed up with, "What kind of response were you hoping for?" George quickly responded, "I want them to offer some suggestions that will help us move forward again."

With a little prodding in the form of a follow-up question from his manager, George began to talk about what he'd recently learned about the group's previous leader. That individual had been even more directive than George. The team had dealt with him by being passive, just following orders. This was new information for George's manager. It gave him a clearer sense of just how difficult the situation was going to be for George. George not only had to learn how to alter his own management style, he also had to learn to deal with a team than had already been trained by a previous team leader to be passive. George finished his initial reflection by stating, "I somehow think that knowing this, knowing how they have learned to treat team leaders, has made me a bit defeatist. I'm trying not to talk over them or tell them what to do, but clearly, I'm going to have to do something different to get them to work with me."

In a coaching dialogue, both participants—not just the coachee—frequently report that they learned something. Yes, the coachee has a chance to step back and examine his or her actions from a somewhat dispassionate perspective. The coaching manager, however, learns more about the employee and his or her challenges. In this case, the manager learned that though he may have assumed that George was solely responsible for the poor quality of the interaction in the team meeting, the situation is more complicated than that. It is as if both employee and coaching manager get a chance together to rerun an imaginary but, ideally, realistic mental video of what has just taken place. Such is the nature of reflection. Reflecting on an event and pondering what has happened, carefully and persistently, allows the individual learner to try and make sense of what has happened and to give it meaning (Daudelin, 1996). The added benefit the coaching manager brings to the process is a sense of connectedness. Learning is a social activity. The presence of another person implies that what is taking place is important, offers encouragement, and at times, provides another perspective (Seibert, 1999).

The coaching dialogue will come to a quick end, however, if the coaching manager doesn't listen. We think of listening as one of the most critical components of developmental coaching because it supports individuals' efforts to reflect more deeply on their goals, assumptions, and actions. The coaching manager needs to demonstrate listening with behaviors such as holding eye contact (when culturally appropriate), not talking, summarizing what has been said, asking clarifying questions, and following up on what the coachee has said.

Failure to listen on the part of the coaching manager encourages the dialogue to evolve into a discussion in which the parties return to advocating the position. One of the most common assumptions on the part of the manager that can interfere with listening is that employees are making excuses when they say they are responsible for only part of the problem the manager may have observed. When the manager isn't ready to listen to and deal with the complexity of a situation such as George's, advocacy and defensiveness almost invariably emerge and the potential for learning is diminished.

Researchers tell us that a sense of autonomy on the part of the learner is necessary if learning from reflection is to take place (Seibert, 1999). Coachees need the chance to stop and think for themselves before managers interject their thoughts. The challenge for coaching managers is to remain engaged with employees and at the same time not rob them of the opportunity to independently make sense of what is going on.

HELP THE EMPLOYEE DEFINE AND
TAKE OWNERSHIP OF THE REAL ISSUE

Having ventilated his feelings a bit and interjected this new information about his team into the discussion, George felt better. However, he still had not clearly articulated how his actions helped or hurt his efforts to be an effective team leader. Interspersed with an occasional "That is frustrating," his manager kept asking questions, encouraging George to think about what he was trying to accomplish and what he might need to do differently. He accepted that George was indeed not talking over people but kept encouraging him to think about whether or not he was doing anything that might still be getting in the way of his effort to generate more useful interaction in the team meetings. After several minutes, George said, "I know I look stiff to them. My wife has told me the same thing. I get that way now especially when I'm frustrated. Others have told me I stop looking at people, you know, making eye contact. It's better than yelling I suppose, but I become very quiet. That probably isn't helping."

George's self-assessment fit with his manager's observation. However, the manager still had to be careful not to step in and either define the problem for George or start giving advice that George might not be able to follow. George is well motivated. However, it isn't easy to change one's leadership style. Whatever action he may plan to take next time to improve the situation, he'll probably be committed to the tough work of following through on the plan if it is his idea or if it will help him achieve a goal that is important to him. And as is often the case in a coaching friendly context, George recognized the problem. There was no need for the manager to offer additional feedback to correct his perception. The manager said, "What you're saying makes sense to me." The manager then used a follow-up question to help George plan his next series of actions: "If you are right, what do you think you should keep doing, start doing, and stop doing?"

George was used to these questions from his manager and found them helpful. He said, "Clearly, I need to keep not interrupting and not lose my temper, I can't go back to that. I think I need to be more patient, though. The other thing I need to do is change the way I respond to them. I have to watch the body language and try to do something to let them know that I do want to hear them out. I have to keep reminding myself that this is going to take some time. If I don't get so frustrated, it should be easier to do something other than frown. That will be tough for me, but I'm sure that I'm sending the wrong message."

Several forces are at work here, and George's synopsis addresses them all. George's body language during the team meeting sent the wrong message. He can work on changing that. However, underlying his behavior was his frustration. His frustration emerged because his team wasn't able to meet him halfway. Now he is more aware that it will take time for his team to develop a better style of interacting in the meetings. George's solution represents an explicit acknowledgement of what he can do to further a change process for his team as well as for himself. Most important, George owns the problem and the solution. Granted, it isn't all of his making, but he sees his own role and is developing a preliminary plan for doing something differently. He is more aware of the role his attitude is playing in the situation and wants to work harder on applying an important social skill: smiling.

Will this work? We don't know. George will have to try it and see. Real change takes time. George will probably have to ease into the new behaviors. It may be quite uncomfortable for everyone if George finds himself smiling throughout the entire next team meeting. The real payoff will not be in whether or not George smiles, but in whether or not his behavior helps move the group toward more effective communications.

George's manager did not have to do much more than stop the action, encourage George to reflect on his own behavior by asking the appropriate questions, and control his own impulse to jump in and "fix" the situation. The connections in George's mind between his own actions and outcomes in his interaction with his team became clearer in the process. Significant learning has taken place.

FOLLOW-UP: ASK THE EMPLOYEE ABOUT USEFUL NEXT STEPS

The interaction we have highlighted here represents one piece of an ongoing coaching dialogue between George and his manager. We can assume that they will continue capturing coaching moments such as this as they move ahead. However, it will probably be very useful for George and his manager to discuss explicitly what kind of follow-up might promote continued progress. George told his manager that he was meeting with the team again tomorrow. He was going to pay close attention to how he was coming across. He wanted to try and be at least a little more patient with the team and be a bit more friendly. He promised his manager that he'd let him know how it went. George's manager believed, on the basis of their previous efforts, that George would indeed observe his behavior more closely and report back to him.

Alternatively, George might have found it helpful to have his manager sit in on another team meeting or even talk with members of the team himself. George's manager would then have to provide balanced feedback, holding up the mirror to give George more information about his behavior. Note that the step of providing formal feedback to George would take place as part of a process in which George was actively engaged.

What if George did not want to actively engage in the coaching process? We remind you again that as George's manager, you would probably have to nurture his participation by creating a coaching friendly context. A high level of openness, honesty, and vulnerability on George's part characterizes the dialogue described here. George has to truly believe that his learning and his success are important priorities for his manager. He also has to get used to the idea that every so often, the action will stop, and reflection and learning will be prioritized.

Practice Cases: Stopping the Action and Starting the Dialogue

In the following cases, consider whether or not it would potentially be useful to stop the action and create a coaching dialogue. If so, what questions might you use to start the dialogue? Read the case first and then read our commentary. These cases are disguised; they are based on scenarios provided to us by human resource and leadership development managers from firms we provided with training in developmental coaching as part of an executive education program.

Case 6.2: Is John Headed for Burnout?

John has been a project manager at a company for the past 2 years. His projects are completed on time and on budget. He is quite gifted technically. He is also very nice when dealing with others—too nice, in fact. He is successful because he is doing much more than his share of the work. He won't push back on his colleagues, delegate more, or hold them accountable for scheduling and workload. Recently, he was looking tired and complained of a cold that wouldn't go away. John is a very proud individual, and he wants to get ahead at the company. But his manager also knows that he'll burn out at this rate. His work style would cause even more trouble at the senior management level to which John aspires. His manager sent John an e-mail asking him to meet for lunch. John sent back a very nicely worded response, thanking the manager but stating that he just didn't have the time right now; he was up to his elbows in work and totally stressed. Perhaps he could call his manager when he got back from the customer site next week? His manager wondered whether or not she should walk down to his office and have a chat with him.

Commentary: This is a difficult situation that many managers know well. One of your most valued resources, a dedicated manager, is probably working himself beyond a level that is wise for him or for the company. Of course, the company is at least partly to blame. The question here is whether or not there is learning potential in the situation, and if there is, is the timing right to stop the action? If the manager decides to stop the action, how can she begin a useful dialogue?

We have had participants in executive education programs take this case in two directions. Is John going to be able to learn from a coaching intervention at this point? The answer may be "no." If he is so consumed with the needs of his current client, it may be very difficult to create a learning opportunity no matter how important the situation might be. Clearly, however, some type of intervention is warranted. We would suggest that the manager let John know that even though the time isn't right, it is important that the two of them talk, and arrange a meeting after his return. The coaching manager in this case has to remember that she can't necessarily fix the problem all at once. She could order John to take a break. Would any learning take place under such a circumstance? Probably not. It isn't clear that John wants or feels the need to change. He is not taking any ownership of the problem at this point. (If the meeting is delayed, the manager should take a few minutes to jot down her thoughts and concerns so that her memories will be fresh when they do meet.)

Alternatively, let's say that the manager was aware that John actually had some health or family problems. She might then order him to slow down a bit, thinking that he would at least comply with a directive. The manager could then have a follow-up coaching dialogue to explore John's interest in changing his management style.

If the manager chose to talk with him that same day, we would recommend that she be respectful of the fact that John had already declined the opportunity to talk. An opening comment such as "John, I know you're busy, but I think this is important" might convey that sense of respect. The manager could undertake the task by asking questions (remember, John already knows how stressed out he is and doesn't need feedback on that point) to help him express what he is trying to do and consider whether or not another approach might help. She would probably know fairly quickly whether or not John was ready to stop the action and reflect on his behavior.

Case 6.3: Samantha, the Frustrated Superstar

Samantha is one of the best account managers on the staff. In her 2 years with the firm, she has consistently performed at or above the level of other "best performers" in the company. She likes the company but fears that it will take forever for her to move up the ranks to program manager. Her manager knows from previous discussions with her that she aspires to a leadership position and wants to have a big impact. (Her work is global, but she and her manager talk by phone for an hour each week and meet when she is in town. She understands the approach to coaching and has made good use of it in the past.)

Samantha has expressed some frustration with how long it takes to move up at the firm. However, her manager also knows that she has a lot to learn about the challenges of sustaining long-term client relationships through difficult times. She is technologically savvy and good with people, but doesn't have a deeper feel for the economic drivers in customer relationships. Her inexperience in this area clearly influenced the results of the project she completed yesterday. Her work was timely and effective, but her failure to mobilize the right team to help her led to some significant cost overruns. The firm will make very little money as a result. Samantha has asked to speak with her manager about the project and her career.

Commentary: This is an important learning opportunity. The timing is right as well. The project is coming to an end, and Samantha has asked to speak with her manager. The tricky problem for the manager is his awareness of her frustration and her desire to move ahead quickly. This is not an unusual problem for a manager with bright, ambitious employees. Such employees are likely to be very action oriented. However, this manager is acutely aware that there are important issues about which his employee must learn more before she can advance.

We would recommend the manager begin by reestablishing rapport (chatting a bit) and letting Samantha know that there are a few items to be discussed, while making it clear that he wants to hear her agenda first. If her career concerns, her desire to move up, are paramount in her mind, it makes sense to deal with those first, by thoroughly hearing her out. By listening in-depth, the manager allows her to take full ownership for her goals and the steps it will take to reach them.

It would then be helpful to outline to Samantha exactly what is required for promotion to the next level and begin to create the dialogue by asking her how she feels she is doing in relation to those promotion criteria. If Samantha and her manager have established an effective coaching relationship, she may be able to talk about the problems she is having in building her own team and in paying more attention to the economic issues in her work. However, it is important that the manager not use the problems on Samantha's most recent project as a weapon against her. Rather than telling her, "You're obviously still having problems," the manager can put the onus on Samantha by opening a dialogue about her own assessment of her strengths and weaknesses in relation to each competency she is required to master before being promoted. Once Samantha has had a chance to offer her own perspective, the manager is in a better position to provide specific feedback to her with regard to the perceptions of others in relation to each criterion.

The goal here is not to "talk some sense into" Samantha or to frustrate her perhaps overzealous career planning. It is, rather, to encourage her to stop and begin to think out loud about how she is doing in relation to her goals. If she is used to the process of reflecting on her work, even someone as aggressively ambitious as Samantha will be able to use the opportunity to consider her career goals and the progress she is making toward achieving them. Action-oriented people can have a tough time with the idea of "stopping the action." One of the greatest benefits of developmental coaching is that it helps them learn this invaluable skill.

7

Focusing on What Is Important

IN THIS CHAPTER, YOU WILL LEARN ABOUT THE FOLLOWING:

- How to help your employees understand what it takes to succeed and what they need to learn: building a coaching mirror

In this chapter and the next, we describe a concept that we call the "coaching mirror." We like the metaphor of the mirror for several reasons. First, it emphasizes the importance of stopping to reflect on what is happening, an idea we describe in detail in Chapter 6. Perhaps more important, we have found the notion of the mirror to be of enormous value in teaching managers about the somewhat abused concept of feedback. A mirror can send us a powerful message, but it can't change us. Feedback at its best isn't designed to change the recipient of the feedback, it is offered as a tool that recipients can use to help them achieve goals to which they are committed.

This makes feedback sound somewhat passive, as tools for change go. However, the coaching manager can greatly enhance the power of the feedback, and therefore the value of the mirror, in two ways. First, the manager can help the coachee focus on what is truly important. Second, the manager can provide the feedback in a way that makes it as useful as possible. In this chapter, we focus on the definition of what is important. In the next chapter, we address ways to provide balanced feedback. As you move through these chapters, keep the idea of a mirror in mind (a high-quality mirror, not the kind from the fun house that make you look too thin—or worse yet, too fat!).

The reason for spending so much time on feedback should be obvious. Although effective coaching requires that coachees learn to reflect on and better self-assess their own performance, self-assessment alone may not be enough. The employee may not be focusing his or her self-assessment on the appropriate issues, actions, or behaviors. In addition, the employee may not have a clear sense of how his or her actions are seen by others.

Shouldn't what is important be obvious to every good employee? Shouldn't coachees just know, according to their job descriptions, what is expected of them? The answer to these questions is "yes"—and "no." It may be obvious, for example, to a first-time engineering project leader that the computer programming language in use in her group is C++. What may be far less obvious to this new project leader, particularly if she comes from another group or company, is how she is supposed to go about integrating the work of three other engineers. Does she use a formal, detailed project-planning protocol developed specially for her company? Does she hold meetings with the other engineers and facilitate a shared effort to integrate the work? Should she forcefully take charge and set deadlines for the engineers? The process by which the work gets done is often a mystery to someone learning a new role. To self-assess and, even more, to comprehend feedback from the coaching manager, the coachee has to understand what it takes to get ahead and to be effective in his or her particular context.

In our coach training programs, we have been told repeatedly that one of the great surprises coaching managers confront is that when they first start coaching, they aren't so sure what is important. Business results are important to the firm and the work group, but understanding the required results doesn't explain what people have to do to achieve those results and how the coaching manager can help them get there more quickly. As we have already stated, what is important to the individual employee matters. The employee's motivation makes learning possible. But the employee is shooting at a very large target even if his or her interests are fully aligned with those of the organization. The manager must know which areas of activity are critical to the success of both the business unit and the employee and then guide the employee toward those areas. In that sense, the coaching manager is also a teacher.

Let us stress, however, that this doesn't mean that the coaching manager has to know more about the employee's particular technical expertise than the employee does. In the new economy, the reverse is often likely to be the case. Even in those instances, however, coaching managers must serve as guides, helping employees determine when and how to use their technical expertise, as well as how they can use it to create value for themselves and the business. Even the most highly trained employees are likely to need help in that regard.

Not Just Process, but Results

Process refers to "how the work gets done." Unfortunately, some managers dislike focusing on the processes by which employees get their work done, as long as whatever path the employee takes is within some reasonable limit. Such managers don't want bright, well-educated employees feeling as though they are being watched under a microscope. Other managers may fear that a focus on process is too "soft" and will reflect a lack of emphasis on results. Nothing could be farther from the truth. Results drive an interest in learning and are absolutely essential to effective coaching. Employees are typically focused on results, too. This is fortunate because results are what you, the coaching manager, and your employees are paid to "deliver."

We are by far not the first people to preach the gospel that if you want to get good, sustainable results, you should also look at the processes by which those results are obtained. Executives like Jack Welch, former CEO of General Electric (GE), insist that in the great companies, results and process are inevitably intertwined: "Values and behavior are what produce those performance numbers and they are the bedrock upon which we will build our future" (General Electric Corporation, 2000, p. 2). Welch defines a number of behaviors and values that he and his managers look for, including integrity, relishing change, self-confidence, learning, and leadership. Each of these is further defined so that everyone in the company understands what is meant when one of these behaviors or values is being discussed. Leadership, for instance, includes the elements of *energy,* or the ability to cope with change; *energizing,* or motivating others; *edge,* or the self-confidence necessary to make tough calls; and *execution,* meaning delivering and never disappointing (General Electric Corporation, 2000). Each of these "four E's" of leadership is further defined with specific behavioral descriptions, stories really, that illustrate how these elements function when they are actually put into practice within the corporation.

Those who show the right behaviors or values but don't achieve the appropriate results are coached or repositioned in other roles. However, those who achieve results but don't show the right behaviors are shown the door. "We have to remove these [employees who produce results but do not demonstrate the right behavior or values] because they have the power, by themselves, to destroy the open, informal, trust-based culture we need to win today and tomorrow" (General Electric Corporation, 2000, p. 5).

There was clarity in Welch's position, although some may argue with his methods. He spent a great deal of effort and by some reports, as much as 50% of his time teaching others what he felt was important. This effort helped managers throughout the corporation understand what to look for, coach to, aspire to, and reward. The coaching manager knows what is important and shares that knowledge with others.

What Should the Coaching Manager Pay Attention To? Competency

You should be paying attention to the behavior, values, or skills that are causally related to the outcomes you and your organization seek. If your employees develop the behaviors or skills linked to organizationally necessary outcomes, they will have learned something valuable while helping the firm. Firms offer their managers and their employees varying levels of help in knowing what to pay attention to. Many firms now have what are called *competency models*, or descriptions of the behavior, values, and skills related to success, for at least the firm's most critical roles. From an individual, process-oriented perspective, competency models capture what is important.

Competency models have been growing in popularity for the past 80 years, building on work from two sources. They were initially developed by the federal government to help define needed skills in the armed forces during the world wars of the past century. In the 1950s, AT&T became one of the first industrial organizations to develop a competency model (though they did not use the term) for the firm's various management levels. The job of the first line supervisor is of course very different from that of the senior vice president. AT&T and its human resource management and industrial/organizational psychology staff studied jobs at each of the firm's management levels and were able to specify behaviors that would be likely to predict success at each one (Bray, Campbell, & Grant, 1979).

This line of analysis was greatly extended by psychologist David McClelland (Spencer, McClelland, & Spencer, 1994). He hypothesized that the techniques then in use for selecting employees, such as unstructured interviews or IQ tests, were not particularly helpful. They were not helpful because they failed to predict success in work or in life. The solution was deceptively simple.

McClelland and his colleagues began to interview and observe individuals in particular job roles who demonstrated exceptional performance in the eyes of their peers, customers, or leaders. They also interviewed and observed individuals in the same roles whose performance was average or adequate, and individuals whose performance was poor. They were able to isolate specific behaviors or skills for various job roles that could differentiate the three levels of performance. Importantly, when they went to confirm their findings by testing their competency models in new settings, they found that the particular behaviors associated with superior performance were consistently related to better business performance. In some studies, superior performance has been demonstrated to yield a 1000% dividend over average performers! The best salespeople surveyed in a study of *Fortune 500* firms produced $6.7 million in sales per person compared with $3 million in sales per person for the average salesperson (Goleman, 1998). The comparison with poor performers was even more staggering.

McClelland and his colleagues defined the behaviors associated with a particular performance as a *competency*. A competency, then, can be though of as an underlying characteristic of an individual that is causally related to effective or superior performance in a job (Boyatzis, 1982). Competency can result from individual characteristics, such as motives (what one wants), traits (personality characteristics), or self-concepts (the way one sees oneself). Competency can also be built from content knowledge and cognitive or behavioral skills. The ability to function effectively as a leader, for instance, is usually associated with certain motives, such as having an interest in power (McClelland & Burnham, 1995). Competency in leadership is also often associated with emotional intelligence and a highly developed set of interpersonal skills (Goleman, 1998). Competency in C++ programming, however, is associated with a talent in analysis (a personal trait) as well as specific learned skills in the language itself that build on that analytical talent.

The potential of describing a pattern of behavior or skills for any particular role that is highly predictive of success has led a number of organizations to spend the time, energy, and resources to build customized competency models for their individual firms. They then use these models as guides in selection, development, and in some cases, even compensation. Naturally, a number of consulting firms have emerged to service this niche market, particularly for those organizations that don't have resources to develop a competency model internally. The list of organizations that have established competency models for their executives, for instance, includes some of the best companies in the world: American Express, Eli Lilly, Hewlett-Packard, PepsiCo, and others (Briscoe & Hall, 1999).

Competency models have also been developed for a variety of middle management, individual contributor, and professional roles as well (Rosier, 1994). The service account engineer competency model for Landis & Gyr Powers, Inc., for instance, includes competencies related to leadership, total quality management, interpersonal skills, and technical knowledge (Rosier, 1994, p. 331). This competency model was built by data gained from focus groups made up of people in the role and those who interfaced with people in the role; they were asked to define effective performance in the role.

A competency model provides focus. In our coach training programs, we work with five simple but powerful competencies: leadership, teamwork, decision making, oral communications, and listening. Each competency is defined by behavioral attributes or examples of what effective, average, and weak performance for each of the competencies look like to a trained observer. The participants in the program who serve as "coaches" know that these are the competencies for which they will give feedback.

Not everyone will agree on the definitions of each particular competency. For instance, many participants in our coach training programs wish to use their own definitions of leadership or teamwork. However, we ask that participants use the definition that we have developed from our own research. Not that it is any better than the one they may bring to the discussion. We simply are asking them to use a definition that can be understood by others. Coaching requires that everybody involved, at least within the same work group, be "on the same page." One of the key roles played by the coaching manager, then, is to make sure, when any kind of competency model is in use, that everyone involved comes to consensus on what effective performance looks like. If the manager doesn't push for (or in some cases dictate) such a consensus, chaos can result. For instance, imagine each telephone representative in a call center using their own individual definition of good customer service.

An important implication of the idea that a competency model can be helpful for focusing on how particular tasks are accomplished is that a competency model has to be public if it is to be useful. Descriptions of competencies represent descriptions of effectiveness that offer employees guidance and goals to which they can aspire. We learn what we think will help us achieve whatever goal we have in mind. But we have to know what to learn. A useful competency model helps in that regard by pointing toward a vision of superior performance in a particular role. Keeping competencies secret doesn't help anyone.

This discussion of competency models is offered with the intent of trying to persuade you toward a point of view that until recently, most managers did not accept: There can be a "right way" to approach even the most sophisticated task. This is true even when the job is brand new. Under those circumstances, competencies such as creativity or learning from experience may reflect the "right" approach. Without some sense of what might work from a process point of view, coaching can be very difficult, if not impossible.

An understanding of what is important is thus the foundation for coaching. Most professionals and managers should come to the job with a basic technical knowledge base in their chosen fields, be it programming, marketing, or human resources, but they also need to understand the process in your organization that leads to success. Next, we'll talk about how to put this idea into practice. We first consider what to do if your company does have a competency model in place and then what to do if your company does not.

If Your Company Has a Competency Model

If your company does have a competency model, you should first try to get a sense of how the model was developed. Competency models are developed by companies in three ways (Briscoe & Hall, 1999). Some firms use a research-based approach similar to that of McClelland and AT&T. This approach involves interviewing individuals who hold particular roles and who are perceived by others in the organization to be superior, not just adequate, performers. These interviews, typically conducted by human resource consultants, ask the interviewee to tell specific stories about his or her performance. These stories are then analyzed and grouped together by themes. For example, highly effective executives in a start-up division may offer a number of stories suggesting that they and their teams are capable of making very rapid decisions. These stories indicate that an important competency might be "the ability to make decisions in a timely fashion."

Whereas the research-based approach describes past superior performance, the strategic approach to building a competency model forecasts the competency requirements for the future. In a highly dynamic work environment, what worked in the past might not work in the future. The strategic competency model describes those skills, attitudes, or behaviors that it is thought will help the business unit move in a desired, often new, direction. A company entering a new market, for instance, will likely be able to predict that certain kinds of marketing skills and the ability to manage change will be important to their future success. When a work group takes on a new task, such as that of consulting with a new type of client, they can likewise predict that the skills sought by the new client are likely to be helpful.

Finally, the managers in charge of a group may believe that certain competencies are necessary as a reflection of their values. Integrity, the pursuit of quality, or a team orientation, for instance, may be critical to success in certain firms; to behave otherwise would be counter to the cultural values prevailing in that particular organization, as promoted by the organization's leaders.

Once you have clarified the purpose of the competency model, as a reflection of how it was developed, you will then need to ask what turns out to be a surprisingly tough question: Is the model actually used? Some companies have well-developed competency models that are poorly understood and/or sit on the shelf. This represents a substantial waste of management or consultant time and company money. However, if the competency model was developed at the behest of managers who are no longer at the firm, times may have changed and the competencies they thought were important may no longer be so important. If that is your current situation, see the section below on what to do if your company doesn't have a competency model.

More commonly, we've seen companies that have what ought to be useful competency models but weren't well understood by managers or employees because of the reluctance of senior managers to engage in teaching. The reality is that unless the model is understood by all those affected by it, it will not serve as a developmental or coaching guide. Beyond that, it is poor management practice to appraise people against particular competencies without their having a good understanding of what those competencies mean.

What can the coaching manager do? Take the competency model off the shelf and talk about it. We've seen coaching managers do an excellent job of drawing everyone's attention to what is important by reviewing the competencies in meetings with employees; they encourage everyone to fully participate in discussing what the competencies actually mean for them, in their particular settings. "Timely decision making" as a competency may seem rather straightforward at first glance. Each word, however, is open to interpretation. To an emergency medical technician or an ambulance crew, "timeliness" means something quite different than it does to a biomedical scientist or marketing director.

The exercise of talking about what the competencies actually mean is not a trivial one. If one believes that superior performance of a particular competency is linked to business results, then it is likely to be worth the coaching manager's time. If the coaching manager can define what the "super person" does to achieve such results and help an average but well-motivated performer move in that direction, the potential payoff can be enormous. Unfortunately, coaching won't be effective if all performers don't know what they are striving for and what competency looks like.

How do you talk about it? We recommend that you start with the orientation of new hires. The coaching managers in our studies often talk with new employees about what it takes to get ahead, as part of their orientation to the business unit. Communication involves more than just giving someone a copy of the model or presenting it on overhead displays in a staff meeting. It means using examples, telling stories, and then making sure people understand when they are doing something right. Recognition lets them know that they are executing around a competency in a way that truly creates value. It may also be useful to talk about the origin of the particular competency. Many people want to know why certain attitudes are thought to be important to success. Does the model say something about the way things have always been done, does it say something about where the business is going, or does it say something about the values of the firm's leadership?

Some firms also use competency profiles as vehicles for career development. Career progression in some consulting firms, for instance, involves movement from consultant to manager to partner. Progress from one level to the next usually involves a number of factors, including (a) time in a particular level, (b) results (of course), and increasingly, (c) the development of a progressive level of competency in skills deemed to be of importance to the firm. The competency of leadership may be defined for consultants as the ability to influence clients and others in the firm to work toward a particular goal without incurring hostility. Competency in leadership for the manager may involve the ability to lead a team. Leadership competency for a partner may involve the ability to set and communicate a vision to outside constituents, such as investors.

Linking a discussion of what is important to career development obviously has the potential to serve as a powerful motivator for ambitious employees. It also helps them understand what they should be learning over time. In the worst-case scenario, the link between competencies and career development can help employees understand why their progress is not as rapid as they may have hoped.

All these effects can be gained from simply talking about what people need to do to be successful and to grow with the firm. If your company has developed such a model, these discussions shouldn't require a great deal of time. The real learning will take place while the competencies are actually in play, and that is where coaching comes in.

If Your Company Does Not Have a Useful Competency Model

If your company does not have a useful competency model, then your task is to develop one. You could go out and hire an industrial psychologist, but you probably have neither the time nor the money to do so. Likewise, the important competencies for your organization may be more future-oriented and strategic, or they may reflect the values of the organization. Rather than thinking that you as manager have to build an elaborate model, we encourage you to think of the challenge as being more along the lines of articulating what you, and probably most of the experienced employees on your team, already know.

We have used an approach toward articulating competencies that can be replicated in a short period of time by business units, both large and small. We call this exercise "Building the Success Manual" (Weintraub, 1996). The steps of the exercise are listed in Box 7.1. The results of the "Success Manual Exercise" can help you identify what is important that is specific in your company or business unit's culture.

Box 7.1

THE SUCCESS MANUAL EXERCISE

This exercise can take place in a staff meeting, or any context in which small groups can address the following questions. If you have a large organization and want everyone to participate, you can break the larger group into smaller groups of four to six. Ask each group to record their answers to the following questions on flip chart paper and be prepared to report to the larger group.

1. What does someone have to do to be successful here? (If your group performs many different tasks, you may have to be more specific, rephrasing the question to "What does someone have to do to be successful at selling to larger customers here?)

2. What results must we achieve to be successful?

3. What are the most important processes for the members of the group to follow that lead to success?

4. What does someone have to do to fail or get in trouble here?

SOURCE: From *The Success Manual*, by J. Weintraub, 1999, Wellesley, MA: Organizational Dimensions. ©1999 by Joseph Weintraub, Organizational Dimensions. Used by permission.

In one of our recent executive development programs, there was near unanimity among the 20 or so participants that "you have to know the details, the raw numbers, to be effective at presenting here." Similarly, there was near unanimity that one had to be "good at working under pressure" to be successful at the firm. The coaching managers at this firm knew that if they were to help their employees develop, they would need to address these competencies. The articulation of these competencies took no more than 2 hours.

This particular method is what might be termed a "bottoms-up" approach to competency articulation. It is particularly useful with experienced individual contributors and other managers. Everyone is knowledgeable and can make meaningful contributions to the discussion. However, if you are hiring large numbers of new employees into a particular kind of position, those new employees may need more guidance. Under those circumstances, we suggest that you partner with managers or individual contributors who have some experience to articulate, through a similar process, the competencies you believe you should be teaching to the new hires.

Tom Gillett is a manager in a large customer service unit of a financial services firm whose mission is to provide value-added services to wealthier clientele. He and his colleagues (other managers in the same organization engaged in similar work) collaborated to develop a simple list of competencies to which they could train and coach newer employees, particularly those coming from outside the firm. Importantly, each manager had intimate and expert knowledge of the customer service processes in question. Over the course of several meetings, they talked about superior performers and ultimately articulated three simple competencies having to do with sales, product knowledge, and customer relationship management. For each competency, they described a set of "anchors," or examples, that illustrate the successful execution of a particular aspect of the competency. Under relationship management, for instance, "listening to the customer" is an important behavior that can help strengthen the relationship.

These competencies are taught to new employees. Tom also makes extensive use of developmental coaching and can use observational data from call monitoring to aid in the learning process. He and individual sales associates review the content of recent telephone calls, each reflecting on the associate's execution around the three competencies. Given the nature of their business, which is to provide a high level of customer service, the most frequently used coaching dialogue question is this: "What else could we have done to please that customer?"

More rigorous researchers may question the validity and reliability of competency models developed by such a method. The reality is that Tom and thousands of managers like him are constrained by time and other resources that make the development of a research-based competency model prohibitive. Perhaps more important, the prevailing attitude in most organizations today is "Let's move ahead." Static competency models that require a great deal of time and money to develop and that look backward rather than forward may in fact lack credibility. What is important is that coaching managers and those who work for them have a practical sense of what effective performance looks like, to the highest degree possible.

The Coaching Manager as Teacher

Teaching about "what is important," then, obviously has to be an important part of the work of the coaching manager. Managers don't necessarily think of themselves as teachers, not having had formal training in that role. Luckily, it isn't necessary. Experienced coaching managers tell us that they develop a "feel" for what leads to success. That "feel" may be very specific to their own particular contexts: industry, work group, culture, or customers. That "feel" can help them teach.

Noel Tichy has described the impact of leaders who have what he calls a "teachable point of view." They are able to use past experience to generate a shareable insight about what works and what doesn't (1997). Tichy found that some leaders, such as Roger Enrico, former CEO of PepsiCo, had actually spent a considerable period of time reflecting on what they had learned from their years in business. They didn't teach from management textbooks. While teaching, they can teach from the heart because they truly understand and believe in what they are saying. They have "been there and done that."

The vast reservoir of knowledge that businesspeople build up over the years may be largely implicit, even to them. It may take disciplined reflection and dialogue with others to make that knowledge explicit and therefore useable in coaching and teaching. Reflection and self-assessment help to develop a clear picture of what led to the coaching manager's success. We suggest that you try the "Success Manual" exercise in Box 7.1, as a way of articulating your own teachable point of view and how you might use what you know.

NetSolve, Inc., is a growing company whose main function is to manage the computer networks of other companies. Customer service is absolutely critical to their success and even their survival. CEO Craig Tysdal has given a great deal of thought to the challenge of understanding what customer service means to his customers and what every employee should know in that regard. He spends significant amounts of time personally teaching his insights to each employee, particularly each new employee (Reingold, 2001). He describes the specific behaviors and actions that seem to work there:

> Always take a problem away from a customer. Don't ever hesitate to fix the prob-
> lem, even if it's not NetSolve's fault. Mimic the customer's own style, except if
> someone is angry—then let him vent. (p. 68)

Again, we can clearly see what success looks like in Tysdal's remarks. The employee gets a clear view of what great performance looks like. It is easier for the employee to then make sense of feedback from the coaching manager. The employee understands that critical feedback isn't a politically motivated attack against him or her as a person but is, rather, motivated by important standards of action to which people hold each other accountable.

Strengths That Are Used

This chapter is written from the organization's point of view: what the organization needs for business success. Coaching managers can't pay attention to everything, so their focus should begin with this. However, we have stressed the importance of encouraging employees to drive the coaching process and their own development. Competency is more than skill. Competencies are skills that are *used routinely*. We all know people who are extremely good at executing a particular task but hate doing it. Managers who insist on focusing only on the ability of an employee to deliver should be aware that the mix of great skill and low motivation doesn't yield sustainable superior results. The best coaching managers appear to be able to manage the tension between the organization's needs and the individual's goals. To understand what the employee wants, you must ask, and you must be willing to listen. We suggest that although you must focus your coaching efforts on what your organization needs, that goal will be best served by making sure that the people who are trying to fulfill those organizational needs are not only good at doing so, but *want* to do so as well.

We close this chapter by encouraging you to engage in the following experiment. Its purpose is to help you assess whether or not you and your direct reports have a shared view of what is important.

Self-Assessment 7.1:
How Clear Are You and Your
Direct Reports About What Is Important?

Meet with each of your direct reports. (You should brief them on why you're doing this so as not to unduly alarm them!) Ask each one to write down, independently, the *three most important things* that they believe they get paid to do. You, the coaching manager, should do the same. Compare your lists.

When we have asked managers who haven't done much coaching to undertake this experiment, they often tell us, somewhat anxiously, that they found that only one out of three are the same on both lists. This strongly suggests a lack of clear consensus about what is important. If that is what you find, try to understand what is interfering with your development of a shared sense of the processes by which important work gets done. A number of factors could be involved.

First, you may not have had this discussion before, even in a performance review. Unless your performance review process involves a discussion of skills or competencies, only the results—not the process by which the work gets done—may have been addressed. Second, there may be a real lack of clarity in the organization itself as to the "right" approach or what people need to be doing to achieve results. For instance, should there be a focus on individual effort or teamwork? Finally, of course, employees may be working in a context of significant change. There may not have been time for consensus to emerge regarding the necessary skills and how those skills should be deployed.

The coaching manager will usually find that coaching helps address all three of these factors. Certainly, coaching serves as an invaluable tool for communicating what is important and making sure that it is well understood by all parties. Second, coaching can help to stimulate debates about "the right approach." As we discussed in Chapter 1, coaching creates learning for both employees and for the organization. Through learning about what employees are doing and why they are doing it, the coaching manager is in a better position to pass that information along to others so that a dialogue about what is important can take place.

8

Observing What Is Important, Effectively

IN THIS CHAPTER, YOU WILL LEARN THE FOLLOWING:

- How a tendency to draw inferences can make it difficult for managers to draw an accurate picture of a coachee's job performance
- How to gather information about the performance of others and make that information useful

In this chapter, we continue to work with the metaphor of the mirror, ultimately as a vehicle for helping the manager provide feedback that will be of the greatest possible value. Unfortunately, feedback often misses the mark for the coachee. In Chapter 7, we addressed one aspect of this challenge: deciding what to focus on. In this chapter, we address what can be an even greater challenge, that of observing what is important, but doing so effectively. This isn't necessarily easy to do, even if you know what to look for.

Most of you have seen "fun house" mirrors, the kind that distort your image, making you too heavy—or better yet, too thin. The best mirrors are quite accurate. They serve to augment what individuals looking in the mirror can see on their own. But does one look in the mirror tell the whole story? You and your coachee have selected the competencies that are most important for you to help your employee develop. Now your task is to be able to help the employee build a clear picture of what his or her performance is in relation to those competencies. That turns out to be more difficult than one might hope.

How many times have you been evaluated by a boss who was using what you felt were erroneous data? We would guess, too many times to remember. Unfortunately, human beings, at least in our culture, tend to defensively conclude that information they don't like is inaccurate. We're a defensive lot, and sometimes it seems as though we have a lot to defend ourselves against.

A friend of ours happens to work as a field supervisor in the road construction industry. He tells of a common experience suffered by the workers who build roads in all sorts of bad weather. They may come on the job at 6 to 7 a.m. and work hard until 9:30 a.m. or so, at which time they, deservedly, take a coffee break. Some drivers (annoyed taxpayers probably) passing by the site during the 9:30 to 9:45 time frame will frequently yell, curse, or make obscene gestures at the "lazy government workers who do nothing all day long except waste good taxpayer dollars." At 9:45, the workers go back to work, doubtless feeling thanked for their toil on behalf of the public.

The drivers see, accurately at that point in time, a group of construction workers who are not working. But they are missing the picture as a whole. What appears to be an accurate perception of what a group of people are doing at that particular time is actually quite inaccurate. To make matters worse, as the drivers drive off, they leave with confirmation of their previously held beliefs: People who work for the government engage in loafing. Consequently, they are likely to make this assumption with an even greater sense of conviction the next time the occasion arises. The drivers have seen a "snapshot," which can leave them with assumptions that are not representative of the more complete and ongoing "movie."

One of the most helpful things that the coaching manager can do for an employee is to provide accurate and useful performance feedback. Feedback alone may be enough for a coachee to improve his or her performance. This is particularly true when the coachee is working on the softer skills, such as leadership and teamwork; when people try to self-assess their effectiveness in these interpersonal areas, they are often poor judges of their own behavior and are prone to inaccurate self-assessment (Clark & Clark, 1996). Once they know how they are coming across to others, however, many people will try to improve their performance accordingly.

Effective feedback is possible only when it is based on *accurate observation (or other kinds of performance data)*. As the saying goes, "garbage in, garbage out." If the coaching manager has bad data, the feedback will be flawed and the result will be a lack of learning and even greater defensiveness on the part of the employee. You don't want your employees feeling like the road construction workers just described.

The challenges of gathering good performance data are relatively well understood by industrial and organizational psychologists. We'll review those challenges briefly before reorganizing them in a fashion more consistent with recent work from the field of organizational learning. We will demonstrate how a conceptual tool called the "ladder of inference" (Argyris, Putnam, & Smith, 1985; Ross, 1994) has been particularly valuable to the participants in our coach training programs. We'll then examine the various means that coaching managers have at their disposal for gathering information about employees' performance and offer some suggestions, as well as a few critiques.

As the story of our hapless road construction workers illustrates, even eyewitness observation is not necessarily accurate. Nevertheless, we propose that in-person observation is the standard against which other data-gathering methods should be judged. We realize that this is a high and difficult-to-achieve standard, particularly in a "virtual world" in which team members operate at a distance from one another and the pace of change is rapid. Viewed in this light, most other methods of data gathering, such as the use of multi-rater or 360-degree feedback, appear to be useful, though with a few cautionary notes.

The reality is that performance data should be viewed by the coaching manager with a certain tentativeness. What you think you see, or the reports that you get from others about a particular employee, represent at best a series of snapshots. Unless you can follow the employee around day in and day out, you will end up with a photo album, not a video. It is important to keep that point in mind. What is the coaching manager to do, then, when confronted with the unreliability of performance data? The answer, we believe, is not to take the burden for making the data more reliable all on your shoulders, but to share that burden with the employee.

While coaching, the manager isn't a judge and jury but is, rather, a facilitator of learning. We stress this perspective because it is different from the traditional model of coaching that is linked to performance appraisal. While conducting a performance appraisal, the manager is like an umpire, calling the pitches as "balls" and "strikes." (And as in baseball, arguing with the umpire can get you kicked out of the game.) Managers use the power of their position to take a stand behind their observations, and employees are often left with no choice but to acquiesce. Under these circumstances, the employee may not be motivated to participate as a "co-investigator" in the process of developing good performance data to aid in the appraisal process. The employee will likely be motivated to give the manager data that put the best possible light on his or her performance.

This kind of interaction may be understandable but should not be confused with coaching, a process that focuses on learning. In a coaching process designed to facilitate learning, both the coach and the employee are responsible for getting the best possible information on which to base their assessments. In a coaching friendly context, the coachee will be motivated to help fill in the gaps in the photo album so that the managers can help him or her learn.

Why Is Performance Data, Even Observational Data, Suspect?

In the discussion that follows, we'll leave out the problems associated with organizational politics or incentive systems that encourage managers to consciously present a distorted picture of an employee's performance. Such contextual factors really should be addressed in considering whether or not the manager has created a coaching friendly context. Our focus here is on the challenges that even well-intended and properly motivated managers face when they try to assess how someone else is doing. This is a problem of perception.

Human perception is influenced by a variety of factors. If you just stop to think about your own effectiveness when observing someone else, several challenges come immediately to mind. First, do you have the right kind of access to the person you are observing? The view from close-in can be quite different from the view in the grandstands. Second, what was the physical context like? Was there plenty of light? Could you hear well? Could you see well? Third, how were you feeling at the time? Were you distracted by other thoughts? Were you stressed or unhappy? Fourth, did you have the time to stop and record what you saw, or are you relying on memories that are several days old? Fifth, how well do you really know the other person? Do you have something in common with that person? Do commonalities or differences tend to make your observations more accurate or less accurate? Sixth, how do you feel about the person? If you dislike him or her, your observations, particularly your interpretations of what you see, may well be biased. Seventh, how has the person done in the past? If you have seen someone fail repeatedly at a particular task, you're likely to be expecting that person to fail again, and this expectation may actually influence what you see. We could go on. What becomes clear while reviewing the variety of factors that can influence our observation of another is how many things can go wrong. Human resource management specialists have defined the following six sources of observer error, which are worth taking into consideration (Dessler, 1999).

The first source of error stems from a *lack of clear standards*. Employee and manager don't know what should be observed. We discuss this in detail in Chapter 7. If you don't know what you're looking for, it is very unlikely that you'll be able to describe it accurately.

The *halo effect* is one of the most common factors that shape the perception one person has of another. Friendly people, attractive people, cooperative people, and people who are effective in one aspect of life are likely to be judged as more effective in other aspects of life. A great scientist may be thought of as a great leader even though his or her leadership skills are lacking. Observers tend to give people who demonstrate a desirable characteristic much greater leeway when it comes to evaluating other characteristics or behaviors. We give them a "halo." We also give them a halo if their most recent work was excellent despite the fact that every other performance was not. This creates a real challenge at appraisal time. Unfortunately, people to whom a halo has been bestowed often come to believe that they deserve it.

Three additional sources of error reflect the specific attitude of the observer. Observers may have a tendency to rate everyone as average, with very few exceptions (the *central tendency* effect), or they may be consistently strict (*tough*), or consistently lenient *(supportive)*. In these cases, the observer's attitude shapes what he or she sees. For example, "I never give anyone the top rating, I just don't believe in it" is the cry of the tough manager.

Finally, various forms of socially constructed or cognitive *bias* can influence what observers think they see while observing others. Age, sex, race, sexual orientation, occupation, and ethnicity all serve to define an individual as a member of a particular group. If we expect stereotypical behavior from members of a particular identifiable group, we are more likely to see the expected behavior. We are also less likely to see behavior that runs counter to the stereotypes we hold. If you hold the assumption, for instance, that scientists don't make effective managers, you may be more likely to see the failings in a scientist/manager and less likely to see the strengths and potential strengths. In reality, each individual is unique, and it is typically a mistake, from a coaching perspective, to judge individual performance on the basis of biases one might have about a *group* of individuals.

A coaching manager in a high-tech company told of his effort to help one of his team leaders do a better job at getting his team on the right track. The leader invited the manager to sit in on a few team meetings. The manager saw one particular woman in the group, an engineer, who seemed to be having a very difficult time making eye contact with, or even looking at, any of the men in the group. The situation appeared to be quite tense. This concerned the manager because he had become increasingly worried that his division was not a hospitable place for women to work.

He also was concerned that the team leader seemed to be doing nothing about the situation. When they held a brief coaching dialogue after the team meeting, the coaching manager who had observed the meeting asked about the situation and expressed some concern about what he had seen. "Isn't there something more that the team leader should do about this to help the team manage diversity?" The stunned team leader expressed some confusion for a moment and then reported that he had talked with all three of them recently. The problem had nothing to do with a gender issue on the team. The two men happened to both have major performance problems during their last project, and the woman had had to pick up the slack for their ineffectiveness. She had confronted them in the last meeting and gotten nowhere. She was completely frustrated with their work, and her frustration was palpable. The real problem for the team leader and for the team was managing conflict and poor performance. The coaching manager, being well intended, had assumed that a gender issue existed, on the basis of the gender of the individuals involved and the behavior he had found himself attending to. Bias causes us to make assumptions about the meaning of what we see. In fact, all of the sources of error create a tendency to assume or to make inferences that cause us to misinterpret what little data we actually have to work with in many instances.

The Real Problem: Our Tendency
to Draw Inferences From Selected Data

In our efforts to formulate a means of helping coaching managers deal with the human tendency to distort the reality of what we see, we have sought out simple solutions. The root problem seems to involve a comingling of data with what may be inappropriate interpretations of that data. Unfortunately, this mixing of data and interpretation seems to occur automatically. It can take place very quickly, can be hard to spot, and can be self-confirming. Like the driver who spots the tired construction worker taking a well-deserved break and leaves the scene feeling more convinced than ever that those who build roads are really goofing off, we look for what we believe to be the case. Next time, we'll be very likely to find it.

Ross (1994) describes this as the problem of self-generating beliefs:

> We live in a world of self-generating beliefs which remain largely untested. We adopt those beliefs because they are based on conclusions that are inferred from what we observe, plus our past experience. Our ability to achieve the results we truly desire is eroded by our feelings that
>
> - Our beliefs are the truth
> - The truth is obvious
> - Our beliefs are based on real data
> - The data that we select are the real data. (p. 242)

This phenomenon is aptly captured by the title "ladder of inference"(Ross, 1994) because it describes how we quickly move "up" the ladder. The steps up the ladder of inference are presented in Box 8.1. Several of the steps are particularly worthy of discussion in the context of the coaching manager.

Box 8.1

THE LADDER OF INFERENCE

Step 7. I take actions based on my beliefs.

Step 6. I adopt beliefs about the world.

Step 5. I draw conclusions.

Step 4. I make assumptions based on the meaning that I added

Step 3. I add meaning to what I see (cultural and personal).

Step 2. I select data from what I observe.

Step 1. I observe data and events.

SOURCE: Adapted from "The Ladder of Inference," by R. Ross, 1994, in *The Fifth Discipline Fieldbook* (p. 243), edited by P. Senge, R. Ross, B. Smith, C. Roberts, and A. Kleiner, New York: Currency Doubleday.

The first step on the ladder involves observation. Accurate observation, much as a video camera might provide, is the goal. However, as we've already said, you can't observe everything, and if you did, you'd have too much data to actually help the employee. On the second step, the observer has to select the data on which to focus. Chapter 7 directly addresses this challenge. If, however, you have not decided in consultation with others what is important and made it common knowledge, you'll immediately find yourself moving up the ladder of inference and out of control. The reason for this is that everyone, including yourself, will have an opinion about what is important and impose that opinion on the choices they make about which data to select.

The third step up the ladder involves the imposition of meaning on the data you have already decided to select. This is the basic inferential step, though you should note that meaning isn't imposed on everything the other person does, it is imposed selectively on what you have consciously or unconsciously chosen to pay attention to. In our previous example, the coaching manager visited a team meeting. He made note of the behavior of a female team member and didn't pay as much attention to the behavior of the males on the team. He then made an inference about the meaning of her behavior. He focused on her because he had, for other reasons, been sensitized to the problems of women in his organization. He was observing the men in the group less intently and didn't even note that they were looking down most of the time, avoiding eye contact with everyone else in the group.

Fortunately, as an effective coach, he tested this assumption in his dialogue with the team leader. He discovered that he had been wrong; something else was actually going on. However, let's assume for the moment that he had not tested his assumption. He might have drawn the conclusion that the firm, or at least this team, was inhospitable to women and then taken actions on the basis of this conclusion. The real problems of the group would have been ignored. His focus would have drawn attention to issues of gender and diversity and ironically, might have left the female engineer feeling unsupported (she wanted the other two, who just happened to be men, to be dealt with).

Our coaching managers have consistently told us that learning to work with the ladder of inference has been of enormous value. It ties together the various forms of perceptual bias that for decades, human resource professionals have been concerned about in the appraisal of performance. Most of our coaching managers have found that a 2-step process, observation leading to inference, is sufficient to help them keep track of data and interpretation and prevent the two from commingling.

We now use a simple observation sheet to aid in making the distinction, presented in the exercise in Box 8.2. The format is based on the work of Chris Argyris (Argyris & Schon, 1978), who developed the use of a left-column/right-column case study tool (for a different though similar purpose). We ask coaching managers to draw a line down the middle of a piece of paper. On the left side of the line, write down what is actually observed. On the right side of the paper, record thoughts, feelings, reactions, or ideas about what is observed. We encourage coaching managers to capture both sides because the feelings, ideas, or hunches that are recorded on the right side, although they are the building blocks from which inferences are drawn, can also be useful.

Box 8.2

EXERCISE: OBSERVATION AND INFERENCE

Make an observation sheet like the one illustrated here. Note that the left-hand column includes actual behavioral observations. The right-hand column includes your thoughts, reactions, hunches, hypotheses, and feelings you have about what you see. Keep the two rigidly separate. We use an example from a coach training program to illustrate. Use the observation sheet the next time you get a chance to observe one of your direct reports in action. Does it help you to organize your thinking in this way? Which side is likely to be most useful as a source of performance feedback to the employee?

• John entered the room, he fixed his eyes on his notebook, didn't look at the other members of the team seated around the table.	• He's angry. Something has gone wrong. This isn't the way to send a message to his troops.
• Several members of the team began to make small talk.	• I think they must have been uncomfortable.

- John interrupted their chatting, and said "we have to get on with this meeting, I have some important new numbers from the CFO that you'd better be aware of."

- John then talked about the report from the CFO. He used an overhead with a lot of writing on it. It was hard to see. He read the facts and figures on the overhead in a monotone. Still not looking at the group.

- Team members start to shuffle paper while he's talking.

- Again, sounded angry, or in a hurry. He needs to let them socialize a bit if he wants them to work well together.

- He's not conveying that this is important, or interesting or urgent. He's losing them.

- He's lost them, and I don't think he'll get them back like this. He's not coming across like a leader.

Discussion: Let's say that your hypotheses on the right-hand side were actually correct. (Again, we encourage you not to ignore your feelings and hunches because such reactions may represent important sources of data, particularly on the impact of the employee's behavior.) You might present this to your coachee by saying: "When you did 'this' I felt 'that.'" Consider the problems associated with providing feedback that is based solely on the data of the right-hand column. Such data are hard-hitting, if not quite critical and evaluative in nature. They are also loaded with a series of inferences. The inferences include but aren't limited to the following:

- John is angry.
- The team is uncomfortable.
- John is angry, again.
- The team will work together more effectively if they have a chance to socialize.
- His team won't hear his message as being important.
- He has lost his leadership relationship with them.

All inferences may be accurate—but they may also be inaccurate. It is imperative that the coaching manager understand the difference before using data from the right-hand column. If you, when coaching, believe that these data represent more of a "maybe" than a sure thing, you will ideally use them in a different way: to help you formulate questions, next steps, areas to explore, or possibilities to consider. Data from the right-hand side can be used "as is," as accurate reflections of what you saw in the meeting. The only problem with the data from the right-hand side is that they represent a "snapshot." John may be ill, he may be having a bad day, or he may be behaving differently for a variety of reasons.

One coach, using this technique, described an observation that she made of an employee new to her group, in a very important meeting: "I just didn't like this guy." This rather intense emotional reaction ultimately proved to be an important source of data. What she realized in retrospect, but couldn't put her finger on at the time, was that the employee, someone from a country and culture different from her own, had made several subtle remarks to a customer in the meeting that struck her as very arrogant. This was particularly troubling given the sensitive and political nature of his work.

Other managers in the very same meeting who had overheard his remarks and with whom she later consulted didn't recall having the same reaction. No one could recall what he actually said. They did, however, feel that he might be having some communication problems because of his cultural background that could give others the wrong impression and ultimately interfere with his performance. They were also making inferences about his behavior, but their inferences were strikingly different from the manager's. She resolved at the next meeting to listen more carefully to what the employee was actually saying and to get some real data before jumping to any conclusions.

Using the additional data, she reflected on her relationship with the employee. She began to consider the possibility that she was having difficulty understanding his cultural framework. She felt that she should get to know him better before intervening so that she could have a clearer sense of what was going on. If she had given him feedback about what appeared to be an arrogant personal style when the issue was really something quite different, she might have provoked considerable defensiveness on the employee's part. She caught herself on the upper rungs of the ladder of inference and forced herself back down to the ground level: the data of observation. Although her emotional reaction does matter, she'll have to wait until she actually talks with the employee to get a clearer sense of the origin of that reaction. It matters, but it is not the place to begin.

Error and Expectations: What You See Is What You Get

The "Pygmalion Effect," also known as the *self-fulfilling prophecy*, is well understood in education and management (Livingston, 1988). Research has shown that children who are expected by their teachers to succeed *are* more likely to succeed. Employees who are expected by their managers to succeed seem to be more likely to succeed as well. Conversely, the reverse can occur. In the "set-up-to-fail syndrome," the manager's expectations of poor performance can resonate with an employee's lack of confidence or timidity, resulting in performance problems (Manzoni & Barsoux, 1998). Both of these outcomes, the good employee doing even better or the marginal employee doing even worse, have to do in part with expectations in the relationship between the employee and the manager. The coaching manager who expresses a belief that the employee "can do it" may find that in an effort to live up to the manager's expectations, the employee actually does it.

The expectations the manager brings to a relationship with an employee are determined in part by how he or she manages the ladder of inference. As we've already come to understand, research on self-fulfilling prophecies, good and bad, suggests that expectations can influence perception. If you expect a problem, you are far more likely to be looking for one and to find data that support your theory that one exists. (This is one reason that employees are aware of the importance of impression management.) If you are aware of this possibility, then you're much more likely to master the discipline of keeping inference and observation separate.

We encourage you to give the exercise in Box 8.2 a try. You can do this exercise while watching a video with your family, sitting in a fast-food restaurant, or watching a team at work. Try the exercise first, though, with someone else present who is watching the same event or group of people that you are watching. Choose your target and document what you see on the left side of the column; record your behavioral observations, theories, ideas, or emotional reactions on the right side. Then, stop and discuss what you have seen with your partner. Did you and your partner see the same things?

When we ask two coaching managers to go through this exercise, we often find that they offer significantly different reports. The reasons for this have to do with the fact that, as stated above, inferences are based on observation but they are also based on the perceptions and background of the observer. Sometimes the observer's "hot buttons" are very potent, leading to quick and erroneous inference making.

We encourage you to start thinking about your own issues, concerns, or "hot buttons." What kinds of people and situations tend to lead you to distort what you see? What kind of inferences do you tend to make? Be honest with yourself. Who do you like? Who don't you like? What groups of people do you have a difficult time getting to know, and what groups are you more comfortable with? What tasks do you enjoy observing, and what tasks do you not enjoy observing?

The ladder of inference is a good tool for keeping an eye on the distinction between data and inference, but it is also a good tool for learning about yourself. The best coaching managers are very self-aware. They know what kinds of issues are likely to encourage them to distort what they see. The emotionally sensitive or team-oriented manager might mistakenly see the task orientation of an employee as a manifestation of poor interpersonal skills. The "big picture" coaching manager might see an employee's focus on the details as a roadblock to change. We make one helpful suggestion in this regard. Personal style assessment instruments, such as the DISC methodology or the Myers-Briggs Type Indicator,[1] can often be helpful to managers who want to better understand their own "default" response as they move up and down the ladder of inference. Knowing something about your personality allows you to understand an important source of diversity in the world, the diversity of personal styles.

Getting the Most From Direct Observation and Other Approaches to Gathering Performance Data

So far, we have explored the problems of data versus inference in some detail but only as they apply to direct visual observation of the employee by the coaching manager. When the coaching manager is forced to rely on data from sources other than direct observation, it stands to reason that the potential for the ladder of inference to distort the data increases significantly. Likewise, data-gathering methods that rely on the reports of others (verbal or written reports, survey instruments, or multi-rater feedback instruments that ask various stakeholders to rate or comment on the effectiveness of a particular employee) may engage more people in climbing the ladder of inference as well.

Strangely, apparently robust methodologies, such as the manager's interviewing others who work with the employee or using well-designed multi-rater or 360-degree feedback, may actually give the manager enough data to make a fairly accurate appraisal rating of an employee—but such data won't necessarily be good enough for coaching purposes. When coaching managers interview other employees or customers who work with coachees, they may find themselves hearing inferences instead of data. Likewise, feedback data provided by formal multi-rater feedback systems can also push people up the ladder of inference. The reasons are simple. Multi-rater feedback surveys ask general questions, such as "Does the employee display effective listening in team meetings?" This question asks for a conclusion about a pattern of behavior (the "video"), not an example or examples. Although most multi-rater reports have a section for qualitative narrative comments from people filling out surveys, if the respondents are untrained, they are more likely to provide general statements than specific examples. If employees are to truly see themselves clearly, they need accurate mirrors with the details included.

What are the implications of this state of affairs? We have to be practical. The coaching manager will often have to make do with the available information. First, we present some practical guidelines for coaching managers and then discuss how the coachee can help (see Box 8.3).

Box 8.3

GETTING THE MOST FROM VARIOUS SOURCES OF PERFORMANCE DATA

1. Always strive for specific examples of work. This is easiest to do when the source of data is your direct observation as the coaching manager. It is the standard against which all other sources of data must be judged.

2. Keep in mind that even observation can be limited by inference and even a specific example represents a "snapshot," not the "video."

3. Always follow up on formal and informal multi-rater feedback assessment activities. Get specific examples from the people involved to reflect the generalizations that are offered by the feedback report.

4. Be cautious of how you interpret unsolicited feedback provided by others that is delivered by e-mail or by hearsay.

5. Differentiate feedback from interpretation. Understand your own ladder of inference.

6. Enlist the coachee in producing the "video" and in taking responsibility for thinking about how individual "snapshot" observations fit into the pattern that he or she is monitoring.

- Seek specific examples. This is true regardless of whether or not the employee is self-assessing his or her performance, the coaching manager is providing feedback based on observation, the coaching manager has interviewed others who work with the employee, or the coaching manager and/or employee are following up on a formal multi-rater assessment. Direct observation, then, must be considered the standard by which all other sources of performance data are judged. Direct observation offers specific examples of work.

- Keep in mind that specific examples represent one "snapshot," not a "video" of the employee's life. Do the specific examples represent part of a pattern, or are they unrepresentative of the employee's ongoing performance?

- After a formal multi-rater feedback process in which the employee has received a report, there must be a follow-up. Employees should go back to those who filled out surveys describing their performance. Typically, the feedback report includes the observations of the person's boss, peers, and direct reports, if appropriate. After thanking those people, employees should ask for input in a positive way—for example, a description in general terms of what appear to be their strengths and their weaknesses. They should then ask for specific examples of times when they have not performed at their best, according to the general feedback from their multi-rater report. They should listen and not become defensive or attack. Employees can bring this data back to their discussions with coaching managers. Unfortunately, they will probably have to accept the fact that every individual who filled out a survey form may not actually remember or be inclined to offer specific examples. Multi-rater feedback reports, especially those that are well constructed, can be of enormous value. However, almost all authors of commercially available multi-rater feedback programs recommend exactly what we have described here. Multi-rater feedback reports are designed to suggest strengths or developmental needs, but they are only the first step. The real work and payoff are in the follow-up.

- Be careful about using unsolicited feedback, particularly if it is delivered by e-mail. Our concern here is that impromptu and unsolicited feedback may be of low quality and may draw heavily on inference. E-mails can be sent impulsively, before the sender has had time to think through whatever is provoking the feedback. Unfortunately, if someone has critical feedback about an employee, they may feel very angry and therefore be motivated to retaliate against the employee. We recommend that unless it is exceptionally clear, unsolicited feedback and feedback offered by e-mail be seen as an opportunity for an in-person discussion, or at least a phone call, so that the coaching manager can ask questions to help clarify the data being offered.

- Using the methodology of the ladder of inference, be sure to differentiate feedback based on observation from ideas, hunches, or generalizations about the coachee's actions. We discuss this in Chapter 9 as representing interpretations of feedback. Interpretations made without consulting the coachee are based on inference. You may have good data that accurately describe someone's behavior, but you don't know why they are behaving the way they do. Our coaching managers stress the importance of keeping an open mind.

The Coachee's Role

The coachee needs to be an active participant in the coaching process. He or she must keep track of the learning goal, results to date, feedback from others, and thoughts about what needs to happen next. Keeping with our metaphor of the "snapshot," the coachee must keep charge of the "photo album." This allows the coachee to make effective use of the observations of others, even if those observations are one-time events. When it comes to learning, the coachee, not the coaching manager, is in the driver's seat. The employee may choose to make a great deal out of an individual observation. On the other hand, some employees would ignore a "video review" of their work even if Steven Spielberg had directed it!

We had an interchange relevant to this challenge with Adam, a participant in an executive education program that we were running. Adam was already well-known to us. He is a high-potential manager possessing enormous enthusiasm and unbridled assertiveness. His behavior can at times resemble that of a good-natured "bull in a china shop." In the classroom, as teachers, we noticed that Adam was exercising enormous and uncharacteristic self-control. Every time he would appear ready to jump into a discussion (without raising his hand), he seemed to catch himself, settle down, and try to listen to what others were saying. Curious about this, we asked him about his actions in the classroom (not wanting to give away our enormous sense of relief!).

Adam explained that about 4 months ago, he had participated in an important cross-functional task force with a number of senior-level marketing managers from throughout his company. The vice president for human resources happened to be at the meeting. The two had never met, but he asked Adam to join him for a cup of coffee after the meeting. Curious, and eager to make a high-level contact, Adam accepted. The vice president took his time and got to know Adam a bit. He asked Adam about his career goals and how he felt about his participation on the task force. Evidently, satisfied that Adam was interested in improving his performance, he then offered to give Adam some feedback he thought might help. He explained that he saw Adam's comments in the meeting as being very much on target and that he clearly had a bright future with the firm, words that Adam was happy to hear. However, the vice president then said that, in his enthusiasm, Adam had interrupted several important people from other parts of the firm, and this limited his ability to build influence with those key players. Adam was perturbed, but felt he had to agree with the vice president's observations. He could see it himself. He knew that, out of his enthusiasm, he sometimes inadvertently ignored the needs or feelings of others. No one had ever directly offered that feedback in such a powerful way, however.

Four months later, as we could see in our classroom, Adam was continuing to work on the issues raised by the vice president of human resources. (The two had not met since.) Adam expressed gratitude about the fact that the vice president was nice enough to be observant and then take him aside to give him the feedback in a way that was helpful. Adam explained that he'd been trying to monitor his behavior because he knew he had to change. He had lofty aspirations and didn't want to get in his own way. He went on to say that some days, he was pretty good at monitoring how he was doing; other days, he was not so good. He was glad that his efforts in our classroom had been noted.

Adam is the keeper of his own "photo album" of ideas and observations about his performance. The vice president is certainly in no position to keep track of Adam's performance. Perhaps his manager is in no position to do so, either—but Adam is. He is aware of what he needs to learn and is in charge of that effort.

The Coaching Manager as Observer: Promoting Learning and Performance, From the Sidelines

It isn't easy to be a good observer, even if you are properly motivated. It is easy to make inferences, and difficult to organize your thinking to focus on data rather than interpretation. It is difficult to watch an employee without thinking in an evaluative way. Perhaps just as challenging, managers like to take action. Observation can feel very passive and unproductive. As we've described, sometimes people find it almost intolerable. Nevertheless, the discipline of observing (or getting observation from others), not imposing your own inferences, and then packaging the data in a useful way for feedback to the employee is hard work. It is one aspect of the work of leadership.

Note

1. The Myers-Briggs Type Indicator is a registered trademark of Consulting Psychologists Press.

9

Providing Balanced and Helpful Feedback

IN THIS CHAPTER, YOU WILL LEARN ABOUT THE FOLLOWING:

- The benefits of feedback
- The problems associated with feedback and "management by guilt"
- The basics of providing balanced feedback
- The factors that shape an employee's emotional reaction to feedback, and how the employee's reaction affects his or her ability to learn from feedback
- How to maximize the value of feedback

Feedback is often thought of as the foundation for all coaching—indeed, for all development. As we've stated, although we do believe it is important, it is only one component of the coaching model we have described. According to most research on learning, feedback offered without the support of the other aspects of the model may not be all that helpful. To be useful for developmental purposes, feedback should target what the employee is trying to learn about. Feedback must also be delivered to the employee in a "helpful" way and in a fashion with which the employee can work. Finally, and perhaps most important, feedback must be delivered by a coaching manager who is aware of (a) the power of the emotional impact that can accompany feedback and (b) how the coachee's reactions can shape his or her ability to learn from the feedback.

The Benefits of Feedback

Although feedback is not without its problems, when feedback is effectively directed at an employee's learning goals and offered in the context of a model of coaching that includes self-assessment, the benefits can be substantial. As such, developing skill in effectively providing feedback to employees should be considered an important goal for all coaching managers. Research on feedback shows that the following are just a few of the most important benefits of providing feedback, particularly to employees who are interested in their own learning and development (London, 1997):

- Feedback helps to keep goal-directed behavior on course. Keeping employees informed about progress as they attend to change or pursue any goal helps them see how far they have come and how far they have to go.

- Feedback helps employees set new and more aggressive goals. On the basis of the feedback they receive, they see what they have accomplished. Those who are motivated will want to push on further.

- Positive feedback, when appropriate, helps employees feel that they have achieved even when their achievement doesn't lead to a material result, such as project completion or a pay raise.

- Motivation theory and research also show that feedback can serve to enhance motivation because employees understand what it takes to be successful. They know the rules of the road. The employee who can say, "Now I know how to get there," is more likely to make the attempt.

- Feedback helps employees develop a greater ability to detect errors on their own. When coupled with self-assessment, feedback helps us better judge our own actions because our ability to observe ourselves has been calibrated by comparison with the feedback of others.

- Related to the last point, feedback also helps employees see what they need to learn. They have a clearer sense of their own weaknesses or learning gaps. Their ability to take charge of their own development is enhanced.

- People who are used to getting feedback tend to seek it out. Effective provision of feedback by a manager is one of the most important tactics for creating a coaching friendly context and the "market for coaching" that should be the goal of every coaching manager.

- Frequent feedback also serves to eliminate most of the conflicts we've discussed between performance appraisal and developmental coaching. As many of our coaching managers have told us, "If the employee is surprised in the performance appraisal meeting about any serious problem with his or her performance, I've failed to give them feedback along the way."

- Finally, feedback helps employees develop what is called a *career identity:* "I know that I'm good at this because my manager told me." Feedback shapes how employees see themselves. One of the authors of this book can point to two specific instances of positive feedback from senior managers, early in his career, which helped to crystallize a view of himself and his abilities that survives some 25 years later. Feedback to employees about their strengths communicates to them that they can make a contribution that will be valued by others.

The Problem With Feedback

Unfortunately, feedback does not always result in such positive outcomes, a fact of life of which we are all too aware. A review of the research on feedback to date has shown that overall, feedback has only a moderately positive impact on performance (Kluger & DeNisi, 1996). Feedback that focuses on personal characteristics ("You are a slow worker") rather than on tasks and behavior ("You took 7 extra minutes at Step 3") and is delivered in a way that threatens an employee's self-esteem ("You're just not as good as the rest of them") appears to significantly undermine its usefulness. Overly negative personal and general feedback is discouraging from a motivational standpoint and is also not helpful from a learning or performance-improvement standpoint. Such feedback leaves the receiver feeling angry and less likely to communicate with his or her manager in the future.

So, who is out there offering unintelligent character assassination as a substitute for helpful feedback? Are most managers really monsters? Certainly some are, but we don't believe that is the most common problem. Too many managers are unsure of the value of feedback, unsure of their skills in delivering feedback, and afraid of being hurtful. This leads to some interesting outcomes. We suggest that if you asked most employees what they considered their worst feedback experience, you'd find them making one or both of the following points:

- "The worst feedback I ever got was the feedback I never got." The employee who is left out in the dark, getting only some sense of how he or she is doing on the yearly performance appraisal day, has a legitimate complaint. Not knowing how you are doing creates a list of "anti-benefits" that is a mirror image to the list of benefits described above. Efforts are not focused, learning gaps are not recognized, motivation is not strengthened, and learning itself is unguided or absent. The most frequent cause for the "no feedback" feedback is probably the manager's fears that the feedback will be responded to negatively.

- "The worst feedback I ever got was the feedback I got thirdhand, because my boss told everyone else but me." Feedback delivered "through the grapevine" leaves employees feeling confused and mistrustful. Such feedback also leaves the employee, and the manager, with none of the benefits described above.

Note that both of these "sins" refer to an absence of feedback, not a personal attack. The underlying dynamic involves the manager either being passive out of fear, or passive-aggressive and afraid to confront the employee directly. Ironically, in our experience, such errors are even more likely to take place in the executive suite than on the shop floor (not that things are always great on the shop floor, either).

Harry Levinson (1986), one of the pioneers of consulting psychology, suggests that managers find that the giving of feedback, particularly critical feedback, creates an unconscious sense of guilt on their part. Some managers fear that they will literally make others hurt or ill by criticizing them and as a result, may withhold corrective feedback. Most of us fear the way others will react to our criticism and don't want to be hurtful. What makes the problem important for managers in particular is that they are in positions of authority. They know that their words have extra weight. Their assessments can affect their employees' compensation and careers. Managers can be vulnerable to such concerns, even though their employees may not see them in that light. But the problem can get worse.

If a manager feels disappointed in the performance of a subordinate and is fearful of the power of his or her anger, the manager tries to avoid thinking about it. The problem, however, doesn't go away. The manager's anger builds and, in what may be a rather unskilled performance, is released in a torrent, all at once. The formerly reserved and compassionate (or downright fearful) manager becomes the tyrant who delivers an explosion of pent-up feedback, threatens the individual's self-esteem, and focuses more on the person than on the actual task the employee was performing, or not performing. This may be accompanied by a trip to the human resources department and demands that "We've got to fire this person!" We were recently told of a situation in which a manager counseled an employee at breakfast for more than a year, trying to be helpful to him but never telling him what the problem was. Their relationship ended on a very angry note.

Is this an issue that emerges only when a manager is working with an employee who has a severe performance problem? The answer is "no." In fact, the conditions for what Levinson (1986) describes as "management by guilt" may be even more compelling when a manager is coaching a good or great employee. That employee may have made significant contributions to the business unit. He or she may have good interpersonal skills. The manager may like the employee and indeed be friends with that person. Many employees, at all company levels, have told us that they didn't get helpful feedback even from managers who really seemed to like them. Fearful of having to provide critical feedback to the good employee, they provided none at all until forced to do so at performance appraisal time.

It is important to remember that the good employee wants to learn and takes the task of learning seriously. "Top talent" is more likely to see feedback, even critical feedback, as helpful. The first step for any manager interested in developing his or her skills as a provider of feedback is to move beyond the belief that feedback, even when properly given, is injurious.

Your Development as a Provider of Feedback

The reality is, learning to give useful feedback takes some practice. Helpful feedback needs to be clear, and the ability to speak clearly about what one has seen is a skill that must be developed. Because developing effectiveness as a provider of feedback also involves learning on the part of the coaching manager, it is probably necessary to get feedback on your feedback! Such a two-way learning process, in which the coaching manager gives feedback to an employee and gets feedback on his or her effectiveness in doing so, is greatly facilitated by a good relationship between the employee and manager—in other words, a coaching friendly context. Our action recommendations on learning to be more effective as a provider of feedback are presented in Box 9.1.

Box 9.1

DEVELOPING EFFECTIVENESS AS A FEEDBACK PROVIDER

1. Decide whether or not this is a developmental goal to which you feel committed.

2. If you hope to improve the feedback you are providing to your employees, share this goal with them and ask for their help.

3. Practice often, with a variety of people and situations.

4. Always keep the dignity and self-esteem of the employee in mind.

5. Work to develop clarity and simplicity in your feedback through rehearsing feedback conversations with others (friends and family).

6. Ask for feedback from your employees. Make sure that your feedback messages are understood and are helpful.

First, make up your mind as to whether or not this is something you want to learn how to do. If this isn't a goal that you can embrace with some commitment, you're not likely to make much progress in learning how to become more effective. (This, of course, is true for any serious developmental goal.) If you feel that you're not that effective at providing feedback, own up to this with your employees. Let them know that this is something you're going to try to do more of and you need their help. Tell them why you're trying to improve your effectiveness at giving feedback; give them the business or personal case for its importance.

The next section, on the basic requirements for balanced feedback, will help by providing you with a set of guidelines for the content of feedback as well as the tactics of providing it. However, consulting on thousands of feedback episodes has convinced us that it is not possible to offer you a fully functioning "cookbook" that will address the contingencies of every situation. Simply put, there is too much variance across individuals and contexts. So you'll need to be persistent in your efforts by practicing them in a variety of situations. Of course, while practicing, always keep the dignity and self-esteem of your employees in mind. If you ask for their help, be prepared to accept it.

As you'll see in the next section, clarity and simplicity are essential to making feedback usable by the employee. This requirement may get at the heart of what you'll need to learn in a project. We suggest that you work on practicing clarity and simplicity with friends, colleagues, or your own coach/mentor. Rehearsing conversations with an uninvolved third party gives you a chance to practice what you want to say and get feedback in a very low-risk context. Rehearsing a conversation in advance has been found to be a particularly powerful strategy while planning for conversations that may be stressful (Weeks, 2001).

After you have delivered the feedback, get used to checking to see whether or not your comments and observations were understood and whether or not the feedback was helpful. Be prepared for some comments, particularly to the effect that "That wasn't clear" or "I don't agree." Don't retaliate; consider what aspects of the message were lost or garbled by you, and try to restate your observations.

The Basics of Providing Balanced Feedback

In describing the basic components of feedback, we will also report on what the coaching managers we have studied have told us works and doesn't work. We'll also try to fit the various components more directly to the model of coaching described throughout this book. In this section, we'll rely heavily on work by Buron and McDonald-Mann (1999).

Before giving feedback, we make the assumption that you and the employee have discussed what he or she is working on and that you have given the employee an opportunity to reflect on his or her own performance. We also assume that you were clear on what aspects of the employee's performance you were trying to observe and what was important in the situation. Finally, we assume that you have had a chance to get some good solid data about the performance of the employee, data that you trust.

We also assume that you have decided what your goal is in giving the feedback. In addition to learning, is your goal to help appraise or celebrate the employee's previous actions? Or is your goal to encourage the employee or provide helpful information as he or she looks forward to the next challenge? Either way, the basic structure of feedback is the same, and the suggestions for how to manage the process are similar. Having said that, the art of coaching, an art that one learns only with practice, is in knowing how to offer feedback in a way that conveys as much useful information as possible. (See Box 9.2.)

Box 9.2

FEEDBACK, THE BASIC REQUIREMENTS

Feedback content should include the following:

- The situation in which your observations were made.
- Your observations of the employee in action.
- The impact of the employee's behavior or actions, particularly on you.

Before offering feedback, be sure to do the following:

- Set the stage for your feedback discussion in a way that will encourage the maximum degree of openness, which is essential to learning. Make sure that the location, degree of confidentiality, and timing are appropriate to the individual and the situation.

Effective feedback is . . .

- Solicited by the employee.
- Focused on what the employee is trying to accomplish or has told you that he or she wants to learn.
- Given frequently.
- Given, whenever possible, right after an action and the employee's reflection on his or her action.
- Given, whenever possible, with a helpful, not an angry, attitude.

- Specific, using behavioral terminology or a comparable description terminology.
- Focuses on the task, action, or behavior, not on the person.
- Is direct and usually begins with "I" statements.
- Delivered without interpretation.
- Checked by the coaching manager to make sure that the employee heard the message the manager wanted to deliver.
- Followed by the question: "What do you plan on doing with this feedback?"
- Followed by the suggestion of a follow-up meeting, particularly if the feedback to the coachee has been negative.

Feedback represents a form of communication, or a message. What should the message include? Feedback content usually includes the following: a description of the *situation* in which you observed the employee; a description of the *behavior* of, or *actions* taken by, the employee you observed; and finally, a description of the *impact* of the behavior or actions of the employee on others or on a relevant business outcome. "Here is what I saw, and here is what I think was the impact of what I saw" is the basic structure of a feedback message. Note what is included and not included in the message. What *is* included is factual information, to the highest degree possible.

What is *not* included is an interpretation. You may have to climb the ladder of inference a bit when describing what you "think" is the impact of a particular action or behavior; but oftentimes, you'll know. You'll know because you can describe the impact of the employee's behavior on you. "I don't know what others might have thought about your approach to this, but I liked it. It really addressed my concerns." If you describe the impact from your vantage point, you're making very few inferences. After all, an individual's manager is a key stakeholder in the actions of that individual. The impact on you, as manager, does count, and the impact you experience from the actions of an employee may be similar to the impact experienced by others. You can therefore state, "This was the impact on me," with real authority.

On the basis of our own research and review of the writing to date on personal learning, we encourage you to always consider the importance of the employee's goals while delivering feedback. If you *focus on what the employee is trying to accomplish or has told you he or she wants to learn,* you have been given license by the employee to be clear and direct. Consider the alternative, as described by one of our former students and coaching manager trainees. The following is a true story:

I just had an illuminating experience regarding feedback that I thought you might find interesting. I contacted a colleague about a job when I was applying for positions in the company he worked for. I sent him my resume and he said he would forward it along to any manager he knew of who might be hiring. Today, I got a two-page response from someone else who works at my old colleague's firm, a complete stranger, giving me "feedback" on my resume. I was completely at a loss for words—not at all what I was expecting and least of all what I wanted to hear. It was interesting to notice my own response to this completely unsolicited and unwanted feedback. Although the author of the feedback letter made very good points, and I am very impressed that he took the time, I could feel my anger rising as I kept reading the e-mail. The anger started with the second sentence that read, "I have a few concerns with the way that your resume is crafted." I was particularly upset at this point because several professional career counselors had worked with me over an extended period of time to write the resume. Because of the nature of the feedback, it is very unlikely that I will implement any of the points. A major lesson learned from this—don't give unsolicited feedback!

(We point out that the author of the above story also learned nothing from this particular manager about jobs in his business unit, which was the author's original goal.) This may seem like a rather small matter, but we strongly believe that it is not. The author of the above quote was a classic victim of the "butting in" syndrome. Every relationship has boundaries, and we violate those boundaries at our peril. If you have taken the time, as a coaching manager, to establish good communications with your employee, gone to the trouble of finding out what the employee wants your help with, and then you veer off course on the basis of your own agenda rather than the employee's, this will often be experienced as a violation of trust.

Granted, you may at times have to speak for the organization. That is okay if you clearly signal your intent with a statement such as "I know this is a bit away from your own agenda, but I have to speak for the company now and give you some feedback on a different topic." On a less formal level, the simple question "Do you mind if I give you some feedback on that?" can also help you seek the learner's permission for changing the boundaries of the relationship. However, it is important when using the latter question to note the power differential between you and your employee. It may be very hard for an employee, particularly someone of lower status (younger, newer, or less experienced) to say "no" to such a question, even if they really want to do so. We recommend using such a question only when you're comfortable that the power and status differential between yourself and the employee is quite small and the level of trust is high.

Set the stage for your feedback discussion in a way that will encourage the maximum degree of openness, which is essential to learning. How and where you set the stage can vary quite a bit. In some situations, the scheduled individual setting is most appropriate. You may have been asked to go out and gather a significant amount of performance data for the employee, or the issues may be quite sensitive. Structure (a scheduled meeting) and confidentiality (away from everyone else) may help the employee focus on what is being said rather than on the reactions of others. In yet other instances, the stage may have been set by your working understanding with the employee. Perhaps the employee expects to meet with you in the hall, right after the big meeting. Particularly once you and your employees are used to the give-and-take of feedback, you may find yourself providing more of it in informal settings. Finally, in a mature team characterized by high levels of feedback, it would seem inappropriate to move the discussion to a private setting, offline. The point we are making with regard to setting the stage is to be sensitive to the employee's needs. When in doubt, ask. If you're not satisfied with the answer, the old rule "Praise in public, criticize in private" should serve as your guide. We encourage you to always set the stage in such a way that the self-esteem of your employee will be minimally threatened.

Setting the stage also involves a consideration of timing. Feedback, particularly if it is based on substantial data collected by the coaching manager, perhaps involving others, may be eagerly sought but anxiously anticipated by the employee. Substantial feedback takes time to absorb. If you are going to engage in a major feedback intervention, make sure you and the employee have sufficient time to thoroughly discuss the issues raised by the feedback.

If feedback is being given to enhance an employee's learning and the employee is trying to build effectiveness in addressing a challenging goal, then feedback from multiple observations will be useful. Your intent should be to give the employee enough data to build a "video" of his or her performance over time. This suggests that it is best to *give feedback frequently* and focus frequent feedback on what the employee is trying to do differently.

Likewise, feedback that is given *right after an action and the individual's reflection on that action* is more likely to result in learning. The events are fresh in everyone's mind. Feedback that is timely is thus important as well. It may be necessary for you to take a few minutes to figure out what you want to say, but don't delay too long.

The feedback you provide should be *specific* and *focused on the task, action, or behavior.* By specific, we mean descriptive. We return to our oft-used metaphor of the mirror. It is important to gather data that accurately reflect the employee's performance. Feedback involves delivering that data in a way that is helpful. The mirror says very little about why things are the way they are. Rather, it simply describes how things are. Use data from the left column of your observation sheet (see Chapter 8) to describe actual behavior.

We've already described the importance for the coaching manager of *having a helpful attitude* while delivering feedback. If the coaching manager runs into the problem described (above) by Harry Levinson, that of being angry, we recommend tabling the discussion until cooler heads prevail. You probably can't do a good job of carefully delivering a focused message when you are angry. The reality is, the tone of your voice, the affective coloring of your presentation (your mood), and your body language will give away your feelings. If you are a typical adult, people can tell. Just ask your friends. If the employee feels that you are angry, he or she will respond to the feeling, not the content of the message.

For the receiver of feedback to be able to make use of the data provided by the coaching manager, the information must be presented *clearly and simply.* The language and style of the presentation should be appropriate to the audience. Avoid nondescriptive or technical terms unless you are sure that the receiver of the feedback can work with those terms and can understand what the terms actually mean.

The best feedback is also usually quite *direct.* Directness usually requires the use of "I" statements. "This is what I saw." Some of us have experienced, and probably all of us have heard about, feedback statements that begin, "We don't think . . ." The reality is that unless the employee knows who you are talking about when you use the word "we," such a feedback statement may have very little credibility. "We" statements can also make the employee feel "ganged-up on" or attacked. If the coaching manager has to provide feedback on behalf of several individuals, it is much more effective to be specific about who said what.

Avoid interpretations drawn from the second, or above, levels of the ladder of inference. For reasons previously discussed, such interpretations are likely to generate defensiveness—and worse yet, are likely to be wrong. Interpretation occurs during the coaching dialogue through the use of questions. Our favorite example of inference masquerading as feedback is "You have a bad attitude." Such a statement is actually devoid of data and represents a pure interpretation. A descriptive statement that would support such an interpretation might be something like "You told the last three customers who walked in the door that you hated working here." Note that such a descriptive statement is in some ways even more hard-hitting than the interpretation. Data almost always carry more weight than the inappropriate use of inference.

After delivering feedback of importance, the coaching manager *asks the employee what he or she heard.* Such a question can seem awkward, but it is very important to make sure that the right message was given in the feedback process. If you are coaching on the fly or coaching under stressful conditions, the effectiveness of your ability to communicate and of the employee's ability to comprehend may be limited. It is important not to leave the employee with the wrong impression and the emotional fallout that may come from the wrong impression. An anxious employee can interpret a simple statement such as "I thought you had a hard time with that" in many erroneous ways. Though not what the coaching manager intended, the employee might walk away from such feedback feeling defeated and unwilling to try again.

Finally, *ask the employee what he or she can or will do with the feedback.* Ideally, feedback leads to additional reflection, and then action. Having delivered the feedback, or after delivering each point of the feedback, the coaching manager should stop, make sure that he or she was understood, and ask for the employee's thoughts about how the feedback can help. Remember that the coaching process begins with a coaching dialogue. It is important to keep the dialogue going by providing plenty of opportunity for the employee to reflect on the feedback you have provided. A little silence during these periods is okay. It is far better to offer some feedback, ask for the employee's reactions, and then wait, rather than hurry on to the next point. Indeed, if the feedback has any real substance to it, it is natural for the employee to need a few minutes to digest what has been said. Make sure you, the coaching manager, don't do all the talking!

After the feedback is given, the coachee may move ahead with future reflection and action. If the feedback is particularly negative or problematic, however, *it may be wise to schedule another meeting to follow up soon after the meeting at which the feedback was given.* Even under the best of circumstances, critical feedback can be difficult for some employees to manage. Very critical feedback will be difficult for many. Follow-up meetings show concern for the coachee and symbolize the coaching manager's commitment to the coachee's ongoing learning.

Before closing this section on the basics for providing balanced feedback, we should discuss in more depth what the word *balanced* is intended to convey. It is not intended to convey the age-old practice of providing a "feedback sandwich." The feedback sandwich begins with good feedback, moves to critical feedback, and then closes with good feedback. Although it is overtly constructed out of concern for the coachee's self-esteem, the need for a "sandwich approach" suggests that the feedback is a surprise and may in part be interpreted as a punishment. The sandwich approach also requires the feedback to offer something positive as well as something critical, which may not be appropriate.

If the employee is seeking feedback on something that he or she has chosen to work on, the coaching manager's feedback may be much more focused. Consider the following comment offered to a team leader who had requested that her manager give her some feedback on how she could help her team make better decisions: "When you said, 'We should come to closure now,' several people in the meeting just stopped talking." The coaching manager is offering these observations in response to the employee's request. Such feedback still needs to be given with the employee's self-esteem in mind, but there is little information to "sandwich" and little need to do so. The employee and coaching manager are focusing on specific, mutually agreed-on developmental goals.

By *balanced*, we mean thoughtful, accurate, and respectful. We said in this chapter that coaching requires practice. It is a discipline, really. Working from a good observational position or on the basis of data provided by others, the coaching manager packages that information and provides it to the employee. The employee is truly interested in the perspective offered by the data and as a result, feels as though he or she has been helped. The employee's learning—not his or her self-esteem—is at issue.

The Emotional Impact of Feedback

Although there are very useful rules of thumb for constructing and delivering feedback, we've come to understand that there is more to the discipline of providing balanced feedback than mastering the mechanics of packaging the data. Learning, as we all know, requires some risk taking, some courage, tolerance for some real defeats and pain, and ultimately, a great deal of persistence. Learning, especially learning that takes us outside our comfort zone, is a very personal affair whether we like it or not. It is probably for that reason that employees sometimes (we hope not too often) hear a carefully crafted task-focused piece of feedback and turn it into a statement about their worth as individuals, even though the coaching manager intends just the opposite.

Feedback, when viewed from a perspective beyond the immediacy of a single manager/employee interaction, includes a rich array of emotional signals that can shape how the coachee experiences and ultimately processes the feedback. Confusion about, or failure to attend to the management of emotionally laden messages that accompany feedback, is perhaps one of the greatest sources of "feedback blowback," the negative reaction to feedback that many managers and employees fear.

One of our coaching managers recently told us a story about a major developmental experience from early in his career. While he was employed by a small but well-thought-of consulting firm, he had somehow managed to get an assignment consulting with what was, at that time, one of the most dynamic and glamorous show business organizations in the world. He spent 6 months working with the senior management of the organization, doing what sounded like a spectacular job. He hobnobbed with the rich, famous, and powerful. He learned an enormous amount about himself and his profession. It was a learning experience that shaped his career. When he returned to his consulting company's home office, no one wanted to hear about it. He was told to write up his personal report and file his expense account. In his performance evaluation several weeks later, he was rated very favorably by his manager, receiving a rating of 4 instead of the usual 3. However, his manager focused only on contribution to the bottom line, not on the young consultant's experience of the work and the learning that had taken place. Having been given that rather uncommon (for this firm) rating, he received a nice bonus for his efforts. His manager felt as though he had been generous with his feedback and helpful to the young man. The young consultant felt unwanted and began to prepare his resume. It wasn't that he didn't like the rating or didn't want the bonus. Rather, he felt there was something missing in the manager's feedback.

The manager provided relatively specific feedback about the consultant's performance in relation to the organization's goals by focusing on the financial contributions that resulted from his efforts. He then rewarded the consultant's performance accordingly. We hope that by this time, the reader will note that part of the problem in this example was the manager's failure to attend to the employee's goals as well as the organization's. In addition, the manager did not consider the emotional meaning of the kind of feedback he was offering—and not offering—for that particular employee in that particular context. We suggest that coaching managers can enhance their own effectiveness by taking into account the emotional messages implicit in their feedback and by trying to match the message to the needs of the situation. That may sound complex, but a simple matrix covers most of the situations most managers will encounter (see Table 9.1).

Feedback describes what just happened. It reflects back to an individual a picture of his or her actions, behaviors, or decisions. However, feedback can be given with a variety of intents in mind on the part of the person who gives it. The intent of the feedback may be to help the employee gain a perspective on what just happened—or to help the employee move forward into the future. A manager may say to an employee, "That was an effective presentation and demonstrated your command of the details," to indicate that it was completed in a satisfactory way, and why. On the other hand, such a statement may indicate that the employee should be aware of what a great job he or she did this time—while planning the next presentation, which will take place tomorrow. The context when added to the comment provides an indication as to how the employee should interpret the feedback. In the latter case, the feedback is given with the intent of building the employee's confidence in preparation for the next performance. Feedback is a response to past actions, but it can also be preparation for the future.

There is, as we have said, an emotional component to feedback as well as a cognitive component. Typically, the way the emotional aspect of the feedback intervention is managed provides information as to how the manager feels about the employee, not just about the action. We have noted several times that

Table 9.1   Managing the Emotional Content of Feedback

	Examples of Coaching Actions or Statements	
	Past Orientation	Future Orientation
Emotionally symbolic statements or actions	Celebration • "Good job" • Superlative statements: "How in the world did you pull that off?" • A formal celebration • Discussing what this means for the employee's career or at least the next step • Helping the employee deal with defeat	Encouragement • "I think you can handle that" • "What additional suports do you need?" • "Try it again"
Cognitively oriented communication	Performance Appraisal • "This is how that situation looked to me" • "These are the final results and how they relate to your work"	Personal Development • "Here is the gap that I saw" • "It looked to me like you might try doing that differently"

feedback delivered in anger can easily be interpreted as a personal attack, for instance, even though the words used in the feedback may be quite appropriate to the situation. Consider the cognitive component of the statement "This is how you did." This statement can be offered for the purposes of providing information for the historical record, information that might be used in performance appraisals, for instance. However, it could also be offered as a *celebration* of what was accomplished. A celebration provides a symbolic way for the coaching manager to meet the emotional need an individual or group might have for recognition, appreciation, or bringing a difficult project to closure.

The emotional message that accompanies the cognitive one has a great impact on what the coachee will hear. The story of our friend, the consultant, illustrates the importance for coaching managers to be aware that the two are quite different. Some people are used to getting an *A*. For them, a report card with "straight *A's*" is perhaps not such a big deal. For others, top grades are a struggle. This young consultant, perhaps unsure of himself, had achieved an important outcome and learned a great deal along the way. This knowledge would soon be lost to the firm, assuming that the young consultant followed through on the impulse to leave. Note that all the while, the manager felt that he was coaching the employee, giving him useful feedback about what it takes to be successful at the company: revenue generation.

What form might such a celebration have taken in this case? Celebrations could have ranged from simple interest on the part of the manager to asking the consultant to stage a lunchtime seminar in which he would describe what he'd learned to other consultants engaged in similar kinds of activities. The failure to do either represented what the employee seemed to infer as a very clear message: "We don't care about you as a person." Granted, the employee may have been unfairly climbing the ladder of inference. Such is the nature of symbolic rather than direct communication, however. Symbolic communications invite interpretation.

Similarly, future-oriented feedback has an emotional component as well. Feedback that says "I think you can do this" is much more potent in this regard than "This is the gap between your current performance and where you need to be." The latter needs to be said, but the coaching manager should consider what kind of emotional message should accompany the cognitive one. Does the coaching manager want to offer encouragement? If he or she does not, the employee may experience the feedback as discouraging, no matter how factually it is offered.

We hope that several lessons emerge from this discussion. First of all, missing or incomplete spoken feedback does not mean that the employee gets no feedback at all. Inaction on the part of the manager is also feedback. The employee will fill in the gaps. The employee will particularly wonder, "Did I do a good job?" and/or "Does the manager think I can really handle this?" Ultimately, like it or not, the employee will be thinking about questions such as "Does he like me?" "Am I cared about?" and "Is this a good manager to be working for?"

Second, whatever else the manager does that is closely related in time to the feedback event may be watched by the employee and incorporated with the feedback itself. Our favorite is something we call the "good feedback that punishes." An employee has a very successful engagement with a difficult customer, for example. The manager is ecstatic about the employee's success. He then promptly assigns her every difficult customer he has had the misfortune to deal with. Ask yourself: Does this kind of feedback communicate a genuine interest in the employee? Of course not. If the coaching manager thinks someone has done a great job under difficult circumstances, he or she should first communicate that fact and then express a real interest in the employee's development by negotiating the next assignment. In this case, the manager should ask the employee if she wants to be thrown back in with the tough customers again or try a different kind of assignment.

Maximizing the Value of That Imperfect Instrument, Feedback

It is interesting to review the scientific literature on feedback and find that even when delivered effectively, it is not a panacea. Our hopes for the power of feedback have grown over the past several decades, encouraged by the research and writing on systems theory and cybernetics. Cybernetic theory holds that systems, including the individual in interaction with his or her environment, can be self-correcting if they are effective at accessing and working with the right kind of information. Typically, this is information from both inside and outside the system. The tremendous emphasis we place on gaining input from the customer is one manifestation of this belief. If we can just figure out what the customer wants and make sure we deliver (by getting feedback from the customer), our organizations will be on track. This is, of course, true only to an extent.

As any CEO or marketing manager will tell you, "Easier said than done." Which customers do you need to get information from? How do you know the feedback is accurate? How do you get customers to take the time to give useful feedback? Most customers don't really want to give you any information; they want to take their product or service, assuming that it works properly, and go home.

A new brand of systems thinkers (Senge, 1990) draws our attention to an additional aspect of feedback in this regard. The gap in time between feedback and action tends, even in fairly tightly coupled systems, to result in a delay in our ability to interpret the impact of any particular piece of feedback. During that delay, the conditions in the system may change. Imagine that you're standing in a shower trying to get the water to just the right temperature. You stick your hand under the shower and find that it is a little too cold (that is feedback), so you turn the hot water up a bit. It is still too cold, so you turn the hot water up some more. Now it is almost just right, so you turn the hot water up one more time, just a bit. Suddenly, it is way too hot! Suppose an employee has been working on building her skills as a team leader and receives coaching help and balanced feedback from her manager in the process. She may try a number of different tactics, for instance, to improve the effectiveness of team meetings.

Unfortunately, it may be months before she or the manager finds out whether or not those tactics actually worked.

Feedback, then, even when effectively delivered, is an imperfect source of information about our work. Despite its imperfections as a learning tool, however, it is still quite important. *We believe that feedback is likely to be most useful when it is offered as part of a systematic approach to coaching.* By a *systematic approach,* we mean following the steps of creating a coaching friendly context, looking for coaching moments, creating a coaching dialogue, knowing what to look for and how to observe, providing balanced feedback, collaboratively interpreting the causes for any gap between actual and desired performance, and setting some meaningful goals for change.

When the coaching manager takes a systematic approach to coaching, the goals of the coaching are fairly clear, the manager's role as a helper is fully established, and the employee's role as a learner who takes responsibility for his or her own growth and development are also fully established. This can be seen in a working relationship between a coach and an athletic team. Coaches and athletes are fully engaged in working together toward a common goal. Athletes know that, given the nature of their competition, they have to improve to achieve that goal. It is a given that feedback is focused toward that goal, and it is offered to individuals who want it (presumably everybody on the team). In such a coaching friendly context, the coach isn't the only one providing feedback. Team members also give feedback to one another. Consider how this takes the pressure off any one particular feedback intervention. Feedback from multiple sources, directed at one particular issue or problem, might have to be given on a number of different occasions to be useful.

Let's say the coach sees that a particular play isn't working. It may not be clear right away what is wrong or what needs to change. Team members struggle to figure out what the feedback is telling them. The problem may not even be clear to the coach. The team may have to discuss, or dialogue, among themselves and with the coach to understand what the feedback is actually telling them. Perhaps it has to do with the way one player is executing the plan or how several players are working together. *Feedback at its best is additional knowledge that will be explored and understood in order to determine what it really means.* Feedback should not be the last word on the subject. It is merely the next step.

10

What Does It All Mean?

Collaboratively Interpreting What Needs to Change

IN THIS CHAPTER, YOU WILL LEARN ABOUT THE FOLLOWING:

- Employing the coaching dialogue as a method for helping you and your employees understand the root causes of the gap between desired and actual performance, and what needs to change
- Some of the most common root causes for a performance gap

Case 10.1: What's Going On With Jack?

Jack was appointed sales manager late last year, and you've been keeping an eye on how he's doing, or at least you thought you had been. You want him to be successful and don't want to just let him hang out there on a limb waiting to see who might saw it off. Jack is an independent sort, though, and although he says he wants your coaching, he really wants to focus on results. You've encouraged him to also think about process, but he feels he can handle staffing, keeping people motivated, setting the vision, and the other demands of leadership.

This isn't one of those situations in which the best salesperson was promoted to sales management but has no management skills. You hired Jack into his sales position with the idea that, on the basis of his work history before coming to your firm, he'd quickly be able to assume managerial responsibilities. He had positions as sales team leader, supervisor, and sales trainer in his last two companies. In preemployment interviews, you asked him pointed questions about issues he'd dealt with as a supervisor, and his answers to every question made Jack sound like a knowledgeable individual who understood both sales and leadership. You brought him in to sell for 6 months while he learned the products and then moved him into the sales manager position, with responsibility for two sales supervisors. Each of those supervisors has 10 field sales representatives reporting to them. Jack was asked to set a new vision for the group and work along with the supervisors to execute it.

Jack knows you are a coaching manager and wanted to work for you for that reason. You talked with him about your leadership style and expectations and made it clear that he must take charge of his learning but that you would be there to coach him. When he responded, "Coach me on results, come in and check in with the staff and customers at the end of each quarter, give me some good feedback, and help me keep improving," you felt very comfortable. The two of you agreed that you should keep an eye on sales, employee product knowledge, and employee morale as key indicators of how Jack was doing. You told him he needed to make the numbers, keep his people motivated and on target, and keep himself happy and growing. All seemed well, particularly given the scope of Jack's job and the 6 months you gave him to get to know the product and the rest of the team.

Unfortunately, Jack didn't make it through the first quarter before you started to get some disturbing e-mails and phone calls, first, from the sales representatives you know quite well and then from one of the supervisors. Each message told essentially the same story: "You have to do something with Jack. He's getting in the way by asking us to generate a lot more paperwork on each sale. He is demanding all the information he can get. After each sale, he wants us to complete an extensive survey having to do with customer type, customer need, financial arrangements, product configuration, literally anything you could imagine. We've tried to accommodate him, and we've also told him that this extra paperwork isn't helping the customer or the company. We don't even know what problem he's trying to solve." Jack had been insistent. In fact, he'd been downright angry when people had suggested to him that there might be another way to handle his need for all that information that wouldn't create so much additional red tape.

You had worked hard to create an environment in which feedback could pass from sales rep to sales rep, from sales rep to supervisor, and on up the chain. You want people to coach one another. You also expect open communications in your organization around any new initiative.

You feel suddenly like kicking yourself. How could you have missed something so important about Jack's leadership style? Yes, he does a lot of the things you want him to do, but you now realize he is doing some other things that really run counter to the work group culture you tried to create. Your mind races to what you are sure is the right diagnosis: Jack is a new, nervous manager, and evidently, his confidence is low. He's having trouble building a partnership with the supervisors, whom he didn't choose himself. You believe that the impact of all this is that he's becoming something of a control freak. He wants every piece of information he can get his hands on. He'll never make it as a manager this way, you think. He's got to trust his supervisors and his reps, listen to them, and learn from them.

You experience a sense of guilt about all this. Did you set him up to fail? You feel certain of what you should do. You have to call him into the office and start giving him more pep talks, start telling him to relax. You feel suddenly more comfortable. You have a plan.

Ah, the view from the upper rungs of the ladder of inference is fine, isn't it? Especially when, relying only on outcome data (angry e-mails) and very little process data, you can generate a solution on the basis of your own experience. After all, what manager doesn't recognize what appears to be Jack's problem? The new manager, even a nice one, becomes something of a control freak during the transition. Sometimes it just goes away by itself, when the "lightbulb" goes on in the new manager's mind. At other times, the manager has to get hit in the head by the proverbial baseball bat. The trouble is, you don't know at this point what is going on. You have a well-educated guess. You and Jack had agreed on what you should help him keep an eye on. However, you don't have Jack's self-assessment, his interpretation of what has been happening and why.

Our coaching managers have told us that one of the biggest hurdles they face is that of avoiding the rush to judgment. In this case, the rush to judgment, which is based on inferences made while gathering performance data, leads to an interpretation stemming from the coaching manager's past experience, not from a dialogue with the coachee. Unfortunately, an action plan, perhaps an informal one, may then be developed that targets issues or problems completely unrelated to the gap between actual and desired performance.

Let's consider some other possibilities for Jack's behavior. (We are not excusing his behavior but are not condemning it, either. We want to understand it.) Jack may indeed be nervous, but he may also be angry. He may be trying to get ahold of what he sees as excessive sales expenses. He may be trying to track customer data for feedback to marketing. He may be fearful that one of his reps is accounting for business inappropriately, to inflate his or her commission. Someone else in the company may be leaning on him to conduct the survey.

This may have been the way other firms with which he has worked always did business. He may come from a cultural background in which employees are expected to obey business leaders and leaders are not expected to have to explain their actions to followers.

The phrase *performance gap*, meaning a gap between actual and desired performance, has a negative connotation, unfortunately. It must be emphasized that such a gap may exist for very positive reasons. Jack may have set up a stretch situation for himself, one that demands even more of his leadership style than he is used to. He may be doing better this time than he had done in previous attempts. Remember that the data you have at this point are "snapshots" when viewed from the perspective of his career overall. You need more information about what this means, and so does Jack. You need to know why—or do you?

Do You Need to Know Why?

You may be saying to yourself, "I don't need to know why Jack is doing this. The fact is, he needs to communicate about this issue with the supervisors and the reps. I'd just tell him he has to do it." We understand your approach. The question here is, does knowing why add any value to Jack's situation and to his learning?

Certainly, if compliance, not learning, is your only concern, you might just tell Jack to explain what he is doing to his supervisors and have them explain it to the sales reps; if you thought Jack's behavior was damaging the integrity of the group or the customers, that would be an appropriate action to take. However, your goal here is to help Jack learn. You'd like him to become a better communicator, if that is in fact the problem.

Make note that this is when you have to display emotional intelligence yourself. If you've just received a significant amount of feedback from others that the person you put in charge is causing trouble, you may feel guilty and angry. You may want to jump into action. Remember Woody Hayes, the football coach, and try to stay on the sidelines. Summon up a helpful coaching attitude and focus on the learning process if that is indeed your goal.

Do you need to know why? Another example suggests an approach by which coaching managers can answer this question on a case-by-case basis. Let's say that you are speaking to a large group of people without a microphone. Someone gives you feedback by saying, "Please speak up." It doesn't really matter in this one instance whether or not you were speaking too softly because you underestimated the size of the crowd, overestimated the acoustics of the room, overestimated the strength of your voice, are shy, or don't know what you're talking about. The reason in this one instance isn't terribly important. You can fix the main problem right away by speaking up. This is a small issue and not central to your overall plan for self-development. You speak up, people seem more comfortable, and your talk proceeds with greater impact.

What if this happens on a regular basis? What if you always speak too softly while addressing a group despite the fact that you are routinely asked to speak up? It then becomes important to get to the root of the problem. Feedback directed only at the offending behavior doesn't lead to change.

Before leaving this example, let's assume that you knew in advance that the CEO of your company—or even the President of the United States—was going to be in the crowd you were addressing. Let's further assume that in addition to speaking too softly, your overhead slides were in bad condition, and you were not terribly well prepared. This is an important situation in which there is a significant gap between your performance and the desired or expected performance. If your boss could control her temper after such a performance, she might find it possible to actually help you understand not only what you did wrong. (We're sure she would inform you about that!) She would ideally try to help the two of you understand why this performance failure occurred. The implications could be significant. Perhaps you are terribly frightened of speaking in front of senior managers because you have had very little exposure to them. Perhaps you know nothing about public speaking and didn't understand how to prepare. Perhaps there is a significant cultural gap between how you believe you should behave and how the manager believes you should behave.

We suggest the following rule of thumb: *If there is a recurring gap between desired and actual performance and/or if there is a gap between desired and actual performance when the performance is an important one, it is important to understand the root cause of the problem.*

Does Jack's problem qualify under this rule? Although you don't know whether this is a recurring one, we would say that this is an important performance gap. His role is an important one. He is early in his tenure in that role. Many people are being affected by his behavior. Perhaps most important, he's very talented. Both you and Jack should expect your efforts to yield more than mere compliance on his part.

The Coaching Dialogue

Once the coaching manager and the coachee have determined that it is appropriate to search for the root cause or causes for any performance gap, a continuation of the coaching dialogue can help both of you look for those causes. The coaching dialogue encourages the coachee to reflect on the feedback the coaching manager has presented. Provide the feedback, ask the employee for his or her thoughts, and wait. See what the employee has to say.

A return to the coaching dialogue is important for several reasons. First, if you tell Jack the "right" answer, it is your answer. It may not be his. Perhaps you tell him that you can empathize with what is it like to take over a new group. He hadn't been thinking about that; he had just been thinking about trying to get a handle on sales expenses. This disconnect between your comment and his mind-set is significant. However, let's say for the sake of argument that when you made the comment indicating you understand how hard it is to take over a new group, Jack says, "I never thought of that. I guess you're right." Is Jack then focusing on the issue that he wants to focus on, or is he focusing on the one you want him to focus on? Giving Jack time to reflect on the feedback you have received encourages him to take full ownership of whatever diagnosis and implications emerge from the dialogue as it moves forward. It encourages him to keep learning more about how to think for himself.

Asking Jack to reflect on the feedback is also more likely to encourage him to consider the range of alternative causes or issues and come up with the right one(s) on which to focus. If his own analysis of the situation dominates, assuming you have created a coaching friendly context in which he can speak openly, it is more likely to be accurate.

The coaching manager can aid in this process, if the coachee is having trouble, by using the basic coaching questions: "What were you trying to do?" "What is the impact of what you did?" "What do you need to do differently to have the impact you're hoping for?" Such questions serve to keep Jack focused on the basic principles of experiential learning: action, reflection to assess the impact of the action, and experimentation with new approaches or different actions. Along the way, the coaching manager can encourage the coachee to consider alternatives other than the obvious.

Root Causes

Behavior associated with any activity is what psychologists call *multideter-mined*. If you decide to go to the store for a cup of coffee, the decision that resulted in that action may have been influenced by a variety of factors. You wanted some coffee. The store was close by. Your spouse wanted to go with you. The car is all warmed up and ready to go. You like the coffee at that particular store, and so on. The same is true for actions at work. Actions are driven by the thoughts and feelings of the individual, what is happening on his or her team, and what is happening in his or her organization. An accurate understanding of the cause of any particular action, and therefore of any particular performance gap, may have to take into account a number of different factors.

For this reason, it is difficult to offer an exhaustive list of factors that the coaching manager and coachee should consider while trying to understand the root cause(s) for any performance gap. Furthermore, because the context of your exploration is action in business and not, say, anthropology, it isn't necessary to use words from a textbook to articulate your diagnosis. Ideally, you use words and phrases that make sense to you as a coaching manager and to your employee.

Nevertheless, we do feel that it is useful for managers to have some sense of the factors that typically show up when trying to understand a performance gap. In addition, two factors that we'll discuss in this section are important to keep an eye on because they are so common: cultural diversity and organizational change.

It is a mistake to focus on the individual employee to the exclusion of all other possible factors as you and the employee try to understand the causes of a performance gap. The gap may also reflect a variety of interpersonal, team, or organizational-level issues. We will start with the individual-level factors and then move to those beyond the individual level of analysis. Again, we remind you that a performance gap can occur for good reasons as people stretch themselves. The diagnosis shouldn't be seen as a criticism. An overview of our nonexhaustive list of root causes can be found in Box 10.1.

Box 10.1

A NONEXHAUSTIVE LISTING OF ROOT CAUSES FOR PERFORMANCE GAPS

Individual level

- Lack of knowledge
- Lack of skills
- Lack of motivation

For a specific task within a role
For the role itself

Culture and cultural diversity level
Team and organizational level

- Poor distribution of talent, attitudes, and resources
- Lack of managerial support
- Organizational changes that make desired performance difficult to define and generate unintended consequences

Individual Factors

Individual performance requires the mobilization of *knowledge* and *skills*. Many if not most individual-level root causes for a performance gap occur because one or both of these factors are undeveloped. We return to our discussion of Jack to illustrate. Let's assume that the root cause in this situation has to do with Jack's inability to communicate his need for the information with his supervisors. Jack may not have *knowledge* of the importance of effective communications. He may not have a conceptual understanding that people are much more receptive to change if the reason for the change is explained in advance. Jack may still be very skilled at communicating. Perhaps he can give a great speech. Being able to do something, or having the *skill*, doesn't mean you know when to do it.

Alternatively, Jack may know that it is important to communicate but may be very ineffective as a writer or presenter. This skill, the ability to execute a desired behavior or action effectively, is absent or underdeveloped. Opportunities for practice, feedback, role models, mentors, conceptual discussions, formal classroom training, and reading can all help to address knowledge- and skill-related performance gaps.

Several other individual-level factors can also create performance gaps. One question that Jack must face is whether or not he actually wants to face the hassles associated with having to communicate every decision to his followers. He may have the ability to communicate, he may know how to communicate, but if he is unhappy with the need to communicate, he is unlikely to be successful in doing so. He may not be *motivated* for the task at hand. Motivation, as we discussed in Chapter 4, is terribly important, particularly for people in challenging jobs. "You have to want it bad," as the saying goes.

Note that individuals may be motivated to tackle most of the tasks associated with a particular role but may still find that certain aspects of that role are distasteful. If Jack is naturally introverted and more comfortable with analysis rather than action, he may not appreciate how much effort he will have to put into selling his ideas to others. The coaching manager and Jack might use several possible tactics to address such a problem. First, Jack might have to "go against the grain" and work on developing a skill that he will find distasteful to use. Unfortunately, he may dislike having to exercise such a skill even if he becomes quite effective at doing so. Some leadership development practitioners insist that when people are in stretch assignments, they will probably need to work on skills they normally don't want to use (Lombardo & Eichinger, 2001). After all, it is possible to become quite effective at laying people off, but who enjoys doing so?

An alternative view suggests that managers will have a bigger impact on productivity by being sensitive to the importance of harnessing what can be described as "enduring life interests" (Butler & Waldroop, 1999). Once the manager and the employee understand the employee's interests, they should work together to shape or "sculpt" jobs that capitalize on those interests. Job sculpting versus going against the grain: Which approach is correct? Both probably have their merits. On balance, if the employee likes the role but dislikes certain necessary tasks, it is probably in their best interest to learn to develop those needed skills, no matter how anxiety-provoking or distasteful. Dale Carnegie and Toastmaster's International are two examples of organizations that have quite successfully helped numerous individuals confront one of the most common workplace fears, that of speaking in public.

Remaking the job through job sculpting is also possible in some instances. Jack might be able to address the need to communicate more effectively with his employees by having one of his supervisors, someone much more outgoing perhaps, take on that responsibility. There are two issues to consider in this regard. First, is there anyone else in the organization with the time and ability to help make up for Jack's deficit? Jack should also consider, however, whether or not he is creating a more permanent deficit in his own competency profile by not addressing the problem now. If Jack's long-term plans don't involve roles that require a great deal of communicating (granted, this is hard to imagine), he may decide that there is no compelling reason to build those skills now.

Employees are often very reluctant to talk about whether or not they actually want to be in a prized role. Admitting that one doesn't want to be in such a role can be perceived as a career-limiting move (or as we say, "CLM"). They fear that such a discussion will leave the manager with the conclusion that the employee wants out and isn't fully committed to the work. The coaching manager then has a real problem. Is it appropriate or even ethical to leave someone in a role in which they may fail, hurting themselves and the company in the process, because they may not want to be in the role? It may take a number of discussions and a truly helpful attitude on the part of the coaching manager for an open dialogue to develop around this issue. Nevertheless, our coaches have told us that if they have created a very coaching friendly context, the question "Do you want to be in this job?" can be discussed. This is particularly the case if the employee trusts that the manager will try to help him or her through what may be an important career transition.

Cultural Diversity

In a diverse world, the coaching manager will frequently have to consider whether or not cultural factors may influence the gap between actual and desired performance. Cultural assumptions, often implicit and undiscussed, can have a significant impact on how people behave by shaping the way individuals view a task and the options for responding to a task. Concepts such as leadership, goal setting, time-management, negotiations, teamwork, influence, assertiveness, respect, and decision making, to name just a few, are defined either explicitly or implicitly in very different ways in different cultures.

It is difficult and often inappropriate to stereotype the behavioral patterns and perceptual outlook of people in any given culture. Nevertheless, some regularities do appear to be worth noting. Geerte Hofstede (1993), in a classic series of studies completed for IBM in the 1980s, found profound differences across cultures, even among employees from the same company, along the following dimensions that are relevant to this discussion: hierarchy or power orientation, comfort with ambiguity, time orientation, and the importance of context.

Hierarchy or power orientation refers to what in the United States might be described as "respect for and obedience to authority." Strong adherence to hierarchy leads individuals to pay careful attention to the statements of their leaders and to adhere to the rules they perceive to be appropriate in any particular situation. In hierarchical cultures, authority is less likely to be challenged. In highly innovative U.S. companies, for example, individuals with a very strong sense of respect for hierarchy might be seen as conservative and unwilling to think "outside the box." They might also be less comfortable engaging in conflict or "getting to the point" if they fear their actions could be seen as a challenge to those in authority. As a coaching manager, you might see someone who is quiet in a meeting as being timid, by virtue of his or her personality. Perhaps the quiet individual even believes that it would be rude to speak up. Although you as a coaching manager encourage the employee to do so, that person is nevertheless unfamiliar with being assertive, or "appropriately" assertive for the situation. Assertiveness is one behavior that can be very difficult to mimic or fake.

Comfort with ambiguity reflects an individual's tolerance for uncertainty. In some cultures, such as the United States, uncertainty tends to be valued. In other cultures, ambiguity or an absence of rules, procedures, or plans can create a significant level of discomfort. Those who seek certainty might look for written directives and be less likely to wade into an unstructured problem without careful study. Note that the very model of coaching discussed in this book requires a fairly high tolerance for ambiguity, because it puts a great deal of the responsibility for learning on the employee and less on the manager or the organization.

The influence of context involves the degree to which protocol and tradition dictate how communication should proceed. In high-context cultures, greater emphasis is placed on protocol, and communication tends to move from the general to the specific. In low-context cultures, communication tends to be more to the point, an approach that can come across to individuals from high-context cultures as rude. An employee from a low-context culture may appear to be quite aggressive to an employee from a high-context culture. For instance, in a recent executive education program in which managers from both the United States and the United Kingdom participated, participants from the United Kingdom described their U.S. colleagues as being "overly direct." The directness of the managers from the United States created significant discomfort, particularly for lower-level U.K. employees. An employee from a high-context culture who is on the receiving end of very direct feedback early in a meeting with his or her boss may feel quite attacked, whereas in a low-context culture, the employee might feel appreciative that the boss is getting to the point.

These examples merely begin to describe the tremendous diversity of personal styles and decision-making processes that emerge from cultural variation. Cultural variation can even be found among employees from the same country. In the United States, "southerners" and "northerners" are thought to have very different approaches from the perspective of values and time management. In addition to learned differences between groups that have to do with cultural diversity, one can add differences that are based on race, age, and gender. The challenge for the coaching manager is to avoid seeing a particular action or behavior as being determined by individual factors when it may also be determined by the employee's cultural or group identification.

How can you tell? If the coaching manager thinks that culture may play a significant role in how an employee is approaching a particular task, it is usually possible to raise that issue as part of the coaching dialogue. We have found that a simple question such as "How might people deal with this in your country or culture of origin?" is often well received by the coachee, who is usually more than happy to talk about the differences in approaches between the cultures. Most businesspeople now know that cultural, racial, and gender diversity can affect communications, marketing, product development, leadership, team effectiveness, decision making, and other business processes. If the coaching manager is tactful in positioning the question and gives the employee time to reflect, most employees will respond by trying to consider the role that cultural diversity is playing in how they view and respond to particular situations. (We can't guarantee this, unfortunately. The impact of culture is felt on an implicit or unspoken level, and as such, some people may not notice it or may doubt its power.)

The important point is this: It is critical to treat people as individuals and try to understand the role that cultural assumptions or membership in any identity group (gender, race, and country of origin) may be playing in the employee's performance and learning needs. Perhaps in no other aspect of coaching is it so important for the coaching manager to always "keep wearing a learning hat" (Schmuckler, 2001).

What do you do if the employee does state that culturally based attitudes may be affecting his or her performance? It is important to keep in mind that with regard to the impact of culture on any part of the learning or performance process, an evaluative stance won't help. After all, if someone is behaving in a fashion that is consistent with good practice in his or her culture of origin, to evaluate that practice punitively would seem confusing at best and very offensive at worst. The reality is that it is difficult for people to unlearn one way of acting, particularly when it brought them success, and then learn another way of being that seems "foreign" to them.

An open discussion of the impact of culture on performance allows the employee to decide what course of action he or she should take. We're not saying that the employee struggling with a culturally defined approach to work that may result in a performance gap is automatically entitled to define the organization's performance standards or processes. The coaching manager will probably need to maintain consistent performance standards at the same time. As in all situations, coachees need to consider what they can or should do to respond to those standards. For instance, a team leader from a culture quite different than the culture in which she is now working has to confront the fact that she can't impose her cultural style on the team without creating a variety of negative consequences. Ideally, the team works together to understand one another's different communications or leadership styles. While working outside your own cultural context, you ultimately have to decide whether or not you want to try to adjust or to help others adjust to you.

Team and Organizational Factors

We end this discussion of possible root causes by stressing that individual action and behavior don't take place in a vacuum. In teams and organizations, *talent, attitudes,* and *resources* are not always rationally distributed to support the work that needs to be done. Giving someone lots of responsibility but no authority, for instance, obviously creates the potential for a gap between actual and desired performance on the part of those involved.

The coaching dialogue creates an opportunity for the coaching manager to gain insight as to what is going wrong or right on a team and intervene as a coach or as a manager. Unfortunately, too often employees have learned to expect that their managers will blame them when something goes wrong, even if the root causes were outside their control.

We have stressed the importance of taking a helpful attitude as you coach, particularly toward those employees in the "good" to "great" categories. These people want to be successful. If these employees say they haven't got the resources to do the job, perhaps they are right. We encourage the coaching manager to listen to such feedback and not immediately conclude that it is an excuse. Yes, you may ultimately decide that you should encourage the individual or team to push on despite the fact that conditions are not perfect, but failure to acknowledge problems at the team or group level can seriously undermine trust.

Unless you are in combat and have to ask people to do the impossible, it is appropriate for workers to expect that they will be given a rough approximation of what is needed to do the job they have been asked to do. If you recall, the second element of the Gallup 12 elements (Chapter 4) linking employee experience and productivity was, "Do I have the materials and equipment I need to do my work right?" (Buckingham & Coffman, 1999). In addition to considering whether or not an individual or team has the right talent for the job, you may need to keep in mind other resources as well, such as financial, material, time, and managerial resources. *Managerial resources* include the time and interest of whatever level of management is ultimately responsible for holding the individual or team accountable.

Finally, it is also wise to consider the degree of *organizational change* that is taking place in the context of the employees you are coaching. The importance of this factor should be obvious. In times of change, which are increasingly the norm rather than the exception, it may be difficult or impossible to adequately define performance gaps. Under conditions of great uncertainty, employees may not know whether or not they performed a task adequately using the appropriate process. Indeed, their manager may not know, either. The employee, team, manager, and perhaps organization are all experimenting. They are learning together through enlightened (we hope) trial and error.

Perhaps Jack's group had been selling a specific set of products in a multi-product company. Product knowledge is everything in such a scheme. Now his firm decides to focus on selling multiple products to each customer through one sales account and one salesperson. Jack has to help his supervisors and sales representatives learn an entirely new approach to relating to their customers. The relationships they build with customers must be deeper and stronger through a longer period of time. Jack may try to match sales representatives with various customers on the basis of their previous experience and on the overlap of their experience with the customer's industry. Is this the right way to go? In discussing such a change with his coaching manager, Jack talks of his uncertainty regarding how to involve his customers in such decisions. He's been asking them what they want. The coaching manager may not know, with certainty, the right answers to such questions.

Jack tries out his plan for customer involvement, and it creates havoc amongst the sales force. Their anger drifts to the manager's level and constitutes the feedback that the manager must now give to Jack. Does this mean that Jack was insensitive to the needs of his sales reps? This was an experiment that he undertook with his manager's understanding. Everyone is being stretched. It makes sense, then, to (a) provide him with the feedback that his reps are starting to rebel and (b) help him think through what he was trying to accomplish and what he needs to do differently as he moves forward. The reality is that *change brings on unintended consequences.* For instance, people involved in leading a change effort may not, for good reasons, be aware of the importance or power of one particular component of the organizational system, such as the very powerful individual contributor who keeps to himself—except for the fact that he is an old friend of the CEO. Under these circumstances, the coaching process and a shared effort to understand the gap between actual and desired performance can generate important learning for the individual employee, as well as for the team or organization as a whole.

The Importance of "Getting It Right" When Interpreting Performance

There are times in life when it may be better to do nothing than to do something poorly. This lesson was brought home to us recently through a story told by an employee working with a very effective coaching manager. This young engineer was evidently known for his ability to solve enormously complex problems and explain those problems in lay terms to business people. He was about to give the most important presentation of his young life in front of his own CEO and the leaders of several important customers.

When the time came, he stood up, and froze. He was absolutely unable to put his thoughts into words or make sense of his own overheads. The CEO was clearly not pleased but said little. In an effort to end the pain, the young engineer's manager stood up and took over. The manager was very upset after the meeting but held her temper in check. The engineer was shocked and fearful. Clearly they needed to talk. The manager, who basically trusted the engineer, asked him what was going on. The engineer was at a loss. Finally, the manager asked, "Is something wrong? Is anything bothering you?" The engineer, who was loath to talk about his personal life at work, confided that he'd just put his mother in a nursing home. Perhaps he didn't realize, he said, just how much that had shaken his concentration. The manager expressed confidence in his ability to handle situations like this in the future. Although he was quite anxious in light of this incident, his manager assigned him to do another presentation several weeks later. Once again, his anxiety did detract from his performance, but not nearly so badly. He got through it and covered the necessary material. His manager noted the improvement and predicted a slow but sure recovery. Over time, that is exactly what happened.

If the manager had criticized the employee after the original incident, she would have been doing so on the basis of an inference that the cause of the problem was perhaps his lack of preparation or even a lack of ability to work with senior managers. Working from such an inference would have undermined her ability to accurately understand the source of the problem. In criticizing the employee, she would also have undermined what little confidence he had left. She would not have helped him develop an awareness of the impact of his personal life on his performance and the need to address work and life stress proactively. (Had she known that he was going through such a major family transition, she never would have asked him to present in such a high-stakes context in the first place.) Ultimately, she might have lost a great engineer.

Most of us can tolerate criticism when it is directed at a real fault, but to be criticized for not being prepared when in fact we are struggling with an overwhelming level of stress can generate long-term resentment. We encourage you to notice how often you rush to interpret the actions of others before finding out the true cause of their actions. To put it another way, *try to precede every conclusion with an open-ended question.*

11

Goal Setting and Follow-Up

Making Change Happen

IN THIS CHAPTER, YOU WILL LEARN ABOUT THE FOLLOWING:

- Development planning
- How to reasonably integrate goal setting and follow-up in your activities as a coaching manager without burdening yourself with additional paperwork
- How people change and how follow-up can help people through the stages of change

Interviews with coaching managers tell us that follow-up is perhaps one of the most underrated tasks of developmental coaching. Effective coaching managers follow up, sometimes formally, but more often informally. Whenever possible, they know who is working on which projects on an ongoing basis. They are aware of who is learning a new Web design technology, who is designing a brochure for the first time, who is leading a project team through a crisis, or who is trying to position himself or herself for a significant promotion. They keep an eye on how these people are doing. They look for *coach-able moments*. Perhaps most important, they help keep people focused on what they need to learn.

The importance of follow-up stems from two basic realities of personal development. Learning, especially learning that stretches an employee, can be quite difficult. Most coachees need ongoing support, if for no other reason than to make sure that they are getting the kinds of assignments that will help them keep learning. Just as important, it seems that if the manager does not follow up in some fashion, he or she is sending a message to the employee discounting the importance of learning. Ideally, of course, the manager follows up because in most instances, the learning in which the employee is engaged is important to the business goals of the work group. Learning at its best is important to the success of the group as well as the success of the individual employee.

Follow-up, naturally, begins with some sort of goal setting. In many cases, we have found that learning goals are not written down until performance appraisal time, if at all. The most compelling goals have been talked about by the coachee and the manager and are relatively well understood on a day-to-day basis.

The idea of having to engage in goal setting and follow-up when it comes to employee development does raise questions in the minds of some managers. Some managers immediately think that goal setting and follow-up mean filling out more forms from human resources (which is not true). Some have mixed feelings about whether or not they should be involved in trying to plan someone else's development. Development seems optional to them, and they may fear that they will come across as micromanaging their employees. Others are concerned that this aspect of coaching may involve taking on a great deal of extra work. Perhaps for these reasons, our research suggests that follow-up may be one of the least-practiced components of developmental coaching.

It is important to understand that follow-up safeguards the coaching manager's return on investment. If you spend time coaching, you want it to have an impact. In this chapter, we examine the process of goal setting and follow-up and offer a few simple guidelines that can help coaching managers successfully encourage the process in a way that is neither bureaucratic nor time-consuming. As with all aspects of developmental coaching at its best, the employee takes as much responsibility for goal setting and follow-up as possible.

Planned Development

Most organizations now formally link development planning to performance appraisal. The development planning form is usually attached to the performance appraisal form, as the last page. There is nothing wrong with linking development and performance management. However, as we have said, the two have very different purposes and their purposes can sometimes conflict. Employees may choose development targets solely because they believe "That is what the boss wants." As you'll see, an employee's development goals should relate to the needs of the business in most cases but should also relate in a meaningful way to the needs of the employee.

Nevertheless, implicit in the act of linking development planning and performance appraisal is the assumption that the tools of performance appraisal, such as stating clear goals and holding people accountable for goal attainment, can be used to promote employee development. Indeed, there is some evidence that holding employees accountable for defined developmental goals is more likely to ensure that they will follow up and that change will take place (Antonioni, 1996). Is this all we need to know about goal setting and follow-up? Consider the following examples.

Patrick looked around in his organization and saw who was getting ahead (which is what he wanted to do). He noted that there were several skills that seemed to characterize those people, among which was the ability to give effective presentations. He set this as a developmental goal for himself and devoted considerable energy to enhancing his presentation skills. He asked his manager for opportunities to present more often and to get feedback from his manager or someone else in the group when he did present. His manager agreed that improving his presentation skills could really help Patrick's career and was happy to support this developmental goal. After all, if Patrick could become really skilled at presenting, he could take on some of the load for the department. (This is an example of a synergistic learning project, meeting the needs of both the employee and the business unit, as we discussed in Chapter 6.)

None of this was ever documented. (We do suspect that Patrick probably put it in his formal development plan, but after the fact. Recording the goal, for Patrick, was not central to the learning project in which he was engaged.) The initial coaching dialogue with his boss, almost totally driven by Patrick, took place over lunch. Probably the most important pieces of work his manager had to do in this case were to (a) establish a coaching friendly context in his department that would make such conversations possible, (b) look for appropriate opportunities for Patrick to make presentations, and (c) make sure that when Patrick did present, he or one of his colleagues was there to offer feedback, until Patrick seemed ready to work on his own.

Is this a "too good to be true" story? The reality is that often, in an environment that encourages development, employees will pinpoint goals that are both important to themselves as individuals and helpful to the business unit at the same time. They focus on that goal with a great deal of commitment. Granted, this requires a clear vision of what one needs to learn and persistence in working toward the learning goal.

Too often, however, this is not what happens. Consider another example. John is an up-and-coming consulting engineer in a large utility company. His boss considers himself to be a pretty good coaching manager to his employees. John is very talented, especially from a technical standpoint. However, he has a pattern of overcommitment of which he and his boss are both aware. In his enthusiasm and desire to get ahead, he takes on too many projects. He jumps in, starts something big, and excites his internal customers, but before too long, he has spotted another opportunity and jumps to that one. The first customer is left without sufficient support, and work on that customer's project flounders while John devotes himself to a second project. Customer number one then complains to John's boss.

Over the course of 6 months, John's boss gave him repeated feedback about the problem. He told John that if he developed a reputation for not following through with customers, internal or external, his career at the firm could be adversely effected. John seemed to see this and did acknowledge that he needed to work on maintaining a focus in his efforts. John's boss laid down a very specific goal as part of John's written development plan: Over the next year, John was to focus on his three major projects and that was all. John's boss hoped that John would experience the benefits of focusing: being able to generate higher-quality solutions while experiencing less on-the-job stress. John agreed with the goal and the explicit limit set by his manager.

Six months later, John's boss was back in human resources complaining about him. John had gotten involved in two more major projects, had stretched himself way too thin, had some more angry internal customers, and was very stressed and angry himself as a result. The human resources manager asked John's boss why he hadn't stepped in and held John accountable for following the plan they had previously laid out. John's boss replied, "Well, to tell you the truth, those other two projects are really important to the company, and if John can make a bit of progress on either or both of them, that would be a help to me."

This story has two morals. First, a formal goal-setting process alone does not ensure that the goals will be accomplished. Neither John nor his boss kept to the plan to limit John's project load. Second, we should not underestimate how difficult it can be to break habitual routines. Trying to limit himself and to focus more may make sense to John on an intellectual level. However, when people try to make significant changes in their work or their lives, they often run into serious resistance. The resistance may come from the individual, but it can also come from his or her environment. A reasonable approach to setting goals and following up has to take the process of change into account.

Setting Goals

The power of goal setting as a means of improving performance has been well understood for several decades (Locke & Latham, 1990). Simply put, a clear statement of mutually agreed-on and clearly specified goals is more likely to result in the attainment of those goals than a less precise or more implicit goal-setting process. At the performance appraisal and business unit levels, the goal-setting process has been institutionalized in many firms as "management by objectives" (MBO) programs. The employee commits to a particular result, with his or her manager, and is held accountable for that result. When executed effectively, the process tends to ensure that the goals of each particular unit in the organizational hierarchy are aligned and relatively up-to-date.

Research on goal setting offers more guidance as to what constitutes effective goals and an effective process for setting goals. A summary of the guidelines described in this chapter for effective goal setting and follow-up are listed in Box 11.1.

Box 11.1

CHARACTERISTICS OF EFFECTIVE GOALS AND GOAL SETTING

The most effective learning goals are described as follows:

1. *Specific and measurable.* Manager and employee should be able to observe the impact of learning. The goal should be stated as a defined outcome: "Here is what I'll do differently."

2. *Time-bound.* Time boundaries that include specific completion dates help employees measure their progress.

3. *Challenging.* Challenging goals are motivating, though they are also naturally difficult.

4. *Few in number.* A relatively small number of developmental goals allow employees to focus.

5. *Developed in a participatory fashion.* Participation encourages ownership and commitment toward the goal.

6. *Aligned with the goals of the business.* Alignment supports all phases of the learning process (unfreezing, change, and refreezing) and supports maximum commitment to the goal.

The coaching dialogue question "What are you going to do differently?" is one way of asking an employee to commit to a particular action or goal. In the previous case, John, in response to the coaching dialogue that followed his feedback, might have said, "I'm only going to work on the three major projects this year, that's it." Such a goal statement meets several of the criteria of an effective goal (Whetton & Cameron, 1998). Effective goals are *specific.* They are unambiguous and measurable. John's commitment to focus on only three projects is unambiguous. There is also a time frame attached to the goal. Measurable goals are *time-bound.* Time boundaries are essential if one is to be able to measure whether or not the goal has been accomplished. Time boundaries also create an opportunity for employees to measure progress incrementally as they work toward goal completion.

Effective goals are also *appropriately challenging*. Challenge creates motivation. However, what constitutes "appropriate" will likely vary from person to person. In John's case, we can infer from the fact that John has had trouble staying focused in the past that sticking with just three projects for a 12-month period might be challenging. Even with a specific and appropriately challenging goal, however, this plan didn't work. John reverted to his previous style in a few months. Perhaps the goal was not motivating enough for him.

In Patrick's case, he made it clear that he wanted to become an effective presenter. Although how "good" an effective presenter is can be somewhat difficult to measure, feedback from his own manager and other colleagues could give him a pretty good idea of how well he was doing. (The same feedback could also help him change his technique and improve his performance along the way.) The goal was, to a degree, measurable. Finally, given its importance to Patrick's career, it was appropriately challenging. He showed a high level of motivation in taking on the task. In Patrick's case, identifying a goal and working toward it worked quite well.

The reader will probably note that in both cases, the goals that were set did not describe how the learning would actually take place. The archetype of the poorly worded development goal goes something like this: "I will take a course on negotiations (or whatever is the subject of the learning goal)." Such a plan doesn't meet the criteria for an effective goal. Taking a course is an action that might lead to the desired outcome, presumably, in this case, developing effectiveness as a negotiator. But one can also take a course on a topic related to a development goal and not achieve any real change. Taking the course does not guarantee commitment.

We suspect that managers resort to such developmental goal statements when they aren't clear about what the individual is really trying to accomplish. A developmental goal implies an outcome or result that is to be attained. Ideally, the coaching dialogue, observation, and feedback have helped the coachee and the manager create a fairly clear picture of the outcome to which the coachee aspires.

An outcome-oriented learning goal might be stated as follows: "I will seek out the input of team members in all cases before making a strategic decision. I will not criticize input from team members in the process." One simple way to think about developmental goals is through the use of these questions: *What should you start doing? What should you stop doing? What should you keep doing?* Based on some initial feedback from his coaching manager, a full description of Patrick's goal was this: "I want to learn to become more effective in giving presentations. I need to make my case using clear and simple language. I need to stop using so much jargon. I need to explain my objectives early in the presentation. I need to stop putting too much information on my overhead slides. I need to keep using humor to make my point." This full statement offers a fairly clear picture of the outcome to which he aspires. The most effective learning goals *clearly define the outcome of the learning.* We stress that attaining goal clarity represents a goal in itself. Patrick was able to describe those specific behavioral goals after his coaching manager had given him a rather lengthy critique of his most recent presentation. He had to synthesize his manager's feedback before he could pinpoint the specific issues he needed to address. It took him and his manager several discussions to get beyond the larger goal of improving Patrick's presentation skills.

The obvious benefits of focusing one's effort suggests that it is unwise to work on more than a few developmental goals at a time. Although there is no preset number of goals that one should address, it is commonly thought that working on more than three goals at any one time may be overly optimistic. In deciding how many developmental goals an individual can address at one time, it can be useful to consider the following questions (Lombardo & Eichinger, 2001):

- How difficult will the goal be to address? An enormously difficult goal, particularly a goal that has an emotional component, will require a great deal of effort. While working on such a goal, it may be difficult to work on anything else. In John's case, his tendency to overextend himself was deeply entrenched. Learning to say "no" and focus on a defined set of projects may be quite difficult. He may find it painfully boring to work through the details associated with executing a project plan and maintaining a team.

- How much support will the coachee have? In the cases of Patrick and John, they both had managers who were more than casually interested in their development. Note than in John's case, however, his manager's attention to John's developmental goal wavered.

- How similar are the developmental needs to one another? Patrick wanted to learn to give more effective presentations. His secondary goal, closely related, was to become more comfortable speaking to senior managers. As a way of working on both goals, it seems appropriate for him to move from presenting to colleagues to presenting to senior managers.

- What is the coachee willing to do? This is perhaps the most important question of them all. How much is the coachee willing to sacrifice to pursue the goal? Patrick was so committed to becoming a more effective presenter that although he knew he would be nervous, he didn't perceive that as a barrier. He was willing to put up with it. John, on the other hand, seemed unwilling to give up the emotional charge he experienced when digging into a brand new set of challenges. When things started to become routine, he wanted to move along and try something new rather than finish what he had started.

The point of this discussion is to alert the reader to the importance of *setting a relatively small number of goals.* Trying to do too much in the way of personal development creates a significant risk that nothing will change. Too many developmental goals can make it more difficult for the individual to succeed, thereby weakening his or her motivation to achieve even one goal. The employee's attention to his or her own needs will be too diffuse to allow the allocation of time and energy to the project.

Finally, the process by which goals are established is important to their outcome. *Participation by both parties,* the employee and the manager, in the setting of the goal(s) is thought to improve the likelihood that the employee will follow through and achieve goal completion (Whetten & Cameron, 1998). A participatory process of goal setting should allow the employee to bring a greater sense of ownership, and therefore personal commitment, to the process of attaining the goal. A participatory process is clearly consistent with the idea that learning has to be driven by the employee.

Patrick proactively pushed the goal of becoming a better presenter. His manager participated by reacting in a helpful way. It appears that in John's case, the goal may have been to some extent imposed on him by his manager. John agreed in general that he needed to focus more, but limiting his efforts to just three projects was his manager's idea, not his. Although he did agree, he may not have taken full psychological ownership of the goal. (Of course, his manager may have needed to impose the goal to achieve compliance if John's tendency to overcommit had created too much damage to John or the business unit.)

How formal, then, should the goal-setting process be? If the development goal is very difficult or complex, if it may take a long time to accomplish, or if the goal will require a great deal of focus, a written goal statement can be quite valuable. However, a written goal statement does not guarantee success, as we see in the case of John. To better understand the problem John is facing, it is useful to consider one additional aspect that often arises during the learning process in developmental coaching: the need to unlearn.

How People Change

It is one thing to learn a brand new skill. The individual studying accounting for the first time typically has no previous conception of how all those numbers work. However, many of the learning challenges people face confront them with the need to change, not just to learn. By *change,* we don't mean a personality change, but we do mean a personal change. People often have to unlearn skills or concepts that have served them in the past but no longer work in their current situation and will not work in the future to which they aspire.

John's situation may be an example of the need to *unlearn*. He had actually developed a reputation as an extremely helpful individual contributor and consultant to other groups. He was always curious. He was very smart and was a fast learner. He could take in large amounts of information by scanning documents, synthesize that information, and then present it to others. This brought him to the attention of a vice president who began promoting him up the managerial career ladder. Note, however, that this very same "strength" could become a weakness if his work required him to focus on a particular problem in greater depth. John's old trick of scanning, instead of making him appear to be a quick study, made his analysis look superficial. To be successful, he has to let go of this "quick hit" style of working. What does this require?

Kurt Lewin and his followers were among the first to describe the change process that addresses John's learning goal (Schein, 1979). Lewin proposed that personal transformation of the type required of John involves three steps: unfreezing, change, and refreezing. Typically, people move through these phases in a somewhat linear fashion, although regression to the previous stage is not uncommon if the personal change is significant or if the environment does not support continued movement through the change process. It is worthwhile to briefly examine each step.

UNFREEZING

Unfreezing requires developing a readiness for change. In the case of Patrick, he knows he needs to change and is ready to begin the work of doing so. (Admittedly, Patrick also has less to unlearn.) John, on the other hand, has an awareness of the need to change brought on largely by critical feedback delivered by his manager. This feedback has begun to unfreeze John; it works in one of several ways.

When John is confronted with the disappointment of his customers, he begins to sees the impact of his behavior in a way that is not consistent with his self-concept. He normally sees himself as being helpful. How could he have made others angry because he wasn't helpful to them? He experiences a *disconfirmation* of his self-concept. He may also experience *guilt* or *anxiety* because of this disconfirmation. However, if he feels only that he has not been helpful, he may react by becoming intensely defensive. He also needs to feel that it is okay to try another way—that it is *safe to change*. His manager stated that he would provide that sense of safety by clearly siding with the change effort. He told John, "No matter what anyone else says, you're on these three projects, and that is it. If they have a problem with that, tell them to call me."

Unfortunately, as we noted, his manager's actions were not consistent with his statements. He saw that John was taking on extra work and did nothing to stop it. Indeed, it seems as though John's taking on the extra work was actually condoned by his manager despite his complaints. Perhaps unconsciously, he wants John to stay the way he was in the past because John's style, though problematic, was also useful. If this is the case, what John thought he experienced as disconfirming wasn't so disconfirming after all. Should John, then, take that apparently disconfirming feedback seriously? Perhaps not.

What if that had not been the case? What if John's manager had reacted at the first sign of John's overextending himself and talked with John about the problem. Such a clear statement might have been sufficient to keep John "unfrozen" and open to the possibility of learning a new way of doing things and of giving up his old habits. One of the most important questions that managers need to consider while working with an employee to set a difficult developmental goal is whether or not both parties really believe that the goal is essential. If either or both do not, then unfreezing is not likely to result.

CHANGE

In the *change* stage, people are more open to learning. Indeed, they have come to accept that the learning is necessary and are ready to drive the learning themselves. They scan their world for helpful information. They may read about the topic at hand and seek out others who can help them. Patrick isn't debating the necessity of change. He's now interested in various approaches to improving his performance in front of groups.

During the learning process, the employee may need access to a variety of resources. Unfortunately, too often in business, managers make the assumption that the only learning resource that matters is the classroom. Classroom learning, reading, videos, and computer-based educational programs are all terribly important. The coaching manager should keep in mind, however, that in all likelihood, the most important learning resources are the opportunities that allow employees to develop their skills at work. Patrick might find it useful, at first, to participate in a class on how to conduct effective presentations, for instance. Ultimately, however, he'll need his manager's help to get up in front of a group and make presentations in a serious business context.

John's approach to the problem, on the other hand, was quite different. Rather than reading about time management or operations or talking with others who had to make similar adjustments to their work styles, John was thinking more about how he could get around his developmental goal. He wasn't really in the "change phase" of learning very long before he began to slip back. His old, ingrained pattern returned. In point of fact, he just didn't want to or wasn't ready to change. Unfortunately, with such an attitude, he was reluctant to reach out for help from his boss or others from whom he might have been able get some encouragement. He became locked in a vicious cycle in which the lack of support he received interacted with his own behavioral tendencies and drove him farther in the wrong direction.

Two implications may be drawn from this discussion. First, people won't really engage in the learning process until they are ready. They often become ready on their own. They may also recognize the need to change as a result of feedback from their environment. Second, while people are trying to engage in the learning process, especially the change phase, they need support. If people don't find the learning resources and the encouragement they need, they may slip back. They may also not signal to the coaching manager that they have slipped back.

Patrick was ready to learn about presentations. He needed two resources from his manager: opportunity and coaching. Given his status in the organization, he could not have arranged for either on his own. If his manager had not been responsive, Patrick's motivation to learn would have been frustrated. One would guess that ultimately, he'd give up. It is interesting and saddening to consider how often this occurs in most organizations.

REFREEZING

One of our training program participants told us an interesting story with regard to the challenge of *refreezing*, or making the connection between the new behavior, knowledge, or skill and the rest of his life. This gentleman had been an unrepentant workaholic. Until he started to suffer from health problems, he would routinely work 80 to 90 hours per week, even when there was no crisis to manage. His own manager told him that he needed to change; this wasn't the kind of behavior that would help the department in the long run. The manager suggested that he cut his working hours from 80 to no more than 50 each week. With the help of his wife and a counselor, he was able to do just that. Unfortunately, everybody at work became angry with him. He wasn't always at his desk when they needed him. He didn't return every e-mail within an hour. He actually delayed the completion date on one of his projects. As he assessed the situation, "These people had a good deal, they got two of me for the price of one." When he cut back in his working hours, his manager did not hire a replacement. The result was that other members of the department became angry at his perceived lack of responsiveness. Over time, their anger gradually eroded his commitment to change. Within 6 months, he was working

80 hours each week again. However, his colleagues were no longer angry with him! In this case, the manager and the employee failed to anticipate that the employee's changes might affect others and to address this contingency.

If the change is not consistent with the rest of the employee's life, refreezing may not occur. Changes must also be consistent with the individual's personality, at least to an extent. Likewise, those in the employee's network of relationships must be able to cope with the employee's newly learned skill or new routine. They may need to change their behavior, too.

Unless his organization changes, we see difficulties ahead for John in the refreezing area. At this point, others need him to be the way he was, not the way he says he wants to become. Patrick, on the other hand, can step into an important role. His ability to present will be very helpful to the organization. This analysis again suggests the importance for the coaching manager of thinking about the following question: If the employee succeeds in learning this new skill, will he or she be using that skill in a fashion that will be truly helpful to the business unit or company? If the answer is unclear or "no," the change, the learning and use of the new skill, may not "take." In the worst-case scenario, the employee may cease to be competent at the particular skill in which he or she and the firm invested so much to develop.

Building Commitment for Learning and Change

Learning requires a commitment on the part of the employee, and it will often require a good deal of commitment on the part of the manager. This is particularly true when the learning goals are challenging. The goal-setting process and its follow-up can be used as a means of determining and reinforcing that commitment. The determinants of commitment to a set goal are well understood. They include several factors external to the individual, as well as several factors relevant to the individual himself or herself.

Most of the external factors that support commitment to a goal have to do with the manager's attitude (Locke, Latham, & Erez, 1988). Research shows that employees are more likely to be committed to goals arrived at through work with a legitimate authority (the manager) who is supportive and trusted. The presence of support in the peer group is helpful as well. Finally, incentives, such as financial rewards or career movement, can (not surprisingly) encourage commitment.

From the vantage point of the employee, commitment to a goal, then, is enhanced when goal attainment leads to a desired reward (Locke et al., 1988). However, the coachee needs to expect that he or she can ultimately accomplish the goal. If that expectation is missing, rewards by themselves won't motivate commitment to the goal. People don't pursue a reward, no matter how valuable, unless they believe that their efforts will pay off (as anyone who has tried to lose weight can attest). Finally, goal commitment is enhanced if individuals pursuing the goal can recognize even incremental progress and give themselves self-administered rewards as acknowledgment of a job well done. If Patrick can recognize that his use of graphics software was better received in his last presentation than in previous efforts, he's more likely to try even harder next time.

As stated previously, research on commitment to a goal is also enhanced if the employee participated in establishing the particular goal (Locke et al., 1988; Whetton & Cameron, 1998). Most researchers note that it is possible to gain commitment to an imposed goal if the employee has the ability to participate in decision making about related discretionary goals. Interestingly, this creates an opportunity for employees to define learning goals in a participative fashion, even when dealing with an imposed business goal. If corporate wants to push a stretch, results-oriented goal of 15% growth, all managers and employees may have to go along. But in the process, they'll probably have to do quite a bit of learning. Commitment to the learning goal, then, may be strengthened if it is attached to the business goal.

The research thus reinforces a commonsense idea. Commitment to developmental goals will be enhanced when they are *aligned, more or less, with the needs and resources of the employee, work group or team, manager, and the organization.* Patrick's goal showed this alignment, whereas in subtle ways, John's goal did not. In considering how much commitment is possible to a learning goal, probably the most important question to ask is this: "If the learning prescribed by the goal takes place, will we be in a better position to meet our business goals?" If there is a high level of commitment to the goal because it is aligned with the task of the business unit or team in some fashion, it is very likely that follow-up will take place naturally, as everyone involved works toward that business goal.

An informal planning and follow-up process can work quite well under such circumstances. To the degree that fulfillment of the learning goal is essential to making progress toward a business goal, employees who need to unfreeze, or unlearn, in order to be open to new learning will find a great deal of support. They are much more likely to be confronted with good reasons for unfreezing during the natural course of their work. In the change phase, learning resources (coaching, classes, or opportunities to use skills) are more likely to be available to support learning because what is being learned is essential to the success of the business. In the refreezing phase, employees are more likely to find that their new skills or knowledge are valued by peers and managers alike.

Conclusions: Goal Setting and Follow-Up

Most coaching managers and employees engage in the real work of development on an informal, ongoing basis, particularly in a coaching friendly context. We suspect that formal approaches to development planning have taken hold as a way to coerce managers into doing some kind of developmental work with their employees. Unfortunately, this analysis also suggests that setting goals in the absence of other considerations (coaching and opportunities to learn and use new skills) may not be all that helpful.

Having said this, we still believe that it can be helpful for both employees and managers to give some serious thought regarding which approach is going to be most helpful in any given situation. Many employees find the structure of a written goal statement to be quite useful. Others know what they want and inhabit a fast-paced world in which they have no time for filling out forms.

The lessons from this discussion are summarized as follows:

- Encourage employees to be responsible for setting realistic development goals and taking action on those goals. Test to see whether or not employees really own their goals and are willing make sacrifices to reach them.

- Consider also whether or not employees are really ready (unfrozen) to take on the tough goals. Assess whether or not they really believe that learning a new approach is essential to their current or future success.

- Encourage employees to focus on a small number of developmental goals. One goal can be overwhelming if it is a challenging one.

- Ask yourself and your employees the tough questions: Are your development goals aligned with what we really need to do in this organization or team? Will it help all of us if you develop that particular skill? If employees' learning will help the team accomplish its business goals, commitment is likely to be high, and the learning process is more likely to proceed successfully.

- Encourage employees to be clear about what they want to accomplish. Help them think about the outcomes of their learning efforts. This may take several discussions as employees and coaching managers pinpoint specifically what needs to happen.

- Be ready to support employees along the way. Access to learning resources, including the opportunity to practice, is a critical aspect of the learning process. Remember, employees may need some encouragement, particularly if the goal is a challenging one.

Setting Developmental Goals: Give It a Try

Managers, particularly those who like to help others, sometimes ignore their own development. In closing this chapter, we encourage you to practice working with the concepts we've described by thinking about your own developmental goal or goals. Through thinking about your own development using the guidelines we have proposed here, you'll also get a better sense of the issues your employees face as they approach the task of setting development goals and following up on those goals. The exercise in Box 11.2 provides a framework for doing so.

Box 11.2

YOUR OWN DEVELOPMENT PLAN

Step 1: Describe your developmental learning goal in specific and outcome-oriented terms.

Step 2: Is this a particularly difficult or challenging goal? (If so, should this be your only developmental goal?)

Step 3: What are the time boundaries for completion of this goal?

Step 4: Is any unfreezing or unlearning required? If so, describe.

Step 5: In what way is your developmental learning goal aligned or unaligned with the business goal of your unit?

Step 6: What kind of resources (Opportunities, feedback, management support, course work, etc.) will you need to accomplish your learning goal?

This worksheet should give you a good sense of what it is like to define developmental learning goals and assess what it will take to reach them. Having done this, you are now in a better position to consider whether or not it would be more helpful to you to define these goals informally or formally, as part of your quarterly or yearly developmental plan for which you will be held accountable.

12

Coaching and Career Development

IN THIS CHAPTER, WE DESCRIBE THE FOLLOWING:

- The challenges of career management in the new economy
- How the developmental coaching model can be simply modified to help the coaching manager deal with career development discussions
- How this model for integrating career concerns into developmental coaching is applied in several different situations likely to arise in a modern organization

Is coaching for career development different from developmental coaching? In many ways, no. The purpose of developmental coaching is to help employees learn and develop new skills and knowledge. Helping employees develop new skills and knowledge is arguably the most important thing a manager can do to help them have a successful and rewarding career.

Yet there are times when career development issues more explicitly take center stage in an employee's life. It could be at the completion of a project; during times of major organizational change, societal change, or crisis; or after a personal milestone, such as a birthday. Some employees think about their careers routinely, particularly those who take a long-term view of their lives. We are amused by senior managers who say, "I don't want employees thinking about their careers or their next jobs. I want them thinking about today."

Our message to those senior managers is this: You can't control what people are thinking about. Furthermore, thinking about one's future is a natural, healthy, and adaptive activity. You can try to suppress their ability to talk about it at work. However, you do so at your own peril. If they are not allowed, indeed encouraged, to talk about their futures from time to time, they will do so with someone else and may end up at a different company. Coaching for career development can be a key retention tool.

Nevertheless, if many managers have a difficult time coaching employees to learn how to do their current jobs better, anecdotal evidence suggests that even more of them have difficulty knowing how to approach employee career discussions. We empathize with them. Coaching managers may run into several important barriers. People sometimes don't know what they want. They may expect the manager or the organization to tell them what to do or give them special breaks. It is difficult for employees to find out what kinds of opportunities are available in many companies—the job postings bulletin board doesn't mention them all. In most medium to large companies, and even in a number of small ones, opportunities for career development emerge informally: A group needs to add someone else quickly, a function is expanding in another building, a task force is coming together to look at supply chain management. These emergent activities are all opportunities for career development if managers and employees know about them. Unfortunately, sometimes they just don't. Such barriers can create a "Why bother?" attitude among many individuals. There is no easy way around most of these barriers, unless the division or organization has developed a full-scale career planning system whose function it is to capture information about all career development activities and make that information available in a useable form to everyone in the firm. Absent such systems, career planning and development do take some work. If everyone can accept that premise and manage expectations accordingly, employees and coaching managers can do a lot to promote effective career development.

If the coaching manager has created a coaching friendly context, employees are much more likely to raise career issues directly. How the coaching manager responds can have an important impact on the employee, the work group, and the coaching environment the manager has worked to create. Setting expectations and creating the right context for career development discussions can help place the responsibility for those discussions and the follow-up work where it belongs: with the employee. The role of the coach is to help, usually not to "do," and rarely to hand-hold. After a brief description of what career development has come to mean in the modern organization, we'll describe a methodology for using developmental coaching to help employees productively address career issues. We'll then use case examples to illustrate several of the most common career issues facing coaching managers today and make some suggestions as to how the coaching manager might effectively intervene.

An Overview of Career Development in the Modern Organization

Career ladders are largely a thing of the past in most organizations. Organizational structures are flatter. Software giant SAS Institute has only four steps between an entry-level engineer and the CEO, for instance (O'Reilly & Pfeffer, 2000). Firms are also less stable due to downsizing and restructuring, making it difficult for them to effectively engage in long-term human resource planning. Some firms now have technical and managerial career paths, but in reality, too often the technical career ladders don't have many rungs. Even the stars of the new economy that did pay attention to career issues, such as Cisco Systems and Sun Microsystems, have experienced substantial staff reductions. These firms were firmly committed to retaining their knowledgeable employees as a competitive weapon. Their inability to do so underscores the fact that we cannot look to organizations alone for career direction. Indeed, most organizations no longer imply that they will take any responsibility for the career development of their employees. The best firms offer guidance, training, and, ideally, coaching but are in no position to take responsibility for the outcome.

The exceptions are those organizations that have developed competency-based career ladders. These are typically consulting firms, other large service firms, and some technology companies. Firms that articulate competency-based career ladders are most likely to describe what it takes to move up and, at the same time, signal a clear message to valued employees that if they gain certain competencies, they will be able to advance. Competency-based career ladders also help employees set their expectations appropriately. Competency models are discussed in Chapter 7. An example of a competency-based career ladder is presented in Table 12.1.

In the scheme laid out in Table 12.1, the coaching manager can help to promote career development, at least for most employees, by making sure that employees get a chance to build skills at each level that will make them ready for the next. (We say "most" employees because some may not want to move up a career ladder.) It is not surprising that the firms using competency-based career ladders tend to be the ones that most value the knowledge of their workers and compete by virtue of their ability to provide high quality service. Retaining the best employees is critically important to these firms, and taking an aggressive interest in their career development is a very powerful way to do so.

The expectations that most employees hold for their careers today are changing. As implied in the introduction to this chapter, most people traditionally took for granted the existence of a career ladder that would either guarantee lifelong, stable employment or keep them moving upward. Those who wanted advancement went as high as they could on the ladder, hit a maintenance or plateau phase, and then exited to retirement. In modern organizations, however, the following conditions are more likely to exist:

• Upward movement is less likely because it is less possible. Flatter, more unstable organizations may have fewer openings "up the ladder."

Table 12.1   Competency-Based Career Ladder in a Consulting Firm

Position	Examples of Required Skill, Knowledge, or Competency
Team leader: Leads small teams within a project. An entry-level management position.·	• Planning for team deliverables • Estimating resource requirements • Managing a budget • Keeping team members focused on the task • Good with details
Project manager: Plans the project and manages team leaders toward project execution.	• Managing client relationships • Project management skills • Effective at influencing stakeholders
Program manager: Manages a number of project teams who are using a particular methodology or focusing on a particular industry. A firmwide leadership role.	• Managing industry relationships • Effective at setting a leadership vision • Able to communicate effectively with global staff

• Moving from one interesting job, in which the employee builds new skills, to the next interesting job is more likely. The popular career development book *Up Is Not the Only Way* (Kaye, 1997) speaks to the variety of options that employees now have. They may choose to pursue the traditional *vertical* career path and try to move up. They may choose *enrichment* in their current jobs through growing in place. They may choose to move *laterally,* in the pursuit of interesting but different work. They may choose to *realign* their jobs, perhaps moving "downward" to make more time in their lives for other pursuits. They may choose *relocation,* moving out of their profession, firm, or industry. The move from internal marketing manager to external marketing consultant is an example of such a move. Finally, they may not know exactly which direction they should take and may choose to continue exploring the possibilities by taking on new assignments.

• Such a highly differentiated workforce seems to fit better with the realities of organizational life. Companies may need employees who are capable of doing all of the above if business conditions change.

Added to the changing nature of organizational careers is the changing set of values that employees bring to their careers. A variety of researchers have confirmed the obvious: Employees are more interested in a work/life balance and other lifestyle issues than ever before (Schein, 1996). The value placed on a work/life balance motivates employees to be (a) more cautious about taking on assignments that require travel and relocation and (b) more interested in jobs that provide reasonable working hours and conditions. Some are willing, if necessary, to accept a trade-off of financial compensation for greater work-place flexibility. The employee who has a good job with an employer of choice may not want to change roles in an effort to develop his or her career but may, rather, prefer to develop in that current job or location.

Ultimately, then, for better or worse (some employees would probably have fared better under conditions of stable employment and traditional career paths), the employee is now in the driver's seat of his or her career. Most employees will have what career scholar Tim Hall (1996) describes as a "pro-tean career." Employees will drive their careers, want or need to reinvent them-selves from time to time as conditions change, and be engaged in continuous and lifelong learning (Hall, 1996). The employee's relationship with the orga-nization will not be characterized by the kind of dependence found in the traditional structure and the old economy. Rather, employees and organizations will be interdependent. They need one another and can help one another.

Coaching is clearly one aspect of helping from the organization's side. We've already discussed the fact that, unfortunately, managers' coaching activities don't often meet employee expectations and needs. From the employee's side, there are problems as well. The concept of mutuality or interdependency sug-gests a relationship between two parties who have fairly clear ideas of what they want. The firm may know what it wants, but the employee may not.

Personal Career Planning

We have mentioned in several places that workers (that means all of us) don't always do a good job of career planning. In our experience, few aspects of modern life are less well understood than career planning. Too many people think that a career planning process should pinpoint a clear target: "I will be happy if I have this job and no other." If most workers felt that way, workforce flexibility would for all practical purposes end. A small percentage of people do have what psychologists describe as a "calling": for example, the youngster who knew from the age of 5 that he wanted to be a doctor and wouldn't be happy with any other career. If the calling is real, he will feel compelled to follow through and may indeed work happily in his chosen role for the rest of his life.

Most of us have a bigger "target area." We have broader interests. An employee might like working with people and also enjoy working with tech-nology. This tells us something if we take such insights seriously (which we should), though it will likely be necessary to fine-tune things a bit. Let's say that an individual knows she is interested in technology. But does she like designing it, or using it? The distinction is important. The individual who likes working with technology might like a role in management information systems. The individual who likes designing technology might like a role in a design engineering group. These are two very different careers and work settings.

An employee can get a handle on these questions with the help of a professional career coach and the use of a variety of assessment tools (standardized inventories that help an individual define interests, values, personal style, and skills, for instance). Although we recommend such an approach whenever possible, the reality is that most people either don't have access to such resources or, for a variety of reasons, won't make use of them. To address the need for more robust individual career planning systems, more organizations are offering such services through their employee assistance programs or through dedicated career counseling services. If those services are available, they can be very useful resources for the coaching manager. Reminding employees that such services are available empowers them and places responsibility on them for following through on defining their career directions.

People tend to choose jobs on the basis of the opportunities they perceive as being available. For the most part, particularly early in their careers, they don't consciously and explicitly stop to think about what kinds of tasks they like to do, what their values or life priorities are, and what they are good at. They may feel there is no point in taking such considerations into account because for economic reasons, they just have to take the first good job that comes along. Some people try to avoid such questions because they have been pushed into a particular role by social pressure, particularly from their families.

Although most people don't go through an explicit process of self-assessment, most do self-assess implicitly. They learn about themselves as they move through a series of jobs and other life roles. The engineering manager in a large firm jumps to a start-up and finds that the time he can allocate for his family diminishes considerably, far below a level with which he is comfortable. He also finds that he doesn't like the frenetic pace and frequent strategic reshufflings characteristic of the start-up life. He decides to return to the more stable and more focused environment of his previous firm. Ideally, he has learned something along the way about his priorities. He will now factor in the questions of family time and his own need to focus when he assesses the next opportunity. Developmental coaching can play an enormously important role in helping employees make this implicit self-assessment explicit and therefore much more useful.

The coaching manager can try to provide new or differing opportunities for employees as they learn more about themselves and what they want. However, we hope that the reader learns one very important point from this discussion.

The manager can't own the employee's career development challenge. The relationship between employee and company has evolved from a dependent one to an interdependent one, in large measure because of the need for firms to adapt to rapidly changing business conditions. We don't anticipate that the rapid pace of change will slow down anytime soon. The manager can help, but in a mutual and interdependent relationship, the employee must take substantial responsibility as well.

The challenge of dealing with ongoing change raises one additional issue that coaching managers and employees should think about when engaging in a career development dialogue. In addition to knowing what they want and developing knowledge and skills in order to contribute in a field that is within their career "target area," it is also important for employees to build relationships with a wider variety of people: a range of bosses, peers, subordinates, customers, suppliers, consultants, and professional associations, just to name a few (Inkson & Arthur, 2001). Relationships are career assets in a rapidly changing world.

Most senior managers, entrepreneurs, and venture capitalists have appreciated for years the importance of a network of relationships. Entrepreneurs need to know venture capitalists, management consultants, bankers, accountants, and professionals who share common interests. These relationships serve as the highways across which up-to-date information flows. Good information is critical to coping with change. In addition, one's network of relationships becomes the vehicle through which mutual aid is sought and offered.

Traditionally, employees have not had to worry about such concerns—and some still don't. They focus their efforts on being successful in their current jobs and building skills for the next jobs without considering the fact that in a highly unstable labor market, they may have to change their plans. If they are to be successful, they may need to have relationships with people in other departments or other companies from whom they can get information, resources, and other forms of help. As most career counselors will note, the worst time to network for a job is when you need the job. The best time to establish a network is when you have something to offer to others. Coaching managers should encourage their employees to develop networks both within and outside their immediate departments or teams.

Using Developmental Coaching to Address Career Issues

Building on the previous analysis, we offer the following tactics, which should be helpful to coaching managers while trying to assist their employees with career development:

- In the coaching dialogue, *from time to time, encourage employees to reflect on what they find satisfying or meaningful about their work.* Ask them how they feel about what they are doing, where they are, and where they want to be. Doing so proactively communicates your interest in the long-term welfare of employees. This doesn't have to be done often, but we do encourage you not to focus your efforts solely on the issues of effectiveness or learning. This step helps employees self-assess what they want out of their careers. When this takes place in a relaxed atmosphere, employees may begin to consider aspects of themselves that are critical to their future job satisfaction but that they may not routinely think about. Of course, it is important not to react negatively to employees' reflections. Listening with a helpful attitude is probably the most important career intervention the coaching manager can offer.

- *Provide balanced feedback whenever possible in your reaction to the employees' reflection.* Your feedback may include your thoughts about employees' strengths and weaknesses in relation to their career interests; or it may include information about opportunities, or the lack of opportunities, that relate to employees' interests. Direct your feedback specifically at areas or issues requested by the employee. Don't offer unsolicited critical feedback or unsolicited support. In a coaching friendly context, some employees will use the coaching dialogue as an opportunity to "think out loud" about their careers. For example, when one of your employees suddenly says, "I think I want to go to medical school," don't immediately assume that he is looking for your help in getting there. Appropriate dialogue questions that can help you determine where to focus your feedback include the following: "What would you like from me?" "How would you like me to help?" or "What kind of feedback would be useful to you on this?"

- *Whenever possible, encourage employees to build relationships with others who work in areas associated with their career interests.* Facilitate such networking opportunities if you can. As stated above, employees may not recognize the importance of doing so or may consider networking to be a form of political manipulation. Employees who are reserved or less socially confident may also find networking to be particularly challenging. You can be supportive, but it is not appropriate to take responsibility for this challenge. The employee has to drive the career, regardless of his or her personal style. You might encourage an employee who feels significant social discomfort at the concept of networking to consult with the company's human resource group or employee assistance program. A number of well-established training programs can be helpful to employees struggling with this challenge.

- *If possible, use "job-sculpting" tactics to reshape the employee's job in line with his or her career interests when possible.* (Butler & Waldroop, 1999).

However, always keep the needs of the business in mind while job sculpting (see Chapter 10). Don't make up a job just to meet an individual's needs. The job probably won't last, and it may not be doable. It is important that coaching managers know what they can and can't do while considering how to define job roles. Do not succumb to any efforts to push you beyond what makes sense for the business.

We've stated here that listening may be the most important intervention the coaching manager can offer. Listening to someone talk about his or her career seems easy on the surface, but this is not always the case. The coaching manager may have a strong reaction when someone says, "What I've learned is that I don't like doing this!" or when the best employee in the group says, "I have to leave to spend more time with my family." We hope such career insights won't be the most common ones encountered by the coaching manager. However, given changing employee values and the fact that employees don't always pursue career opportunities wisely, the coaching manager should be prepared. In our experience, it is difficult to predict where a career discussion will lead unless you have very thorough knowledge of a particular individual.

- After listening, it is important not to jump into helping. *Encourage the coachee to define a goal or a need and a next step.* You may then be able to provide useful feedback on the basis of your understanding of what the business unit or organization can offer. You may be aware of other people who could help the employee. Respect your own limitations and those of your firm and do so without guilt. In the next section, we'll see how these four components of the developmental coaching model work in practice while dealing with career-related issues.

Coaching for Career Development

Every employee has his or her own career story. There are too many possibilities for us to offer specific advice for every contingency. We have chosen here to discuss four of the most common career concerns that managers face today. These examples are all true, though they are disguised. The real-life case examples that we present here all illustrate common principles: the importance of the coaching dialogue, a careful and helpful response to the employee, an awareness of what you can and you can't do, the use of job sculpting whenever possible, and the value of linking people up with other resources that can help.

Case 12.1: The Good Employee Who Has Become Bored With Her Job

Joyce had been working in customer service for more than 3 years. She was amazingly effective at her job. She had good interpersonal skills. She seemed unflappable no matter how angry the person on the other end of the line was. Joyce clearly liked helping people, had great product knowledge, and was able to bring most calls to a speedy and successful conclusion. Last year, she was awarded the CEO's coveted Employee Recognition Award for her service to the company and its customers. Her manager was very proud of her. Nevertheless, Joyce's manager knew it couldn't last forever. It was obvious that Joyce was quite intelligent and sophisticated. In recent discussions with her manager, she revealed that that she was getting very tired of doing the same thing, day in and day out. No matter how successful she was, she found herself losing enthusiasm.

Her manager wasn't at all surprised and empathized with her, saying, "I'd feel the same way." Normally, her manager would begin to think about how to move her up to the next step, perhaps into a supervisory role. Unfortunately, the firm had an ironclad policy regarding the educational background expected of supervisors. They had to be college graduates. Joyce had finished only high school. She also had major family commitments and was in no position to begin college at nights, even though she once told her manager that she'd love to. At age 45, she felt that when she wasn't at work, she had to attend to her family.

Joyce's problem is a common one, known to managers in many comparable organizations. Certain jobs tend to be quite distinct from the normal network of jobs in a corporation. Telemarketers and customer service personnel are often chosen for their interpersonal skills and natural intelligence. Their pay is relatively low. They are taught firm-specific or product-specific knowledge, along with customer service or sales tactics, and are put to work. If the firm has done a good job of hiring, these employees will be successful for a period of time; then they become bored. They may look around for alternatives but find few natural paths outside their current role. Often, they start to express frustration with their low pay, though this doesn't seem to be the primary problem most of them report. In all likelihood, the job has lost its challenge.

The problem of lack of challenge can occur for any employee who has been in a role for an extended period of time and has successfully conquered its demands. In Joyce's case, the loss of challenge is compounded by the normal personal concerns of mid-life (Hall, 1986). Mid-life and mid-career bring with them an awareness of the limitations of one's life. There seems to be little time left to start over and to build a new career self. Responsibilities for the family are often overpowering and leave little time for personal ambition. Aging and health concerns emerge for the first time.

The desire to do something challenging, perhaps even special, can intensify. Most people still have powerful needs for growth and psychological success (Hall, 1986). If the coaching manager has created a coaching friendly context, she'll know that Joyce's feelings about her work have changed. She can't change Joyce's reality, but she can encourage Joyce to think about what kinds of challenges she might want to undertake. It is not unusual to find that employees, particularly if they have spent a lifetime battling to maintain a basic economic living standard, have never had someone whom they respect express an interest in their careers. The opportunity to reflect and consider what growth might mean can represent an important breakthrough in and of itself. The importance of the coaching dialogue between coaching manager and employee, which rests on empathic listening, can be extremely important to a successful outcome.

The coaching manager can give Joyce feedback regarding her strengths and encourage her to consider how she can use those strengths in other ways. She may need additional information about alternatives to develop a picture of what is possible. There may be activities within the firm, for example, task forces, United Way drives, and new product launches, in which Joyce can use her skills without bumping up against the (essentially bureaucratic) requirement that she have a college diploma. Workshops and courses held at the company may help her fill specific gaps in her education and qualify her for lateral roles that could reinvigorate her sense of challenge. The act of searching for more information and beginning the process of establishing an informal network of contacts may give Joyce a sense that progress is possible. Meanwhile, her manager may be able to help her redefine her role in the organization without running into the organizational policy that threatens to keep her stuck in her current role. (We have seen coaching managers go to the CEO and get a policy waver on occasion, though such an intervention will not always be possible, or wise.)

Why do anything at all? There are really two answers. The first is a human one. Once the coaching manager has integrated helping into his or her management style, helping becomes the natural thing to do. Second, and of far more pragmatic interest, Joyce has been a top talent for the firm and can probably do much more. She is an asset. However, the "asset" will lose value for the company if it is not managed properly. Helping her restart the engine of challenge is the right thing to do for all stakeholders in the business, customers, other employees, and owners.

Case 12.2: The Employee
Who Wants to Move Up (Too Fast!)

Samantha is one of the best team leaders in her division. She has a real command of the tactical, day-to-day demands of her job. In her 2 years with the firm, she has consistently performed at or above the level of other "best performers" in the company. Her manager has recently heard rumors that she may be thinking about leaving. Samantha likes the company but fears that it will take forever for her to move up the ranks to program manager, a more strategic position responsible for building longer-term customer relationships. Her manager knows from previous discussions that Samantha aspires to a leadership position and wants to have a big impact. However, he also knows that she has a lot to learn about the challenges of sustaining long-term client relationships through difficult times. She is technologically savvy and good with people but doesn't have a deeper feel for the economic forces that can affect a customer relationship. Unfortunately, it seems as though her previous manager did little or no coaching. Samantha was given an assignment, executed the plan, and was sent on to the next assignment. She did a good job, but, from her point of view, her work wasn't viewed in a larger context. Her manager wants her to stay with the firm and would like to see her advance, but he also needs to help her understand what she needs to learn and the value of the experience she is getting as she moves up in the ranks.

What should the coaching manager do in such a situation? Should he be the bearer of bad news and confront her on her "incompetence"? Is Samantha's desire to move up before she is ready a manifestation of arrogance or just a natural expression of her ambition and self-confidence? Sometimes arrogance can be a problem. Very smart people don't necessarily have a great deal of self-awareness just because they happen to be smart. Is it your role to tell her that, in essence, she needs to lower her expectations?

We suggest a number of alternatives to consider before jumping in with a great deal of unsolicited critical feedback. First, the coaching dialogue needs to be handled sensitively. If Samantha feels that her manager is not interested in her growth and ultimate promotion, she will likely go elsewhere when the opportunity presents itself. The coaching manager can encourage her to reflect on her readiness by carefully reviewing with her the requirements for promotion.

Let's assume that the career ladder in Samantha's firm is comparable to that described in Table 12.1. Movement to the project manager level requires her to have a greater understanding of customer relationships, as well as the ability to build influential relationships within her own firm. Some firms also have a "years in role" requirement that the coaching manager may not be able to influence; but the key barriers to Samantha's promotion are a lack of skill in two relatively specific areas. If she can understand those requirements and reflect on her knowledge in relationship to them, she may begin to build a clearer picture of what she needs to accomplish to move ahead. The interchange with the coaching manager now changes. It moves from one in which there is the potential for an adversarial relationship—Samantha says she wants something, and the manager says "no"—to one in which Samantha articulates her needs, and the coaching manager tries to help by considering how he can provide her with opportunities to learn the required skills. Samantha can focus her on-the-job development efforts on goals that will take her in the desired direction. In our experience, most employees, even those who are most ambitious, can show patience if they have a "line of sight" between what they are doing now and their ultimate goals.

The problem, then, is a lack of understanding of the real requirements for promotion. In some cases, this may also reflect a failure on the part of the business to define those requirements. (See Chapter 7 for advice on how to develop an informal description of the skills required for a particular role if your company offers no such guidance.) If that is the case, the coaching manager will need to take up the task of spelling out those requirements clearly and thoughtfully so that the employee can identify the learning gap.

If the firm doesn't spend some time trying to define the requirements for jobs, particularly new ones, and communicating those requirements to people in the firm, the promotion process will appear to be political. Under such circumstances, minority candidates and women in particular are likely to assume that the process is unfair, and they may well be right. The coaching manager, assuming he or she has some integrity, can do two things under these circumstances. First, the coaching manager can try to influence the firm to develop a more rational approach to defining jobs. Second, the coaching manager can help employees develop the right relationships so that they have a chance of moving up in the firm when opportunities arise.

Case 12.3: The Employee
Who Is Good at His Work but Hates It

David went into accounting because his parents told him he'd always be able to support himself comfortably if he did so, and because he was good with numbers. Being the good son, that is exactly what he did. As a chief auditor (the top individual contributor position in the firm) in his public accounting firm, he is known for his precision and thoroughness. Clients like him because he gets along well with them, even when the audit uncovers sensitive problems. Several times, he has talked about possibly moving into management. During the last discussion with his manager, he seemed visibly upset. He was coming off of a particularly difficult assignment. Finally, he said, "I just can't stand this anymore. I hate this work. I despise the grind and the details."

His manager was surprised but not shocked. His intuition had signaled to him some time ago that David wasn't happy. The manager saw David as a "people" person. Sometimes he wondered what in the world David was doing in accounting. After David had vented his anger a bit, the manager asked if he had given any thought to what he really did want to do. Did he want to move to the consulting side of the business, perhaps? David responded that he really wanted to go into human resource management. Unfortunately, he had no technical training in that field. David also knew that there were few openings in that department at the time. Besides, if he did go into human resources, he'd have to start from the bottom and take a substantial salary cut as well.

As we discussed previously, people may be pushed into jobs for which they do have the skill but which don't interest them or complement their values. David is a "go to" performer in the eyes of others but doesn't see it the same way himself. Unfortunately, when someone has invested heavily in a career and has reached a certain earning level, it is very difficult to move backward and start over again if the move involves substantial economic or status sacrifice. It can be done, but most people can't tolerate the level of disruption that such a major change creates in their life.

Again, David's manager can't solve this problem for him. He likes David's work and doesn't want him to leave. What can he do? A better question is, what can David do if his manager is willing to help? David's coaching manager continued the dialogue: "It is hard to break into human resources these days. Have you thought of any other options if you want to stay here?" David hadn't thought about other alternatives beyond moving into management, which would at least get him more involved with others, require him to take some responsibility for human resource activities, such as performance appraisal and coaching, and offer him some exposure to human resources task forces that form from time to time. Such a compromise may be closer to David's career "target area."

His manager did have a team manager opening in the near future and felt that David was more than ready for it from a skills perspective. He was concerned, of course, that soon after taking the manager position, David might find a human resources position opening somewhere else and leave the company. The two proceeded to talk about what kind of commitment they wanted from each other to make a promotion to management appropriate. David agreed to commit to at least a 1-year tenure if his manager would assist him in getting involved with work related to human resources when the occasion arose. At the same time, he said he wanted to use the company's tuition reimbursement program to start an evening MBA program with a human resources focus.

His manager was comfortable with the deal because he knew David, felt him to be a person of integrity, and also felt that this compromise could meet both their needs. The manager wanted a good "people person" in the management slot. He also knew that he was going to lose David eventually. That is the risk you take with every hire or promotion. Something may happen, and plans may change.

This bit of "job sculpting" (Butler & Waldroop, 1999) may resolve the problem for now. But what if the manager has little to offer the employee in the way of job-sculpting opportunities? Perhaps there are openings in human resources that would be appropriate for David, or perhaps David would be willing to start over because he felt passionately about pursuing his new direction. In each of these cases, the manager loses David, though the company does not. Alternatively, he may end up in human resources or at another company. David, the former employee, now friend, will spread the word about the coaching manager and the coaching friendly context he created. Ideally, new talent will be lining up at the door to take the place of David when he moves on.

At a minimum, an unhappy but very capable employee has identified the nature of the problem through his own reflection and the coaching dialogue. He is now taking an action to correct the problem and feels supported by his manager, even if only on an emotional level. More serious performance problems that might have arisen, should David's unhappiness have become chronic, have been avoided. The ability of David's manager to listen without judging made it possible for both of them to confront the problem. Consider the likely outcomes if David and his manager had never openly discussed his career!

Case 12.4: The Employee With Work/Family Concerns

John was one of the best consulting engineers in the senior product support group. He had the talent and drive to move to the very top of the firm in 5 years. Since the birth of his second child, however, he's been increasingly concerned about the long working hours required to keep up with the rapid pace of technological change in his product area. Over the course of his career, however, he has been "taught" to keep such concerns to himself so as not to appear less than 100% committed to the company. His new manager has encouraged the people in John's group to be open about their concerns and needs. Unfortunately, John's previous experience has made it more difficult for him to take up such an offer. His productivity has declined, and his own team has begun to express concerns about his effectiveness. His manager, frustrated at John's lack of openness, prepared critical feedback for a constructive confrontation meeting with John. Once John heard the feedback, he began to reflect on the fact that the demands of his growing family were worrying him. He felt he was failing on both fronts.

John's problem is extraordinarily common (Vincola, 2001). Many employees have trouble balancing the demands of work and family. Furthermore, many develop the belief, through experience in other organizations, that to talk about their difficulties, especially at the senior level, can ruin one's career. This may be particularly true for men. Such a belief can make it extremely difficult for the coaching manager to start a coaching dialogue. The lack of such a dialogue can lead to disaster. In one study of how managers and employees deal with work and family conflict, in every case in which the employee brought up the problem with his or her manager, the manager was able to engage in some type of problem solving with the employee and find a solution that made it possible for the employee to remain in the firm. However, in every case in which the employee did not bring the problem up to his or her manager, a performance problem resulted (Hunt, 1994).

The implications of this perspective should be clear. The big problem with work and family conflict issues is the failure of employees and managers to have a conversation to address the problem. Once such a dialogue takes place, work and family concerns may cease to look like career issues. Granted, the manager will not be able to offer concrete options, such as flexible work schedules or telecommuting, in every case. Most good performers don't want a work/life balance problem to force a career change. They are motivated to work with the coaching manager and will often negotiate in good faith until a compromise solution can be met. If the employee is good, it is in the interest of the manager to bargain in good faith as well. Consider that 80% of the effort of a great performer may still yield an economic output that is several times greater than that of a mediocre or poor performer.

Work and family career issues don't usually last forever. Luckily, time is on everyone's side. Children grow up, crises pass, and the demands on employees are not always uniformly overwhelming. The coaching manager with a long-term focus can usually compromise, at least around the issue of time, for a period.

It should be stressed, however, that many employees, particularly those who are ambitious and are working at middle to senior levels, have been encouraged to believe as John did that bringing up work/family problems could hurt their careers. We encourage the coaching manager to be particularly sensitive while responding to the employee's family concerns and to handle those concerns with as much privacy on the part of the employee as is possible.

John's manager encouraged him to talk with several different people. His firm, like many firms, had a work/life resource program that could provide John with information and referral to a variety of additional services. In addition, he encouraged John to have coffee with several other senior managers who met regularly to discuss work/life balance issues. These executives were thinking through strategic options that the firm might consider most helpful in retaining good employees, such as John, who were having difficulty with work/life balance. The executives were interested because they had been through similar struggles themselves.

Conclusions: Developmental Coaching and Career Development

Addressing career concerns is the logical outgrowth of developmental coaching. Employees want to learn for a variety of reasons, one of which is to help them prepare for their next roles, whatever they might be. The tactics are simple: Encourage employees to reflect on their career interests and goals, and respond by offering balanced feedback, job sculpting, or contacts with others, which can help employees move toward their career target areas. Offer these resources when they are aligned with the needs of the business. Finally, be prepared to let go. You are in the people development business, and at the end of the term comes graduation.

13

Developmental Coaching and Performance Problems

IN THIS CHAPTER, WE DESCRIBE THE FOLLOWING:

- The difficulties of applying developmental coaching to performance problems
- Some of the root causes for performance problems and persistent gaps in performance
- Guidelines for using developmental coaching as part of a systems-oriented approach to helping the employee with a performance problem improve his or her performance.

An initial gap between actual and desired performance is not usually a problem. While people are learning a new skill or trying to use a skill in a new way or context, their performance, naturally, will not be expert. At some point, however, with practice and learning, the gap should disappear. It may take time. Learning a complex symphony may take years. Learning a new programming technique may take a day. The employee may move on to the next challenge, and once again, a gap between actual and desired performance may reappear. This is the nature of the connection between learning and performance. Such a pattern does not reflect a performance problem when viewed from the perspective of developmental coaching in a coaching friendly context. This being said, what does constitute a performance problem?

We propose several commonsense answers. At the simplest level, the hallmark of a performance problem is an *ongoing gap* between actual and desired performance, a gap that is not closing and may be worsening. Even the worst performers will be successful on occasion, but for those with performance problems, the gap is there much more often than not. Almost anyone can close a deal sometimes, but organizations need salespeople who can close deals consistently. If someone in a sales role can't sell consistently after he or she has had an opportunity to learn the job, with appropriate support, a performance problem exists.

Performance can also deteriorate. On occasion, a gap may reappear. A performance gap may be observable in an activity that the employee seemed to have mastered. For example, someone who used to be able to sell no longer does so routinely, even though few other conditions have changed.

We have put forth the proposition that developmental coaching is most effective with good to great performers who want to learn. Don't people with performance problems want to learn? One would imagine so; after all, it is in their interest to do so. However, the answer to this question is, unfortunately, sometimes "yes" and sometimes "no." Sometimes the person with the performance problem wants the problem to go away, wants to deny the problem exists, or just wants to survive until the end of the day.

The problem has to do in part with the person and his or her context. As we'll discuss below, many performance problems are influenced by factors over which the manager and even the employee may have little or no control. Performance problems can be driven by personal problems, personality, team dysfunction, and even organizational change.

Performance problems often have to do with the simple fact that we are who we are; and we may be in roles that require us to be someone we are not. We cannot change our personalities or the personalities of others. Psychoanalysts tell us that we can come to understand ourselves better and perhaps channel our energies more effectively (no small accomplishment), but in terms of interests, intelligence, and personality-driven behavior, we can't change all that much.

In Chapter 11, we described the 3-stage learning model: unfreezing, change, and refreezing (Schein, 1979). The model is extremely useful but has its limitations. Not every problem can be unfrozen. People will try, however. The process of trying to help the individual with a performance problem has some unintended consequences of its own.

If the job of an individual whose performance is persistently problematic is to be salvaged, he or she will likely be on the receiving end of highly critical feedback from his or her manager, or others. Even in the most difficult of situations, there may be no other way to communicate to the employee that a serious performance gap exists and must be addressed. After a time, it can be difficult for any employee, no matter how mature, not to feel attacked. Sometimes, if the person is sensitive and/or the problem is serious, that feeling of being attacked will lead the employee to become very defensive. Such defensiveness can be overt or covert. People want to keep their problems hidden if they can, out of pride and self-preservation. As problems worsen, both the employee and the manager may feel threatened. The context for developmental coaching, which demands that the manager be nonjudgmental, can become poisoned. Both manager and employee can become very angry. The person with the performance problem may not be trusted by his or her manager or other team members.

Developmental coaching is only one tool at the disposal of the coaching manager. Others tools include performance appraisal and a variety of direct and indirect rewards and sanctions. In addition, in most organizations, the coaching manager can call on additional resources outside his or her business unit for help. Human resource managers, training and development managers, outplacement firms, and occupational health and employee assistance program (EAP) counselors may all have roles to play in helping the coaching manager work with a performance problem. We recommend that the coaching manager consider a diverse set of approaches for dealing with performance problems. In this chapter, we provide more background on some of the most common performance problems and in doing so, develop a set of recommendations that may help.

Before moving ahead, however, it is probably worth raising a question we've explored before, regarding other matters: Why bother? Most coaching managers we have met would probably be aghast that we ask such a question because they see it as their job to try coaching whenever a problem exists. This outlook fits their values, and it is important for them to be true to those values. Trying to help the performer with a problem can allow the manager to sleep better, a not unimportant outcome. And of course, their efforts may work, despite the cautionary tone of this chapter. We have seen people successfully address chronic performance gaps on a number of occasions. Finally, if the manager has established a coaching friendly context, other people in his or her organization will expect performance problems to be addressed. One of the expectations that people hold in a coaching-rich environment is that people will help each other out. It is the coaching manager's job to continuously model such a helpful attitude. It will pay off in the long run, if not in every case. So for a number of very good reasons, most coaching managers tell us that they will try coaching even if they aren't sure it will work. For these reasons, it is worth considering some of the root causes for serious performance problems.

Causes of Performance Problems

The causes of poor performance are numerous. We present here an overview of the most common. This overview is meant to illustrate several important points. First, it is important to note how much performance-related behaviors are multidetermined. There are likely to be several causes for any particular behavior outcome.

We discuss this as a general principle in Chapter 10, but it is probably even more relevant here. The "system" in which a performance problem emerges can be viewed as including the individual and his or her relationships with all aspects of his or her life, including the self, work roles and relationships, and nonwork roles and relationships. They each have a part to play, and they influence one another.

The net result for the manager is that a performance problem may be beyond his or her coaching influence. The problem may involve aspects of the individual's "system" that the manager is unable to reach. Therefore, intervention strategies that affect multiple roles or aspects of the employee's life (bringing in human resources, health services, or employee assistance, for instance) should be considered. From the perspective of most coaching managers, this is a hard-learned lesson. Business people with a "can do" attitude like to be able to solve problems. The second point we hope the reader will take from the discussion is that the coaching manager should actively seek the help of others when dealing with a significant performance problem.

Poor Managers and Poorly Communicated Expectations

The Gallup study argues convincingly that one of the most important determinants of an individual's effectiveness is the quality of his or her immediate supervisor (Buckingham & Coffman, 1999). Consistent with the Gallup findings, which we discuss in detail in Chapter 4, our experience leads us to believe that the first two core elements are key:

1. The employee needs to know what is expected of him or her at work.

2. The employee needs to have the material and equipment need to do his or her work properly.

Poor managers are often poor communicators. The following quote comes from a senior-level individual contributor who had been referred to us by his manager. This individual had been labeled as having a performance problem. "You'd be working along, thinking everything was fine for a month or so, and then she [the manager] would call you into her office, after refusing to meet with you for weeks. She would start telling you everything you had done wrong in the past month, mostly mistakes that you didn't even know were mistakes. She would change her mind about what she wanted, or would just lie."

We were fortunate in being able to get both sides of this story. This senior-level employee was in fact not performing up to the company's expectations for his particular role. Unfortunately, he didn't understand what was expected of him until his work came to be seen as a problem. The reader may empathize but wonder what this case has to do with coaching. We found out when we interviewed the manager. She was angry about this particular employee and wanted to know what she could do to coach him to more adequate performance. This was the right question for her to ask. However, she went on to explain that she didn't feel she needed to tell this employee what he needed to be doing. He was senior enough and old enough and ought to be able to figure that out for himself.

In this case, we decided that coaching was needed—for the manager. What her employees needed was something more basic than coaching: clear direction. Even though the members of the team were quite senior, they still needed to get a clear sense of where she wanted them to go. They needed her to be more available so that they could talk with her to address the inevitable ambiguities that emerge when people are trying to do something important or innovative.

The moral of this story is that one of the first things the manager should consider when dealing with a performance problem is whether or not he or she has contributed to the problem by failing to execute some of the basic tasks of management. The coaching manager must make sure that he or she has clearly set expectations as a first step in examining what appears to be a performance problem.

The Wrong Person in the Wrong Job

We've mentioned in several places throughout this book that developmental coaching requires that employees and their organizations have at least some overlapping goals. Furthermore, an employee in any role needs to have a foundation of strength for that role if he or she is to learn and grow to become a superior performer. Developmental coaching cannot turn a great engineer into a great engineering manager unless the candidate also has a foundation of interpersonal skills, an ability to work with a variety of people, and an ability to plan and organize the work of a team. Some people, including some great engineers (or salespeople, creative marketers, or counselors, etc.), may not have that foundation.

Unfortunately, sometimes companies knowingly put the wrong person in the wrong role. This can occur for a variety of reasons, including a labor shortage or a well-respected employee's wish to move into a different role for which he or she is not suited. Companies may give such an individual a "try" out of a misguided sense of loyalty, a payback for many years of superior service.

One of us recently consulted with an extraordinarily creative optical engineer who had become quite depressed. She had somehow come to believe that the only way she'd ever get the status she wanted was to go into management. Her company reluctantly went along with her request. She then found herself doing performance reviews, managing a budget, and dealing with interpersonal conflicts. She began to fail at all this and became increasingly upset with herself for doing so. The reality is that she had a severe performance problem in the manager's role. It didn't take much encouragement for her to go back to her manager and renegotiate her role, returning to individual contributor status. She was relieved, as was her family and the company. There was an immediate improvement in her mood, and in a short period of time, she developed a new product design that resulted in several patents. All the developmental coaching in the world would not have helped this individual turn her situation around as long as she stayed in a management role. In fact, it might have made things worse.

In our view, the key to addressing this problem is *prevention*. Organizations and managers need to keep in mind the power of identifying the right talent and fitting that talent with the right roles. Many organizations now hire more for personal or cultural fit than for technical skill in some roles. Although this practice sometimes makes a great deal of sense, it requires that companies and employees carefully consider employees' technical potential for new roles to which they might be assigned once they work in the firm. The "stretch" assignment should be acknowledged as such. Prior to taking such a stretch, the employee and company should carefully consider whether or not the potential is there for the employee to learn and be successful in the new role. Just being a team player does not mean that one can be a super salesperson or an effective manager.

Personal Problems

The fact that personal problems can interfere with performance comes as no surprise to most managers who have been on the job for any length of time. Divorce, alcohol or drug abuse, mental health problems, problems with children, medical illnesses, and other personal issues can all affect an individual's ability to perform. What does come as a surprise to most managers is just how prevalent these problems are. Using depression alone (a medical illness affecting mood and cognitive functioning) as an example indicates the scope of the problem. A study funded by the Washington Business Group on Health demonstrated the potential impact of depression on behavior in the workplace (Vaccaro, 1991). Each year, 10 million people will experience the symptoms of affective illness, the medical name for depression. One-year prevalence rates for major depression at Westinghouse were 17% for women and 9% for men. This survey was taken in a managerial/professional workforce. If we consider, in addition, the impact of other comparable personal problems, such as alcohol addiction, drug abuse, and other serious stress-related problems, it is easy to see just how important this factor is.

Unfortunately, people often have difficulty talking about emotional problems at work because of the powerful stigma attached to them. In addition, some problems, such as alcoholism, drug abuse, and domestic violence, are denied by those with the problem. They don't see it in themselves, and they don't make the connection between their problems or actions and their poor performance. This greatly delays their taking positive action and seeking help. Denial and delay mean that performance problems that don't have a great deal to do with work can affect the workplace. The substratum of the problem could be a medical illness or personal dysfunction of which the coaching manager may not be aware.

In addition, the coaching manager must be very careful about intruding into an employee's personal life, particularly if such intrusions are uninvited. The coaching manager needs to also keep in mind that he or she is not a clinical diagnostician. What looks like a psychiatric problem may in fact have more to do with an employee's drinking. The employee who smells as though he or she has been drinking may actually have a medical illness. If managers try to intervene in such problems, they run the risk of provoking a legal response, such as a lawsuit, on the grounds of defamation of character, or worse. Because performance problems driven by personal problems are so common, we present an example in Case 13.1. The case is fairly representative of what a performance problem driven by a personal problem is like for the manager and the employee.

Case 13.1(a): What the Manager Sees

Barbara is a 29-year-old sales representative for a large high-tech medical products firm. Her duties require her to introduce expensive medical equipment to hospitals and biotech companies. She has been working at the company for the past 2 years, having been hired right after completing her undergraduate degree. For the first year, her performance was outstanding. Six months ago, she began to work for her current manager after a reorganization. Her manager meets with her monthly and stays in touch by phone every few days.

Almost immediately, her manager began to hear complaints from customers who reported that Barbara had made technically confusing and even unfriendly sales calls. One customer complained that she had become angry when he balked at signing up for the latest release of the company's software. Another reported that she was late for their meeting and seemed disorganized. She had been slow to complete her expense reports, and her sales reports didn't seem very well put together, either. Finally, at the last sales meeting, she expressed a great deal of anger at the most recent reorganization. Her angry comments became louder and more vociferous after a few drinks.

At this point, the nature of the problem wasn't clear. Some sort of performance decline was clearly in evidence, but her manager had heard nothing about this from her. The manager speculated that the problem might have to do with the reorganization, her reaction to his management style, or something going wrong in her personal life. He decided to talk with her and bring up the customer feedback. Consider how you might start such a dialogue. That interchange yielded the following information.

Case 13.1(b): What the Manager Hears

In the manger's conversation with Barbara, she reported that she was somewhat mystified at the customer complaints. She blamed the customers, seeing them as particularly difficult. She also expressed the feeling that others in the organization were trying to get her out because she didn't like the recent changes at the company. Then she told the manager that she has been under a great deal of stress because of her daughter's ongoing bout with a serious medical illness. She stated that she was a single parent (which her manager knew) and got no help from anyone else. Finally, she said she was angry at her manager for raising these problems with her and wondered whether he wasn't one of those who wanted to move her out of the company. The meeting terminated on a very sour note.

Though Barbara seemed profoundly defensive, it is difficult not to feel sympathetic to her plight. After all, many of us have experienced serious personal problems at one time or another. To make matters worse, this was a medical problem with a child. The dilemma for the manager was significant. He needed

Barbara to get her performance back up, a need that she didn't recognize at that point. At the same time, he wanted to help her deal with her personal problems and didn't want himself or the company to be seen as uncaring.

If the manager is in a firm with an EAP, an employee counseling service, an occupational health nurse, or physician, he could encourage her to get help. In most companies, he could call for consultation on how to help Barbara himself. He might also encourage her to talk with their human resource representative or see what other support the company might offer, such as family medical leave (unpaid federally mandated leave available in the United States to employees with a medical or family problem). Ultimately though, he still needed her to perform. The manager could try being supportive up to a point, but if customer complaints kept streaming in, he would need to do something.

This case illustrates the importance for the manager of being clear as to what the employee with such a problem needs. In this case, is Barbara going to be open to learning? Would the manager and the employee be better off if the manager simply pressed her to comply with certain basic performance standards? Barbara appeared to be in no mood for learning at this point. She was probably consumed by the demands of day-to-day survival. However, given the problems she was having with her customers, her manager needed her to comply. The manager might have been able to achieve compliance by clarifying expectations, providing direct and even critical feedback, and using performance management tactics up to and including taking some type of disciplinary job action against her in the worst case. At the same time, if he could offer support, Barbara might be able to salvage her current job and her career. In this case, the manager tried to do just that and, fortunately, Barbara accepted his suggestion that she call the EAP.

Case 13.1(c): What the Manager Never Knew

Barbara initially asked the EAP counselor for help in dealing with the stress that she found so overwhelming, but in their conversations she revealed something else just as serious. She had experienced a recurrence of cocaine addiction, a problem she thought she had solved years ago. In her worry over her daughter, she turned back to drugs to make herself feel better, and soon she had the additional problem of her addiction. Because she had successfully participated in treatment in the past, she could see the problem more clearly and was able to discontinue cocaine use. With additional support, she was then in a much better position to deal with her daughter's illness and continue her job. Once the cocaine addiction was being treated and she ceased drug use, her job performance quickly improved.

The reader may feel a bit tricked by the presence of this underlying, quite serious personal problem on top of the very real problems she was willing to talk about with her manager. Unfortunately, such "tricks" occur frequently in life, and they can wreak havoc with the coaching manager's efforts to help an employee.

The moral of this story is twofold. First of all, when someone admits to a personal problem, don't try to deal with it yourself. Get help from your own manager, human resources, health, and employee assistance services. Second, if you try coaching when you believe that a personal problem may be interfering with performance, pay careful attention to whether or not you are able to see progress. If you don't, the coaching may not be working. In Barbara's case, developmental coaching might have delayed the manager's "tough love" stance and in the process, delayed her seeking help.

Character

Character is the manifestation of an enduring set of behavioral tendencies: the way individuals habitually interact with the outside world, how they defend themselves, and how they treat others. If problematic performance is driven by a personal problem, the manager is more likely to see volatility in the employee's performance or a pattern of performance decline. If the problem is driven by the individual's character, the employee's behavior will be more consistent.

Harry Levinson (1978) was among the first to draw our attention to one of the most difficult characterological presentations in the workplace, the "abrasive personality." The abrasive personality may be thought of as the "porcupine" of the business world. The dynamics that lead to the development of an abrasive personal style are varied, but the process begins in childhood. The symptoms include a tendency toward being condescendingly critical, needing to be in complete control, dominating meetings, being quick to attack, being quick to debate, being preoccupied with status and power, taking credit for oneself when success is due to the work of others, and appearing cold and distant or intimidating. The abrasive personality is also likely to be an "overestimator" whose behavior tends toward arrogance, as we discuss in Chapter 4.

The coaching challenge is probably clear to the reader. This constellation of behaviors could wreck the career of even the most talented employees, particularly if their work calls for them to interact with or lead others. The underlying need such individuals are expressing through their habitual behavior is the need to see themselves as perfect.

If individuals assume that they are perfect, or more likely, have a need to see themselves as perfect, it is very hard for them to open up with their managers and define learning goals about anything, let alone how they come across to others. The process of coaching is blocked by the employees' personalities, just as their personal styles block other effective interpersonal processes.

Levinson (1978) suggested that the only hope a manager has of coaching such an individual is to approach him or her frequently, with a helpful attitude. The abrasive character's style can easily provoke anger in others. The coaching manager should try not to fall into such a trap. The manager's expression of anger will lead to the employee's angry reaction to the manager's anger, leading to a vicious cycle in which very little learning takes place.

The coaching manager must then repeatedly hold out the coaching mirror, using balanced feedback to reflect back to the employee the observed behavior and its impact on the manager and others. Inaccurate or overly general feedback will be discounted as reflecting some sort of bias on the manager's part. Ultimately, such employees have to begin to see that their behavior is negatively affecting their own goals or running counter to their self-concepts. Coaching managers are in the difficult position of trying to affect behavior using rewards and punishments (Waldroop & Butler, 1996). To even consider changing, the abrasive personality may have to endure such negative feedback that it is ultimately punishing. No one could tolerate it if there wasn't the promise of something better at the end of the ordeal. The promise of something better is the opportunity for the individual with a significant character flaw to have the impact he or she wants to have. Once the employee realizes this, he or she can take more ownership for the coaching work to follow.

Dan was a brilliant product manager but was routinely disrespectful of the people who reported to him. If he didn't like their work, which happened frequently, he would lash out at them in public. He picked on one individual in particular, who ultimately complained to the company's CEO. The CEO was sympathetic but slow to act because of Dan's potential contribution to the firm. Finally, Dan berated a customer who didn't seem to understand the marketing plan Dan was pushing. The customer's CEO complained to Dan's boss and the company decided to take action. Dan was told by his CEO that such outbursts were not going to be tolerated. He could easily be promoted if he controlled himself over the next year, but he would be fired if he did not. He was offered the help of an executive coach and/or a therapist if he so chose. Confronted by a bad job market for executives at his level and the need to support his family, Dan decided that he'd better respond to his CEO's feedback. He began to show some ability to exercise control over his outbursts in his dealings with others. Complaints to the CEO ceased and Dan kept his job, but he was not promoted. He often stated that he was keeping his feelings to himself merely to "stay out of trouble with the boss." He never took ownership of the need to learn how to influence others without incurring hostility. Ultimately, it was clear to all that although he was complying with their directive, he could not be trusted in a higher-level and more independent role.

Could developmental coaching help employees like Dan? On occasion yes, but as with other interventions, we suggest that coaching managers monitor and evaluate their impact thoughtfully. Most coaching managers would like to believe that people like Dan can learn a new way, but they may merely show compliance. Psychotherapy might have helped Dan better understand his need to be perfect.

We should also add that this is tough, time-consuming work. Many coaching managers have told us that they never like to give up on an employee, but sometimes there is no other way. On occasion, setting a limit on an employee, even a limit that ends up in the employee's departure from the company, can be helpful. We know of very effective managers and individual contributors who freely admit that if their previous managers hadn't had the courage to fire them, they may never have confronted the problems that were destroying their effectiveness.

Team Problems

Serious performance problems can also be rooted in team problems. This is particularly true when there is a relatively high degree of interdependence between team members. If two people need one another to complete their individual tasks, both have to perform. Assessing the impact of team functioning on individual functioning becomes more important as organizations seek to enhance innovation and improve communications by purposefully bringing people together to work. Of note, the people being brought together may be from different occupations, each with their own distinct approach to their work, or from different cultures, each with their own set of cultural assumptions.

It is extremely difficult to assess individual performance problems under such conditions. Unfortunately, it can also be the case that individual performers with problems, such as the abrasive personality mentioned in the previous section of this chapter, can cause team problems.

Coaching, then, may need to involve a two-pronged approach. The coaching manager may need to spend some time coaching the various individuals on the team while intervening at the team level to address team-level problems. It could be that the team has not adequately sorted out individual roles, has trouble as a team dealing with conflict, doesn't have an appropriate mechanism for members to communicate with one another, or does not have adequate resources to do its job. Any of these team-level problems, and others too numerous to mention, can cascade down to affect individual performance. In this case, then, it may not be accurate to say that developmental coaching won't work. It may be more appropriate to suggest that developmental coaching may need to be supplemented by other activities.

Organizational Change

Finally, organizational change can also create performance problems that won't always succumb to developmental coaching. When organizations change, the rules change. We recently talked with a brilliant and innovative operations person who had a spectacularly successful career in a manufacturing organization because he was able to introduce new ways for the company to make its products. His world-class innovations helped the firm take a leadership position in product quality and time to market. Even though his approaches required considerable investment on the part of his company, the payoff made his work economically viable. Then, due to changes in the company's market, the company's strategy changed. The business began to focus on cost cutting and the standardization of operations. Our innovative engineer continued to push for more innovation and increasingly found himself alienated from a senior management group that had once been big fans. He was subsequently terminated.

Organizational change had created a person-to-role misfit that had not previously existed. Note that the job description and title did not change. We could argue about whether or not the company was wise in taking this new tack in their strategy, but the point is, cost cutting was the direction they chose. The engineering manager could not find it in his heart to embrace the new strategy. Ultimately, his lack of commitment to the new vision was obvious. His presence began to do more harm than good from the business perspective, leading to the decision to terminate. He is now doing very well in another company, in which he can exercise his creativity in a fashion that is valued. To be helpful to this individual, developmental coaching would be more oriented toward helping him define his career goals and assisting him in meeting those goals, even if it were to mean leaving the company.

Addressing Performance Problems: Some Coaching Guidelines

The coaching managers we've talked with don't tend to give up easily, as we stated earlier. Perhaps that is as it should be. Their success rests on their having a helpful attitude, and they need to follow that impulse wherever it takes them. However, they have also told us that they have their limits, which is a sound insight to keep in mind. We hope that the following guidelines will help the reader intervene in serious performance problems as effectively as possible:

- Make sure that the employee with the apparent performance problem clearly understands what is expected of him or her. Ask yourself whether or not you are part of the problem.

- View coaching as an experiment. Honestly assess progress. If progress is not forthcoming, consider the possibility that coaching may not be working.

- Seek input from others who may have knowledge of the employee and the performance problem. Don't go it alone. You want to be sure that bias and various perceptual distortions aren't clouding your assessment. (Remember that perceptual biases can work both positively and negatively.) A side benefit of consulting with others is that your own learning can be enhanced.

- It may be necessary to alter the balance between self-assessment and feedback. In the developmental coaching model presented in this book, reflection and self-assessment by the coachee are critical to encouraging employee learning and ownership of the issue at hand. Unfortunately, an individual with a performance problem may need more feedback to promote "unfreezing" than an individual who is more oriented toward learning. Feedback may also be useful if the only option is to insist on compliance, even in the absence of learning. However, take special care to make your feedback balanced, accurate, and respectful. Your own attitude while delivering the feedback is important. If you are trying to coach, even under difficult circumstances, a helpful attitude is a must.

- Encourage the employee to consult other resources. Even though employees may associate the company EAP with the stigma attached to emotional problems, most EAPs offer a range of help, including career counseling, family counseling, and referral to external resources. Typically, they are also confidential. With additional support in a confidential setting, the employee may be able to let go of some of his or her defensiveness and engage in a more productive self-assessment. We offer one caveat, however. Senior executives are sometimes reluctant to take advantage of an in-company EAP for a variety of good and not-so-good reasons. If that is the case, the senior human resources manager can often locate other resources, external to the company, with which the executive might feel more comfortable working.

- Follow-up is absolutely essential. Your only hope is that unfreezing can take place. As discussed previously, when unfreezing is necessary, the employee may need frequent feedback and frequent assessments of the impact of their actions. It is essential that employees at all levels be held accountable for their actions. Otherwise, unfreezing or other approaches to resolving performance problems are unlikely to occur.

• Make sure that your coaching efforts are aligned with other organizational factors, such as job design, compensation, and team functioning. As we showed in Chapter 11, sometimes follow-up is not successful because other factors in the organization are working against the coaching effort. When dealing with a performance problem, it is probably more important than in any other kind of coaching activity that the entire system surrounding employee and manager be aligned.

14

Using Coaching to Leverage the Investment in the Classroom

IN THIS CHAPTER, WE DESCRIBE THE FOLLOWING:

- The challenge of transferring learning from the classroom to the workplace
- A set of guidelines that coaching managers can follow to help facilitate the transfer of learning

The authors have spent considerable time and energy creating educational experiences for practicing managers, frequently in a classroom format. We've also talked with numerous individual contributors and managers about workplace-based educational efforts, as well as with human resource development professionals responsible for improving the performance of employees and businesses. There is considerable hope for and yet some frustration with classroom education as a vehicle for promoting developing business talent. The legends Bill Gates, Steve Jobs, and Ed Land (none of whom graduated from college), among others, remind us that the classroom alone is not the ticket to greatness that it was once thought to be. Does it still have a place? Biased though we are, we insist that it does but that the interaction between the classroom and the workplace often breaks down and has to be repaired.

Developmental coaching by managers offers a powerful vehicle for greatly leveraging the benefits of classroom educational experiences while at the same time, ameliorating the frustrations, at least to some degree. We encourage any manager whose employees participate in either on-site or off-site classroom learning, even on an infrequent basis, to pay special attention to the advice offered in this chapter.

The Nature of the Problem

Enormous sums are spent by businesses throughout the world on classroom training each year. In 1998, the total training expenditures in the United States amounted to 2.0% of payroll, up from 1.8% the year before (McMurrer, Van Buren, & Woodwell, 2000). This figure includes expenditures on all types of training and development activities, such as technical skills training, diversity training, and leadership development.

That may not sound like a great deal of money (and indeed, the figure is higher in some countries) until one stops to think of the size of the payroll in the United States. Two percent of $3 trillion is a lot of money. Indeed there is some evidence, though it is not causal, that firms that do the most training demonstrate better economic performance.

At the same time, on a day-to-day basis, employees and managers report an uneven level of satisfaction with the impact of classroom training. One of the more common complaints issued by both is that even though a particular classroom experience was extremely well done, it may not meet the actual needs of the employee or the business. In that case, the content of the training isn't put to good use.

In Chapter 1, we described the basic model of experiential learning. Learning is thought to take place when an individual acts and then has a chance to both reflect and receive feedback on the action. Classroom education enhances the ability of the individual to learn from reflecting on his or her experience because it provides concepts against which actions can be judged. In the classroom, participants can learn a new approach to selling a particular product. They can then assess their previous performance against the model they learned in the classroom. They may then choose to use aspects of the sales model learned in the classroom to enhance their performance in the field.

What if the participant makes no direct connection between the classroom and practice in the field? Learning can be extinguished in a devastatingly short period of time if what has been learned in the classroom is neither used nor rewarded (Noe, 1999). Note that this is an example of the "refreezing" problem discussed previously. The learning doesn't fit that well with other aspects of the learner's situation.

The link between learning and action is particularly important for most adults. Adults learn differently from children (Knowles, Holton, & Swanson, 1998) and typically exhibit the following behavior:

- They need to know why they are learning something.
- They are more self-directed in their learning. Adults do much better when they take responsibility for the learning goal and the learning process.

- They bring more work-related experience into the learning effort (which means that they may need to unlearn, or be unfrozen, if they are to be open to learning).
- They enter into the learning experience with a problem-centered approach to learning. They learn to solve problems or meet challenges. Some individuals certainly love to learn for the sake of learning throughout their lives, but they are less common than those who learn to help themselves address specific questions or concerns.

It is for this reason that study after study has shown that the most important lessons executives learn are the ones they learn on the job (McCall, Lombardo, & Morrison, 1988). Executives retrospectively report that they learned the most from job assignments, particularly their first supervisory assignment and assignments that were difficult and challenging. They also report learning a great deal from other people (good bosses, bad bosses, or mentors) and from facing personal and business hardships. Some classroom experiences were quite helpful. However, the experiences recalled as helpful were seen as such because they addressed the problem or challenge the executive was facing at the time the course was taken. The classroom experience, in other words, provided the executives in this study with concepts they could use immediately.

Transfer of Learning

The challenge of putting learning into practice is described by human resource development professionals as that of *transfer of learning* from the classroom to the workplace, which is the ultimate goal of any workplace-sponsored learning (Noe, 1999). This is what most employees want to see happen as well, particularly those who want to grow and succeed.

Transfer of learning involves taking specific elements or concepts from the classroom and being able to use them at work. Employees learning C++ (a programming language) should be able to use the identical programming techniques developed as they solved practice problems in the classroom when they return to the workplace. The executive completing a leadership course should be able, at the next board meeting, to use the new ideas he or she developed about influencing others. Such a transfer of learning is facilitated by a number of factors. Obviously, it is facilitated by similarity of content between the classroom and the challenge the individual faces at work.

However, other factors can serve to facilitate or inhibit the transfer of learning as well (Rossett, 1997). A poorly designed or poorly executed classroom experience won't provide much learning to transfer. Mandatory training experiences that don't address the individual's goals or needs obviously violate the principle just described. Compensation systems, as well as other policies, procedures, or organizational-level cultural assumptions and norms will also exercise powerful constraints on the possibilities for using new learning. Executives who participate in classroom training on leadership frequently hear about and come to believe in the value of teams. However, when they try to implement a team-based activity in their companies, they may run into significant obstacles, such as cultural norms and compensation systems that discourage the use of teams, the sharing of responsibility, and the rewarding of teams in addition to individual performance.

Finally, the attitude of the learner's manager and, to an extent, his or her peers can also play an important role in determining what learning is transferred from the classroom to the workplace. If the learning is seen as not being aligned with what the boss and the other employees value, the boss and the peers are likely to be indifferent or hostile to what has been learned.

The result is not merely a failed investment of time and money in the educational process, but significant employee cynicism as well (Rossett, 1997). The employee/learner ends up feeling cynical about the organization's waste of money and his or her manager's lack of interest in performance improvement. Ultimately, and even more sadly, the employee may feel cynical about training and development in general, believing that it is not helpful. Employees who are ordered to undergo training that takes time and teaches them content that runs counter to what it actually takes to get ahead in their organizations are likely to see the training experience as punishing rather than developmental because of the time lost from work, for which they will be held accountable.

The reader will note that the problem of lack of alignment between employee goals, organizational goals, and classroom training is quite comparable to what we described in Chapter 11, goal setting and follow-up. Learning takes work—and not just on the part of the learner. The learner's manager and peers are more likely to put in the time and effort necessary to make the investment in learning pay off when it is aligned with what they generally need to do to be successful.

Effective transfer of learning is probably most readily observed in technical skill-building programs. If a group of employees is going to be working on a new assembly line, their tasks will, for the most part, be delineated before they ever see the line in person. The detailed assignment for each station on the line is developed by manufacturing engineers. The tasks associated with each role are carefully described. Each task is then matched with a description of the skill needed to complete the task. (Soldering a particularly hard-to-reach wire requires knowledge of soldering as well as fine motor coordination and patience.) Employees know that they must learn the particular set of required skills to be successful in these new positions. Even though the training is mandatory, a context that can sometimes discourage transfer of learning, in this case, the value of the training is clear to employees.

Each employee will be trained in the classroom on each particular skill and then be expected to perform the same skill under nearly identical conditions, once the assembly line begins operation. Their manager needs them to use the skills they learned in the classroom and stands ready to support them with coaching once work on the assembly line has begun. Because it is an assembly process in which the workers must depend on each other in order to be successful, they help each other learn through peer coaching or emotional support. Finally, they are rewarded financially and with recognition if they successfully perform the newly learned skills.

It should be noted that such alignment is somewhat easier to achieve because of the relative certainty and stability of this type of operation. It is clear what has to be done. There is little room for discretion on the part of employees or their manager regarding the performance that is ultimately required for success. This is not always the case. Frequently, the correct way to undertake a particular task or role is less clearly defined. This is particularly true in rapidly changing contexts such as those faced by managers, business, and technology professionals.

In the new economy, there is debate about everything from how to write a strategic plan to how to negotiate. A company may order everyone to attend training in cross-cultural sensitivity, for instance, without having clearly articulated a desired outcome beyond that of mutual respect. Just as frequently, employees may be encouraged to take a course that, although relevant to their developmental goals, lacks any real assessment as to whether what is to be learned will fit in with the workplace when the employees return. The net result is that employees can end up enrolling in classroom learning programs without either manager or employee having a real sense of what will be learned or whether or not the learning fits in with the needs of the workplace. This problem is compounded when employees are ordered to undertake "40 hours of training" each year without sufficient guidance and without considering whether or not what will be learned is aligned with the needs of the business, manager, peers, and employees.

Cases 14.1 and 14.2 illustrate the challenge of building alignment that can support the transfer of learning from the classroom to the workplace. Case 14.3 offers a specific illustration of how developmental coaching was used after a classroom program had been completed.

Case 14.1: The Wrong Executive Education Experience at the Wrong Time

Jack came from a rough-and-tumble family business in a rough-and-tumble industry. He was told that he must attend an executive education course in leadership as part of the preparation for moving up to the chief operations officer role (COO) in his firm. He ultimately attended the program recommended by his firm's bankers. One of them had attended the same program previously and found it to be quite useful. The leadership model presented in the program was based on the concepts of shared responsibility and distributed leadership. Program content emphasized the building of trusting relationships and working on the subtleties of one's leadership style

Unfortunately, leadership practices in Jack's family business, and indeed the entire industry in which they competed (nothing like banking, to be sure), were characterized by a lack of trust between labor and management. Order was kept through the use of ruthless and highly manipulative leadership practices.

Jack got something out of the program, though he was very concerned about his ability to put the ideas he had learned into practice. Returning to his family's business, he discussed what he had learned with other firm executives, who proceeded to ridicule him for some of the changes he proposed.

Not all leadership education programs are alike! The public seminar Jack attended is very well-respected because it is excellent. However, if Jack, his father, and other executives at his company had stopped to reflect on what Jack really needed to learn, they might have chosen a very different course. Case 14.1 illustrates a very important point for all coaching managers and those they coach. Leveraging time and money spent in the classroom requires some advance thinking as to (a) what needs to be learned and (b) which, if any, classroom experiences will facilitate that learning.

If Jack, his father, the CEO, and the company's advisers had talked about what Jack needed to learn, they may have decided that negotiation skills, for example, were much more important than team leadership. They might have gone one step further and looked for a negotiations program that others in his industry had found to be effective. This advance work could have created the kind of alignment that would have ultimately rewarded Jack for his learning efforts, rather than leaving him feeling quite punished.

Some might reasonably argue that Jack needed to learn a new approach to leadership that was quite different from the one that had previously been successful in his business and industry. In some cases, that can be an appropriate course of action. Indeed, the classroom can provide new ideas that can help the learner challenge previously held assumptions and consider innovative approaches to old problems.

In most cases, however, the coaching manager and the learner will have, and should have, discussed this in advance. They may agree that the employee's goal in participating in the classroom program is to bring back innovative and possibly controversial perspectives. Both need to acknowledge that transfer of learning to the workplace may face significant barriers. The employee may need the coaching manager's concrete assistance and support in addressing those barriers. Job designs may need to be altered. Compensation plans may need to change. Customer relationships may be affected. New information can be revolutionary; it is in that sense very exciting to go to the university or the industry conference and return with the latest ideas from across the globe. In the process of transferring those ideas into new practices, remember that it may be necessary for other employees or the entire business unit to go through the stages of unfreezing, change, and refreezing. This is really an organizational change problem. Classroom experiences alone are rarely sufficient to accomplish organizational change.

Case 14.2: Leadership Education That Helped

A worldwide real estate management company brought the heads of each of their local territories together for a series of classes on business strategy and leadership. Employees and managers throughout the company were made aware that a change in business conditions required local managers to assume more autonomous and strategic roles in the firm. Instead of relying on the regional vice presidents for building a local business strategy, the local managers would be expected to develop a business plan and execute it. As a result, the local managers needed to build new business skills as well as develop new mind-sets about their work. They needed to learn to see themselves as leaders rather than as followers. Prior to the program, each local manager defined learning goals for the classroom portion of the change project with their regional vice presidents, as part of the formal (written) development planning process.

Every regional vice president attended the last 3 days of the classroom program. They talked with faculty, sat in on classes, and attended a half-day meeting with other regional vice presidents. The topic of that meeting was coaching. They talked about their local managers' development goals and discussed strategies for helping to leverage the work that had taken place during the classroom period when the local managers returned to their home territories. They brainstormed ideas for follow-up to keep the learning process going. After the classroom program was completed, the managers met weekly with local managers, in person or by phone, for developmental coaching sessions. They worked with redefined development goals that each local manager articulated at the close of the classroom experience. Some of their goals had shifted on the basis of input from class faculty and other program participants. The regional vice presidents and the local managers agreed that they all had to take responsibility for transferring what had been learned back to the workplace

Case 14.2 is, of course, the kind of story that management educators love to hear. We suggest, however, that the real beneficiary of this kind of effort is the company. The company obviously believed that it was important to the business for their employees to develop new business competencies.

Learning goals were specifically defined for each participant. Note that it isn't possible to specifically design classroom program content or processes to meet those needs. The classroom experience can't meet the exact needs of every participant, because the class is taught to a group. However, if the content of the program was chosen with a degree of care, participants will emerge with some insights that are specifically relevant to his or her own learning needs. They will gain some serendipitous insights or perspectives that they may not have gone looking for, but were worthwhile, nevertheless.

Individual coaching attention, before and after, can help the employee and the organization take the most relevant and useful insights or skills gained in the classroom and think through how they can be used in practice. One local manager who went through the classroom program described in this case faced some very specific challenges.

Case 14.3: The Challenge of Becoming More Strategic

As a "hands-on" local manager, George was comfortable with tactics, managing existing accounts, and keeping clients happy. However, he missed important opportunities to expand his unit's portfolio of business. For instance, his geographical area had become home to a number of emerging companies, some of which had quickly become quite large. He did not immediately see the opportunity to put together a real estate management program for emerging technology companies or consider other strategies for proactively reaching this market. Several important potential accounts were lost to the competition. In his newly redefined role, he would need to think about potential business opportunities differently and instill a more proactive attitude in some of his direct reports as well. In the past, the corporation would have done most of this kind of marketing. Now it was up to the local team.

Given his hands-on management style, George knew that this would be a real challenge for him. In the classroom, he developed a clearer understanding of what strategic marketing really means; and through his discussions with other participants, he realized he'd have to spend at least 20% of his time scouting out other opportunities and less time monitoring current accounts. He proposed this shift in his own job description to his regional vice president, who heartily agreed. George felt he could handle the reallocation of his weekly schedule on his own, but he was still new at evaluating and responding to more strategic opportunities. Not being confident in this key aspect of his new role, he felt very unsure of his ability to communicate effectively to his own employees, who looked to him for direction. He and his regional vice president agreed that helping George learn more about evaluating business opportunities would be the focus of their work together, going forward. They also agreed that if George had a deeper understanding of how his group needed to assess and respond to business opportunities, he would be in a much better position to communicate the task more effectively to his team.

The classroom offers insight. The coaching manager works with the coachee to prepare for the classroom and to help the coachee apply what has been learned in practice.

The examples in Cases 14.2 and 14.3 show an alignment of employee learning goals, business goals, classroom goals, and company goals in a large firm engaged in a major organizational change project.

To further enhance this alignment between classroom and workplace, companies are increasingly creating shared learning experiences for groups of employees that rely on "action learning" to facilitate learning transfer (Conger & Benjamin, 1999; Dotlich & Noel, 1998). Action learning projects involve teams of employees working together to address specially chosen, but very real, business challenges. Action learning team participants may be from a single business unit but more commonly involve employees from different units or geographies. Diverse team participation can promote the integration of learning across functions and areas through the building of relationships, a major challenge in most large companies. The shared interests of team members can create a coaching friendly context that supports peer coaching even while the individuals and/or the team receive coaching from a manager, corporate team sponsor, or external coach. Classroom help is provided on a periodic basis and is usually targeted at the specific skills or concepts that team members need to fulfill their team's charter. What is learned in the classroom is then immediately relevant and directed squarely at learner goals and needs. Action learning and team coaching represent another thoughtful approach to effectively making use of what should be of great benefit to the employee and the business: time spent in an appropriate and helpful classroom learning experience.

Making the Most of Classroom Learning

We are now ready to draw out a series of simple but important practices that can help the coaching manager and employee get the most out of an investment in formal classroom education. These practices are described in Box 14.1. They address three overriding concerns: the need to properly define the learning goal or goals, choose an appropriate program, and follow up to ensure that the transfer of learning from the classroom to the workplace is facilitated.

Box 14.1

PRACTICES THAT SUPPORT THE TRANSFER OF LEARNING FROM THE CLASSROOM TO THE WORKPLACE

1. First, define the learning goal(s). Will a classroom experience be helpful? It is likely to be helpful in the following situations:

    - The employee has to learn new skills or concepts, particularly in a short period of time.
    - The employee is "stuck," and an educational intervention can address the specific problem that is causing this.
    - It would be particularly helpful for the employee to be working with others who are addressing similar learning needs.

2. Choose the right program:

    - Make sure it is aligned with the employee's learning goals.
    - Also consider whether or not the content of the program is aligned with the needs and culture of the business unit. If it is not, proactively address any barriers that may make transfer of learning more difficult.

3. Provide coaching follow-up to the employee on completion of the classroom experience:

    - Immediately after the learner returns from the program, set aside a 1- to 3-hour block of time during which you and the learner review the content of the program. Discuss what the learner thought, saw, and/or felt that might be relevant to his or her performance or the organization. It is likely that some of the content will be helpful and some will not.

- Either at the end of this meeting or within the next day or two, ask the learner to describe one to three personal learning goals that emerged from his or her experience in the executive education program. (See Chapter 11 on goal setting.)
- Help the learner define what effective performance would look like if he or she were successful in attaining the goal(s).
- Consider whether or not you are the best person to provide the learner with appropriate follow-up coaching. You will need some knowledge of the content area related to the learner's goals and some opportunity to gather performance data and provide the learner with balanced feedback. If you're not the right person, help the learner identify and solicit help from someone who is.
- Support the learner by helping to make sure that he or she has meaningful work related to the learning goals the two of you have identified. Only by using the skills on the job will the learning "stick."
- Follow up with the learner on a regular basis to assess progress.
- If a group of employees have attended a program, bring them together to discuss what they learned, jointly.
- Congratulate employees when they have achieved their goals.

Defining the Learning Goal

The practice of defining a learning goal or goals should be an outgrowth of the developmental coaching between manager and employee that has taken place prior to the program. In a coaching friendly context, both are thinking about learning and progress toward the development of new skills. Classroom education may be appropriate when several different contingencies arise:

- *The employee has to learn a new set of concepts.* If an employee needs to learn something about which he or she knows very little, or if the employee has to learn a great deal in a short period of time, the classroom can be an effective means of addressing the learning need. A focus on learning with the aid of subject matter experts who are also skilled teachers allows for the presentation and digestion of a large amount of information in a short period of time.

- *The employee is "stuck" in his or her learning, and no one in the workplace is able to help that individual get "unstuck."* If an employee is having trouble dealing with a highly conflicted team and the coaching manager's feedback isn't being particularly helpful, taking the problem into the classroom can be useful. The employee can work on the situation with subject matter experts, gain perspective on his or her own approach through reflection and self-assessment, and develop concrete ideas for approaching the problem in a new way.

- *It could be useful for the employee to work directly with others who are addressing a similar set of issues.* The development of certain skills, corporate entrepreneurship or leadership, for example, can be aided by working with others engaged in the same task. The employee may be the only one on his or her team thinking about leading a new product development group. He or she may not be "stuck" but may still find that there is a great deal to be learned from others, particularly peers from other business units or companies.

These simple guidelines are meant to suggest only that it is useful, before deciding on a classroom experience, to consider whether or not such an approach is most appropriate for the particular learning goal of the employee. The classroom offers a great deal. However, it is inappropriate to expect it to be helpful in every case. The employee with a serious personal problem, for instance, will not become a more effective leader by attending a leadership class.

Choosing the Right Program

Cases 14.1 and 14.2 illustrate the importance of choosing the right program. The program should address the learning needs of the participant. The employee, with the coaching manager's help, needs to move beyond the "brand" of the educational institution offering the program, the program's title, or the glowing recommendations of previous participants. The employee should find out in advance whether or not the content is specifically related to his or her goals. In the case of external educational experiences, such as those offered by universities or consulting companies, the employee should carefully examine program brochures and Web sites and, if necessary, call the program faculty directly. (Most will be happy to hear from any potential participant.) Describe the learning goal and ask the faculty member how the content of the program will relate to the goal. It is in the interest of most faculty and trainers to have a realistic discussion about this issue because they are more likely to be successful if the appropriate participants are in their programs.

Following Up

Follow-up begins with setting aside a meaningful block of time shortly after the employee returns from the program and reviewing the employee's experience in relationship to his or her learning goals. We recommend that a follow-up meeting take place within 5 to 7 days of the employee's return. Check for any serendipitous learning that may have occurred as well. Participants in external programs may pick up an idea unrelated to their learning goals but very useful to the group.

The coaching manager should ask the employee to revisit those learning goals and choose several on which to focus for a time. If the employee has learned a new approach to negotiations, for instance, and thinks it will be helpful, discuss how the employee can use the new approach in his or her work. Ask the employee to consider what success would look like if the new approach to negotiation were to become part of his or her repertoire.

Finally, discuss what kind of coaching the employee needs going forward. Ideally, the coaching manager will be in the right position to provide follow-up, but this may not always be the case. For example, suppose an employee has learned a new software language, a language that others on her team, including the coaching manager, don't know. She may need to find a connection with another expert in the organization with whom to consult as she attempts to work with the new language. The coaching manager's role is to help her locate such a resource and support her efforts to build a relationship with that individual.

If an employee's usage of what was learned in the classroom is likely to encounter serious barriers, more follow-up with the employee will be necessary. Remember that if refreezing does not occur, regression to actions that rely on previous learning will take place almost automatically. If the employee is really trying something new and different, follow-up support (as we describe it in Chapter 11) is essential.

The Classroom and the Coaching Manager

The process we have described should sound fairly simple. We believe that it is. Unfortunately, too many managers don't take such a direct interest in the impact of classroom learning (with the exception of technical skills training) on the employee and on the business. This may be a manifestation of the unaddressed split between learning and working that exists in most organizations. Most companies pay for at least some classroom training for their employees and then, strangely, do little with it back at the workplace. The coaching manager can lead the way in this regard and learn quite a bit in the process.

Epilogue: Coaching and Organizations, a Final Word

We like to pride ourselves on being pragmatic about coaching. We know that business leaders have a job to do, and the economic, marketing, and operational challenges they face are the focus of their attention most of the time. Business managers have little tolerance for bureaucracy and no time to fill out another batch of forms from the human resources department. Developmental coaching takes place in formal meetings, but even more often, by the watercooler, at the airport, over lunch, and right after the big meeting. We believe that this is a practical view of what is possible and what most managers can achieve. It is based on what is happening right now.

However, as we have noted several times throughout this book, the simple truth is that far too many managers offer no coaching to their employees at all. "Sink or swim" rules the day when it comes to the development of employees in many organizations. (We say this with apologies to the many readers who will be saying about now, "But hey, I do a lot of coaching." Our reply is, "Stop and think about just how competitive this makes you in comparison with other managers! Congratulations.")

So perhaps the real truth is that we are pushing the rock up the hill. Maybe it just isn't going to happen. Especially when times are tough, employee development is often the first thing to go. The reason so few managers coach is that organizations just don't encourage it, and that isn't about to change any time soon.

We believe that "tough times" are really nothing more than a shallow excuse for doing nothing. In 2001, the airline industry was in terrible shape. Layoffs, bankruptcies, bad service, and cutbacks in the number of flights due to lack of demand were common. A notable exception was Southwest Airlines, known for its focus on choosing the right people and then developing them as a sustainable competitive advantage. Southwest was not quick to resort to layoffs and was seen as having a good chance of remaining profitable (Sanders, 2001). SAS Institute, the software giant with a similar focus on people, saw a sales growth of 12% in 2001, a terrible year for technology companies. Their focus on helping people get the most out of their careers continued to pay off (Schu, 2001).

The business case for spending at least some time on talent development is hard to dispute. The moral case is even stronger. Despite how well the firms we just cited have done during a difficult economic period, the reader knows, as do we, that even these great companies can offer no guarantee to their employees. Any firm can run into problems that just can't be overcome. It is very difficult for business firms to offer loyalty to their employees in a capitalist economy. So what is the firm that takes a humane and even a moral view of the employment relationship to do? We believe that the only answer to this question is to keep people learning and growing so they can take care of themselves if and when something happens. The relationship between firms and employees has been changing since the 1980s when, during rounds of layoffs, it became clear that lifetime employment was no longer a viable human resources strategy at the organizational level. Sweeping change and globalization had made it a thing of the past. What, then, would be the substitute?

A "new psychological contract" between firms and organizations was to supplant the old (Altman & Post, 1996). In this new contract, employees would be offered mobile financial rewards (401Ks instead of pensions, for instance), challenging work, and an opportunity to keep their skills current, to become "career resilient" (Waterman, Waterman, & Collard, 1994). The firm would no longer take responsibility for the employee's career but would help by providing continuous learning, particularly on-the-job learning. This kind of relationship sounds similar to what we're advocating here, but with one small difference. We propose that companies honor their end of the bargain, something that to date, many have not done. Companies find it easy to offer challenging work. However, most have not shown a commitment to on-the-job learning. If they had, the findings we have cited regarding the lack of coaching would be quite different.

Many of the coaching managers we have talked with get little or no support from their organizations in their efforts to help their people develop. Indeed, this book is targeted at individual managers, not at corporations. We have taken this stance because that is where the action is. However, one of the implications of the Gallup research, we have cited several times in this book is that an individual focus by itself is limiting (Buckingham & Coffman, 1999). Organizations should work hard to overcome the organizational as well as the individual barriers to creating a coaching friendly context.

The organizational barriers to on-the-job learning, which really means coaching by managers, are well-known. At the personal level, managers aren't trained to coach, and even if they are, they get little or no ongoing support for their development as coaches. They don't get on-the-job help to become better at coaching. At the business level, the barriers include a short-term focus on quantitative results and compensation systems that reward short-term results. Many organizations encourage their managers to coach but end up punishing them for doing so. The punishment can be direct or indirect. Direct punishment includes telling managers that although coaching seems like a nice idea for others, if they spend too much time coaching others, it will hurt their careers. Indirect punishment takes the form of loading more work on managers to the point that any time they spend coaching their employees will come out of what little time they have to devote to their life outside work.

Management scholar Jeffrey Pfeffer picks on one particular industry's set of productivity measurements as an example of how businesses can create environments that essentially extinguish learning:

> Many [consulting] firms, perhaps most, have some measurement system which is really utilization, and utilization when you think about it is really a wonderful way to make sure no learning goes on because every minute you spend learning you're not being utilized on some engagement. (Pfeffer, 2001, p. 40)

We add one additional barrier reported by many of our coaching managers: a lack of role models. As one of our coaching managers said: "I didn't even know there was such a thing as coaching. I'd never seen it done. Nobody cared about it. I didn't have a chance at learning it until I knew I needed to learn something."

Given what we know about coaching, about the need for organizations to learn and adapt, about how coaching can improve performance, and about how people need more from their work than just money, will senior management and their boards respond appropriately? The answer is not clear. Some are hoping that the core processes of coaching, processes that rely on the relationship between manager and employee, can be augmented by other resources.

Will Technology Help?

Work groups and teams are now more geographically diverse than ever. Technology is a critical enabler of this global form of teamwork. E-mail, the telephone, and increasingly, videoconferencing do provide opportunities for people to have meaningful conversations over long distances. A more in-depth discussion of the role of technology in coaching is beyond the scope of this book, for the following reason: We found our coaches using very little technology while actually coaching. When they do coach at a distance, that old standby, the telephone, is by far the most popular form of technology.

In all fairness, many coaching managers use e-mail to gather and disseminate information in support of their coaching efforts. One of our coaching managers described how, at the end of each project, she uses e-mail to do a kind of After Action Review (AAR) with global project teams. She asks each individual to e-mail responses to the following questions: What went well? What should you (we) do differently? What did you (we) learn that would be valuable to others? She then tabulates the results and sends the entire list back out to the field. This particular coaching manager has done an excellent job of creating a coaching friendly context. People in her group trust that they can be candid in their responses to her. While coaching individually, however, she uses face-to-face and telephone-facilitated coaching. Her employees know what she wants and feel safe talking about their learning needs with her.

Another coaching manager told us that she would never use e-mail for distance coaching, only the telephone. Her reasoning was simple. It is too easy for misunderstandings to occur through e-mail. Her approach to distance coaching starts with a face-to-face meeting. She does no coaching until that has taken place. She then sets up weekly or biweekly telephone meetings with anyone she is coaching. In this sense, her coaching efforts with those away from the home office are somewhat more formal than is typical for her, but this has to be done for the parties to connect properly. She treats each coaching discussion like a face-to-face meeting. She stays away from her own computer and paperwork so she can focus fully on what the coachee is saying.

We collected many such stories from very technology-savvy managers. It is not that they don't like technology. Many use technology intensively. Some make technology. Rather, they have a strong belief in the face-to-face meeting or the telephone when it comes to coaching. This seems to us to be quite sensible, though subject to change as our culture becomes more accustomed to using existing and emerging technology for communications.

Coaching requires a great deal of trust. Subtle cues, often given nonverbally, assure the coachee that it is safe to open up. Feedback from the coaching manager can be critical at times. These managers don't want to hurt their employees, they want to help them. They watch and listen carefully to get a sense of how the feedback is coming across. They strive to be fully understood, to hold up a "clean mirror." It is obviously much more difficult to do that without at least being able to hear the other person's voice.

One obvious technological solution to this problem is the use of videoconferencing. As of this time, the technology is still developing and is not widely available. Although we believe it does hold great promise, it will probably be difficult to assess its value until the technology is near to being as widely available and as comfortably used as the telephone. Coaching managers are busy, as are their employees. Technology that supports coaching needs to be very convenient.

Software packages that describe lists of competencies, development tips for working on those competencies, and competency-specific coaching advice are now readily available and may be helpful to coaching managers. In some firms, such as Cisco Systems, coaching and development support of this kind are available on the corporate intranet. In our experience, however, the degree to which such programs or Web sites are used depends on their alignment with the needs of the individuals in the firm and the culture of the firm or business unit.

Many companies have career development planning tools on their internal Web sites, for instance. The most heavily used are those that are perceived by employees and managers as truly helpful. The experience of organizations that have used technology to support career development offers a lesson as to what we might expect technology can do to facilitate coaching. The following observations recount the introduction of an online career development technology at a Silicon Valley company:

> It turned out that workers wanted to use the software as a just-in-time technology resource when they were at an inflection point in their careers. This could be something as basic as preparing for an annual performance discussion with the manager, as traumatic as dealing with the fear they might be laid off, or as positive as their determination to get promoted or to move in a more satisfying career direction. What I saw was that some of these needs could be met quite well with technology tools, but that a significant number of users wanted to take the software results to a manager, mentor, or career counselor for additional insight and assistance. (Epperheimer, 2000, p. 93)

Employees used the software because it was integrated with other human resources and management practices that support people in doing their jobs. However, career planning, like the learning of a new skill, is a very idiosyncratic task, and the process must be tailored to the needs of each individual. Technology can help, but it can take the individual only so far.

Our conclusion, then, is that although technology can aid coaching, the coaching dialogue itself will likely remain a "high-touch," rather than a "high-tech" endeavor. We realize that at the organizational level, this doesn't necessarily help reduce the barriers to coaching. Many people are more comfortable dealing with difficult or emotionally charged matters by e-mail. And technology now keeps us at our desk, in front of the terminal. Coaching requires getting up and walking down the hall, on occasion, and holding a face-to-face conversation.

Can Coaching Be Delegated?

Whether coaching can be delegated is another important question. There are two trends in this direction: peer coaching and mentoring, and executive coaching. The conceptual foundation of executive coaching is of interest to those concerned with the development of nonexecutive talent as well. If individualized expert coaching is helpful to executives, it may offer a model for the provision of developmental relationships that is distinct from that provided by an employee's boss. Indeed, some consulting firms (not those previously mentioned by Pfeffer) now use formal mentoring or coaching programs in which the mentor is distinct from the manager. At Boston Consulting Group, for instance, new hires are assigned a mentor whose responsibilities include providing objective counsel, interpreting the feedback from performance reviews, and advising the new consultant on career development (Underwood, 2001). The foundation for this relationship is its safety. The mentor is in a role that does not require him or her to make judgments about the consultant and has little to do with the new consultant's performance review.

Executive coaches or other specially designated internal coaches can offer focused, convenient, and relatively inexpensive education and consultative services to help employees learn new skills, develop new competencies, deal with difficult challenges, and plan their futures (Witherspoon & White, 1997). They may be drawn from inside or outside the organization, depending on the specific need and the context in which the employee is working. Human resources roles in some firms are now defined to include coaching as an essential job task. We believe this innovation in the delivery of education and training has merit, and we hope to see it continue.

However, in our personal experience, executive coaching without the active participation of the individual employee's manager may lack something important: the view of the boss who is there, in the action, with the employee. Ultimately, the manager and the employee have to decide what is important and which goals the employee should work toward. The employee can discuss such concerns with an external coach, and such discussions may be useful, but in the absence of input from the manager, they can also take the employee in the wrong direction. For example, if an employee, in the eyes of his manager, needs to learn to be more modest and self-effacing to deal with a delicate political situation and at the same time, is discussing his desire to be more assertive with the executive coach, tension will obviously be directed into the learning process. Indeed, to which goal should the employee direct his attention?

Beyond that, even if employees and the coach are working on the right goals, where will employees get feedback on the changes they are trying to make? They have to get that from people "on the ground" when they are doing their work. In most instances, the external coach won't be there. The coaching manager, and perhaps other members of an employee's team, will be in the best position to provide the feedback necessary for the employee to gauge his or her progress, or lack thereof.

Most executive coaches are keenly aware of the importance of continued coaching by an employee's manager, for exactly the reasons cited here. They would be the first to declare that coaching, to a significant degree, cannot be delegated. Additional learning resources, internal or external coaches in this case, work to supplement the efforts of the coaching manager and employee, but they can't supplant those efforts. At the end of the day, the responsibility for learning falls on the manager's shoulders.

Peer coaching takes place in all organizations at all times (Kram, 1986). Employees will routinely help one another unless strongly discouraged from doing so. The power of the peer coach is driven in part by the level of trust that exists between peers. One of our daughters recently reminded us of the importance of the competitive advantage of peer coaching as she recounted how a friend taught her to ride her bicycle: "You know a friend and you trust them more. If you don't trust them, they can't coach you as well because you don't know whether what they're teaching you is right." When employees need advice about dealing with difficult political situations, tough customers, technology that doesn't work, and almost anything else that transpires in the workplace, they turn to one another. It is safe to do so. It is also safe to listen to a trusted friend because you don't believe they will steer you in the wrong direction. While talking to a peer, there is far less perceived need to engage in impression management.

Peers, unless highly competitive with one another, readily create a coaching friendly context. For the most part, they aren't in the business of evaluating one another. But we note that this view of peer mentoring can suggest the image of an environment in which employees turn to one another for help because that is safe, whereas going to the manager is fraught with peril; peers coaching one another on how to deal with a hostile boss; or worse yet, peers coaching one another because they get no coaching from the boss. In a coaching friendly context, peer coaching is not required as a tonic for a toxic boss but is rather another manifestation of an environment in which coaching is part of the fabric of all relationships in the group. Peer coaching isn't a substitute for the coaching manager but is stimulated by the coaching manager's emphasis on learning and helping.

The Relationship With the Coaching Manager Is the Key

Whether augmented by technology or other innovative tactics that help employees learn, there can be no doubt that the coaching manager is indispensable to the effort if we are to take on-the-job learning and development seriously. The manager is there. The employee's relationship with his or her manager sets the tone for how the employee feels about the work and the organization. The power of that relationship is not to be underestimated. We're not saying here that the employee is solely dependent on the manager, but that ideally, when the two work together to create learning, exciting things can happen.

We add that employees are much more likely, in our view, to be loyal to the company through the manager. The stronger the personal connection with the manager, the less of a problem, on balance, retention is likely to be. Note that employees choose to remain in such a relationship not just because the manager is charismatic or fun, but because the employee is getting something invaluable from the relationship: learning and growth. Ultimately, we suggest this is a mature basis on which to build a relationship.

What Should Organizations Do?

Most of the answers to this question are well known: Create an open and honest culture in which people can talk freely, without fear of reprisal. Encourage people to take manageable risks. Don't punish innovative failures—reward them. Show interest in new ideas. Stay current as a firm. Make sure all levels of management are paying attention to their industry, community, and the larger business world. In other words, show that you value learning in general. Obviously, it is critical for the firm's leadership to make sure that its compensation practices don't actively discourage coaching and learning. However, an organization can also be more proactive in encouraging coaching.

Coaching is a skill. Most managers don't know how to coach. They will need quality training to get a basic sense of what coaching is and how to do it. Most organizations are capable of providing the basic training for their managers. However, as in most adult learning, on-the-job learning is what counts the most. Coaches in our training programs have consistently found that the ability to work and talk with other coaches is probably the most helpful thing they do. Coaching is not a conceptually complex task. It is a complex task in execution. Each coaching encounter is different, just as each relationship between manager and employee is different. The learning for coaching managers comes from thinking about the specifics of each case: What can I learn from this effort to help this specific employee?

Coaching managers can help each other with this kind of reflection, simply by drawing on a rudimentary knowledge of coaching and a basic knowledge of people and the business. It is a common practice for the senior management of some companies to spend a few hours each quarter talking about how the top 50 or so people (or, in small firms, the top 3 or 4) below their level in the organization are doing. They review the assignments of the "high potentials," what they are learning, what they will be ready for next, and what kind of help they need along the way. (If management doesn't do this, they should.) Consider the implications of driving such a process all the way down the organization: bringing groups of managers together who work in related areas to reflect on and talk about their talent, how these people are doing, and what they need to learn to prepare for whatever is coming next. Would such a discussion be worthwhile? We suspect that it would. We propose that creating such a process is likely to be one of the most important steps that an organization can take to create a coaching friendly context.

A Final Word for Our Coaches, Old and New

The implications for you of this last discussion are that you should never forget your own need to learn. You are probably coaching because you enjoy the processes of helping and of discovery. Those who teach generally like to learn. Coaching managers like to receive coaching. Find others who share your interest and spend some time reflecting on your good works and what you need to do to keep on going.

We hope that we have given you some "new and improved" ways to coach. The key to becoming a coaching manager is to start using the techniques on a day-to-day basis. If you'd like to stay in touch with a community of coaching managers, please go to our Web site: www.coachingmanager.com. We invite your comments, ideas, and stories. The Web site will help us help you by sharing those stories, as appropriate. Good luck.

References

Altman, B., & Post, J. (1986). Beyond the social contract. In D. T. Hall and Associates (Eds.), *The career is dead, long live the career* (pp. 47-71). San Francisco: Jossey-Bass.

Antonioni, D. (1996, Autumn). Designing an effective 360-degree appraisal feedback process. *Organizational Dynamics*, 24-38.

Argyris, C., Putnam, R., & Smith, D. (1985). *Action science*. San Francisco: Jossey-Bass.

Argyris, C., & Schon, D. (1978). *Organizational learning: A theory of action perspective*. Reading, MA: Addison-Wesley.

Ashford, S. (1986). Feedback-seeking in individual adaptation: A resource perspective. *Academy of Management Journal, 29*(3), 465-487.

Baird, L., & Kram, K. (1984). Career dynamics: Managing the superior/subordinate relationship. *Organizational Dynamics, 12*(4), 46-64.

Beer, M. (1997). *Conducting a performance appraisal interview* (Case No. 9-497-058). Cambridge, MA: Harvard Business School Press.

Boyatzis, R. (1982). *The competent manager: A model for effective performance*. New York: Wiley-Interscience.

Bradford, D., & Cohen, A. (1999). *Power up*. New York: Wiley.

Bray, D., Campbell, R., & Grant, D. (1977). *Formative years in business*. Huntington, NY: Kreager.

Briscoe, J., & Hall, D. (1999, Autumn). Grooming and picking leaders using competency frameworks: Do they work? An alternative approach and new guidelines for practice. *Organizational Dynamics*, 37-51.

Buckingham, M., & Coffman, C. (1999). *First break all the rules*. New York: Simon & Schuster.

Buron, R., & McDonald-Mann, D. (1999). *Giving feedback to subordinates*. Greensboro, NC: Center for Creative Leadership.

Butler, T., & Waldroop, J. (1999, September). Job sculpting: The art of retaining your best people. *Harvard Business Review*, 144-152.

Clardy, A. (2000). Learning on their own: Vocationally oriented self-directed learning projects. *Human Resource Development Quarterly, 11*(2), 105-125.

Clark, K., & Clark, M. (1996). *Choosing to lead* (2nd ed.). Greensboro, NC: Center for Creative Leadership.

Conger, J., & Benjamin, B. (1999). *Building leadership: How successful companies develop the next generation*. San Francisco: Jossey-Bass.

Daudelin, M. (1996/Winter). Learning from experience through reflection. *Organizational Dynamics*, 36-48.

Dessler, G. (1999). *Essentials of human resource management*. New York: Prentice-Hall.

Dotlich, D., & Noel, J. (1998). *Action learning: How the world's top companies are re-creating their leaders and themselves*. San Francisco: Jossey-Bass.

Edmondson, A. (1996). Learning from mistakes is easier said than done: Group and organizational influences on the detection and correction of human error. *Journal of Applied Behavioral Sciences, 32*(1), 5-28.

Edmondson, A. (1999). Psychological safety and learning behavior in work teams. *Administrative Science Quarterly, 44*(2), 350-383.

Ellinger, A., Watkins, K., & Bostrom, R. (1999). Managers as facilitators of learning in learning organizations. *Human Resource Development Quarterly, 10*(2), 105-134.

Epperheimer, J. (2000, Fall). A different view from business. *Career Planning and Adult Development Journal,* 93-97.

Evered, R., & Selman, J. (1989). Coaching and the art of management. *Organizational Dynamics, 18,* 16-32.

Garvin, D. (2000). *Learning in action.* Cambridge, MA: Harvard Business School Press.

General Electric Corporation. (2000, June). *GE Annual Report.* Fairfield, CT: General Electric Corporation.

Goleman, D. (1998). *Working with emotional intelligence.* New York: Bantam.

Goleman, D. (2001, April). Leadership that gets results. *Harvard Business Review,* 78-90.

Greenleaf, R. (1998). *The power of servant leadership.* San Francisco: Berrett-Koehler.

Hall, D. T. (1986). Breaking career routines: Mid-career choice and identity development. In D. T. Hall (Ed.), *Career development in organizations* (pp. 120-159). San Francisco: Jossey-Bass.

Hall, D. T. (1996, November). Protean careers of the 21st century. *Academy of Management Executive, 1*(4), 8-16.

Hicks, M., & Peterson, D. (1997). Just enough to be dangerous: The rest of what you need to know about development. *Consulting Psychology Journal, 49*(3), 171-193.

Hofstede, G. (1993). Cultural constraints in management theories. *Academy of Management Executive, 7*(1), 81-91.

Holland, J. (1992). *Making vocational choices.* Odessa, FL: Psychological Assessment Resources.

Hunt, J. (1994). *The impact of work group culture on work and family stress.* Unpublished doctoral dissertation, Boston University.

Inkson, K., & Arthur, M. (2001). How to be a successful career capitalist. *Organizational Dynamics, 30*(1), 48-61.

Kaplan, R., Drath, W., & Kofodimos, J. (1991). *Beyond ambition: How driven managers can lead better and live better.* San Francisco: Jossey-Bass.

Kaye, B. (1997). *Up is not the only way* (2nd ed.). Palo Alto, CA: Davis-Black.

Kluger, A., & DeNisi, A. (1996). The effects of feedback interventions on performance: A historical review, a meta-analysis and a preliminary feedback intervention theory. *Psychological Bulletin, 119*(2), 254-284.

Knowles, M., Holton, E., & Swanson, R. (1998). *The adult learner.* Houston, TX: Gulf Publishing.

Kram, K. (1985). *Mentoring at work.* Glenview, IL: Scott Foresman.

Kram, K. (1986). Mentoring in the workplace. In D. T. Hall (Ed.), *Career Development in Organizations* (pp. 160-200). San Francisco: Jossey-Bass.

Kram, K., & Bragar, M. (1992). Development through mentoring: A strategic approach. In D. Montross & C. Schinckman (Eds.), *Career development theory and practice* (pp. 221-254). Springfield, IL: Charles C Thomas.

Levinson, H. (1978, May-June). The abrasive personality. *Harvard Business Review,* 86-90.

Levinson, H. (1986). *Ready, fire, aim: Avoiding management by impulse.* Cambridge, MA: The Levinson Institute.

Livingston, J. (1988, September/October). Pygmalion in management. *Harvard Business Review,* 121-130.

Locke, E., & Latham, G. (1990). *A theory of goal setting and task performance.* Englewood Cliffs, NJ: Prentice-Hall.

Locke, E., Latham, G., & Erez, M. (1988). The determinants of goal commitment. *Academy of Management Review, 13*(1), 23-39.

Lombardo, M., & Eichinger, R. (2001). *The leadership machine.* Minneapolis, MN: Lominger.

London, M. (1997). *Job feedback.* Mahwah, NJ: Lawrence Erlbaum.

Manzoni, J., & Barsoux, J. (1998, March/April). The set-up-to-fail syndrome. *Harvard Business Review,* 101-114.

McCall, M. (1998). *High flyers: Developing the next generation of leaders.* Cambridge, MA: Harvard Business School Press.

McCall, M., Lombardo, M., & Morrison, A. (1988). *The lessons of experience: How successful executives develop on the job.* New York: Lexington Books.

McClelland, D., & Burnham, D. (1995, January). Power is the great motivator. *Harvard Business Review,* 126-135.

McGregor, D. (1960). *The human side of enterprise.* New York: McGraw-Hill.

McGuire, G. (1999). Do race and sex affect employees' access to help from mentors? Insights from the study of a large corporation. In A. Murrell, F. Crosby, & R. Ely (Eds.), *Mentoring Dilemmas* (pp. 105-120). Mahwah, NJ: Lawrence Erlbaum.

McMurrer, D., Van Buren, M., & Woodwell, W. (2000). *The 2000 ASTD state of the industry report.* Washington, DC: American Society of Training and Development.

Nannus, B. (1992). *Visionary leadership.* San Francisco: Jossey-Bass.

Noe, R. (1999). *Employee training and development.* New York: McGraw-Hill.

O'Reilly, C., & Pfeffer, J. (2000). *Hidden value.* Cambridge, MA: Harvard Business School Press.

Peter F. Drucker Foundation for Non-profit Management. (1998). *Lessons in leadership* [Videotape, featuring Peter F. Drucker]. San Francisco: Jossey-Bass.

Pfeffer, J. (1998). *The human equation: Building profits by putting people first.* Cambridge, MA: Harvard Business School Press.

Pfeffer, J. (2000). *Hidden value: How great companies achieve results with ordinary people.* Cambridge, MA: Harvard Business School Press.

Pfeffer, J. (2001, October). Economic cure all: Take care of your clients. *Consulting,* 38-40.

Phillips, K. (1998, March). The Achilles' heel of coaching. *Training and Development,* 41-43.

Reingold, J. (2001, September). Teacher in chief. *Fast Company Magazine,* 66-68.

Rosier, R. (Ed.). (1994). *The competency model handbook.* Lexington, MA: Linkage, Inc.

Ross, R. (1994). The ladder of inference. In P. Senge, R. Ross, B. Smith, C. Roberts, & A. Kleiner (Eds.), *The fifth discipline fieldbook.* New York: Currency Doubleday.

Rossett, A. (1997, July). That was a great class but. *Training and Development,* 19-24.

Sanders, L. (2001, October 18). Southwest weathers tough quarter. Retrieved from the World Wide Web on 10/20/01 at: CBSMarketwatch.com

Schein, E. (1979). Personal change through interpersonal relationships. In W. Bennis, J. Van Maanen, E. Schein, & F. Steele (Eds.), *Essays in interpersonal dynamics* (pp. 129-162). Homewood, IL: Dorsey.

Schein, E. (1996, November). Career anchors revisited: Implications for career development in the 21st century. *Academy of Management Executive, 10*(4), 80-88.

Schlender, B. (2000, May). The odd couple. *Fortune,* 106-126.

Schmuckler, J. (2001). Cross-cultural performance feedback. *OD Practitioner, 33*(1), 15-20.

Schu, J. (2001, October). Even in hard times, SAS keeps its culture intact. *Workforce,* 21.

Schwab, G. (1999, December 18). Woody Hayes: TKO vs. Clemson. *The Charlotte Observer.* Retrieved from the Word Wide Web on 8/14/01 at: Charlotte.com

Seibert, K. (1999, Winter). Tools for cultivating on-the-job learning conditions. *Organizational Dynamics, 1,* 54-65.

Senge, P. (1990). *The fifth discipline.* New York: Doubleday.

Senge, P., Ross, R., Smith, B., Roberts, C., & Kleiner, A. (1994). *The fifth discipline fieldbook.* New York: Doubleday.

Spencer, L., McClelland, D., & Spencer, D. (1994). *Competency assessment methods: History and state of the art.* Boston: Hay/McBer.

Sperry, L. (1993). *Psychiatric consultation in the workplace.* Washington, DC: American Psychiatric Press.

Steinberg, M. (2001, September 23). *Master violinist Isaac Stern dead at 81.* Associated Press State and Local Wire. Lexis-Nexis® Academic Universe Document.

Tichy, N. (1997). *The leadership engine: How winning companies build leaders at every level.* New York: Harper Business Press.

Underwood, S. (2001, August). The nurturing bond. *Consulting,* 42-47.

Vaccaro, B. (1991). *Depression, corporate experiences and innovations.* Washington, DC: Washington Business Group on Health.

Van Velsor, E., McCauly, C., & Moxley, R. (1998). Our view of leadership development. In C. McCauley, R. Moxley, & E. Van Velsor (Eds.), *Handbook of Leadership Development* (pp. 1-23). San Francisco: Jossey-Bass.

Vincola, A. (2001, June). Helping employees balance work/life issues. *Workspan,* 26-33.

Waldroop, J., & Butler, T. (1996, November-December). The executive as coach. *Harvard Business Review,* 111-117.

Waterman, R., Waterman, J., & Collard, B. (1994, July). Toward a career-resilient workforce. *Harvard Business Review,* 87-95.

Weeks, H. (2001, July-August). Taking the stress out of stressful conversations. *Harvard Business Review,* 113-119.

Weintraub, J. (1999). *The success manual.* Wellesley, MA: Organizational Dimensions.

Whetton, D., & Cameron, K. (1998). *Developing management skills.* Reading, MA: Addison-Wesley.

Witherspoon, R., & White, R. (1997). *Four essential ways that coaching can help executives.* Greensboro, NC: Center for Creative Leadership.

Wolfe, D., & Kolb, D. (1984). Career development, personal growth, and experiential learning. In D. Kolb, I. Rubin, & J. McIntyre (Eds.), *Organizational Psychology* (4th ed., pp. 124-152). New York: Prentice-Hall.

Yammarino, F., & Atwater, L. (1997). Do managers see themselves as others see them? Implications of self-other rating agreement for human resources management. *Organizational Dynamics,* 25(4), 35-44.

Index

About the Authors

**Dr. James M. Hunt** is Assistant Professor of Management and the Charles E. McCarthy Family Trust Term Chair at Babson College, in Wellesley, Massachusetts. He teaches management, strategic human resource management, and leadership. James is also a faculty member of the Leadership and Influence Program at Babson's School of Executive Education. Previously, he served on the faculty of Clark University's Graduate School of Management. He is a Faculty Co-Director of the Coaching for Leadership and Teamwork Program at Babson. The Babson Coaching Program provides developmental coaching for Babson students working toward enhancing their competencies in leadership and teamwork. Each year, the faculty train over 500 Babson alumni and MBA students in coaching techniques and development planning. His recent paper on coaching (with Dr. Joseph Weintraub) was awarded the "Best Management Development Paper" by the Academy of Management, the largest professional association of business school professors in the world.

Dr. Hunt is also a founder of Hunt Associates, a career and leadership development firm that provides executive coaching, career counseling, employee assistance programs, and strategic human resource consulting. Since 1990, Hunt Associates has worked with companies such as the Bose Corporation, 3Com, Genzyme, and Stratus Computer. He graduated from the Massachusetts Institute of Technology with a BS degree and received a doctorate in business administration from Boston University's Graduate School of Management, where he studied career and leadership development and work/life balance.

Dr. Hunt can be reached at: Hunt@coachingmanager.com

Dr. Joseph R. Weintraub is the Founder and Faculty Co-Director of the Coaching for Leadership and Teamwork Program at Babson College, where he is also an Associate Professor of Management and Organizational Behavior. At Babson, he developed the Human Resource Management and Leadership courses and is a Faculty Director at the Babson College School of Executive Education. He is also President and Founder of Organizational Dimensions, a leadership development and human resources consulting firm based in Wellesley, Massachusetts. He is a past President of the Human Resources Council, a Boston-based society of human resource executives. His work has appeared in many publications, including *Fortune, Entrepreneur, The Wall Street Journal,* and *The New York Times.* He has been featured on several syndicated television programs, such as *Evening Magazine* and *The Bottom Line.* His paper on coaching (with Dr. James Hunt) was awarded the "Best Management Development Paper" by the Academy of Management, the largest professional association of business school professors in the world. Dr. Weintraub is also one of the developers of Star-Teams Insights,™ a Web-based assessment report providing developmental feedback in the areas of leadership, teamwork, and work style.

Dr. Weintraub has consulted with many organizations, including Fidelity Investments, Dunkin' Donuts, Bose, Marriott, Duke Energy, General Electric, and the Los Angeles Dodgers. Much of his recent activity has been focused in the areas of leadership and coaching. He is currently working with companies in both Japan and the United States to combine the teaching of leadership, coaching, and teamwork with the playing of baseball and other sports. He received his BS degree from the University of Pittsburgh and both his MA and PhD degrees in Industrial-Organizational Psychology from Bowling Green State University.

Dr. Weintraub can be reached at: Weintraub@coachingmanager.com